Voices of Inquiry in Teacher Education

Voices of Inquiry in Teacher Education

Thomas S. Poetter
Trinity University

with

Jennifer Pierson
Chelsea Caivano
Shawn Stanley
Sherry Hughes
Heidi D. Anderson

LEA Lawrence Erlbaum Associates, Publishers
1997   Mahwah, New Jersey

Lawrence Erlbaum Associates, Inc., Publishers
10 Industrial Avenue
Mahwah, NJ 07430

Cover design by Kathryn Houghtaling

Library of Congress Cataloging-In-Publication Data

   Poetter, Thomas S. (Thomas Stewart), 1962–
Voices of Inquiry in Teacher Education/Thomas S. Poetter with
Jennifer Pierson...[et al.] ; [foreward by Thomas J. Sergiovanni].
       p. cm.
   Includes bibliographic references and index.
   ISBN 0-8058-2378-6 (p : alk. paper).— ISBN 0-8058-2689-0
(c : alk. paper)
   1. Action research in education—United States. 2. Teach-
ers—Training of—United States. 3. Student teachers—United
States.
   I. Title
   LB1028.24.p64 1997
   370' .7' 2—dc21   96-54813
                                                      CIP

Printed in the United States of America
10 9 8 7 6 5 4 3 2 1

"Somehow educators have forgotten the important connection between teachers and students. We listen to outside experts to inform us, and consequently we overlook the treasure in our very own backyards: our students. Student perceptions are valuable to our practice because they are authentic sources; they personally experience our classrooms firsthand. As teachers, we need to find ways to continually seek out these silent voices because they can teach us so much about learning and learners."

—*Soohoo, 1993*

Contents

CB ◆ ∞

Foreword

CŽ ◆ ŁO

You have heard it before. Inquiry should be at the heart of teacher education. Why? Because inquiry is seminal in preparing teachers as artisan-professionals who will respect the knowledge base as a treasure of insight for informing their practice. Inquiry is seminal in preparing teachers who will use intents, contextual indeterminates, and nuances of practice as key factors in deciding how teaching and learning knowledge will be used in practice. But how do we do it? What is the struggle to develop artisan-professionals like? How do teacher educators place inquiry at the center when novice teachers have so many other pressing concerns? How do novice teachers learn to inquire and to benefit from this inquiry while also trying to learn the basics of teaching? Once novice teachers decide to give inquiry a try, what does this struggle look like in practice? How do teacher educators and students alike place inquiry at the center when today's teaching environment seems so inhospitable to the idea?

Tom Poetter and his five co-authors provide some answers to these questions by telling their stories—stories of struggle, insight, and hope. Poetter is a teacher educator working with teacher interns as part of Trinity University's 5-year Teacher Education program. His coauthors are fifth-year students teaching full-time in a professional development school. The medium is stories that weave together a penetrating and expansive journey of challenge, triumph, and defeat. These are stories that teach readers important lessons as to what inquiry is like on the chalk line, how inquiry works, and how it can work better.

Chapters 1 and 2 set the stage by providing an engaging analysis of how inquiry fits into the teacher education picture, a compelling review of related literature, and a vivid picture of how the work described in this book evolved. From the beginning Poetter acquaints readers with storytelling by immersing himself as a person and as a person-professor into the discussion. Getting to share his struggle almost firsthand is an important strength of this book. Championing inquiry in teacher education, one soon discovers, is not an abstraction but a personal journey for teacher educators who decide to put their shoulder to the wheel. It is as much a struggle for them as it is for the students who will be involved.

Chapters 1 and 2 have punch because they bring to life real people and real events. The major players are Poetter, his students, and the mentor teachers who provide the students with daily supervision. Particularly interesting is the initial resistance of the teacher interns to the idea of researching their practice, the reactions of Poetter, and the gradual warming up to the idea by the interns.

Chapters 3 through 7 tell the stories of the five teacher interns. Consistently engaging and overflowing with insight, they lay the foundation for the analysis that follows in the remainder of the book. They deal with the use of manipulatives and technology in teaching mathematics, developing a perspective on teaching journalism, understanding connections between teachers and students, teaching at-risk students, and gender bias in the classroom.

In the last four chapters, each masterfully written, Poetter tries to make sense of the stories. Chapter 8 provides a moving description of how Poetter and his students manage to work out their differences about the nature, viability, and usefulness of the inquiry project. Particularly useful for me was to read about the many ups and downs these novice teachers experienced as they journeyed through their internship year and the wonder they experienced when they finally arrived at a comfortable place at the end. They had defined for themselves a sense of competence and commitment that told them when they were reflective teachers. Chapter 9 deals with the thorny task of defining a problem worth investigating, and then developing a strategy for its investigation. Chapter 10 catalogues the learnings teacher-interns and professor alike experience as a result of the inquiry project. Chapter 11 examines inquiry in its broader context, focusing on implications for teacher education.

In these concluding chapters, Poetter digs deeply into the teaching lives of the students and into his own work as a teacher of teachers. The yield is an alive picture of what is involved in teaching novice teachers about inquiry, in helping them to inquire, and then in helping them to make sense of it all. Despite the challenges and difficulties, the experiences of Poetter and his students are reassuring. Inquiry from the beginning is not only a good idea, but a doable one.

Voices of Inquiry in Teacher Education will be helpful to teacher educators everywhere who are interested in placing inquiry at the center of what they do. Teacher education students who are being asked to try inquiry will find in this book some friends to lean on, to learn from, to laugh with, and to cry with. This book is a welcome addition to the literature on teacher education.

—*Thomas J. Sergiovanni*

Preface

ભ ✦ ৪১

I wrote this book with the co-authors for several reasons. First, it is an attempt to show that preservice teacher knowledge is substantive and should be part of the wider database of knowledge about teaching and learning in the field of teacher education. Although I attempt in places here to interpret the intern teachers' work, their writings ultimately stand on their own as separate chapters. In the end, their chapters and their teaching experiences constitute quality pieces of research in their own right. Second, performing inquiry projects during teacher education experiences is becoming a more widespread practice; we wanted to share how our experiences looked and felt in order to inform a wider audience about the possibilities and pitfalls of preservice teacher research. Third, what started out as a smaller attempt to describe what happened to us as a teaching and learning cohort in this preservice teacher education experience (an early version of chapter 2 entitled "From Resistance to Excitement" first appeared in *Teaching Education*, Fall/Winter 1996) grew into a bigger story as I began to see implications for our work and experiences for a wider audience, including teacher educators, students of teaching, school administrators, and university researchers interested in the processes and uses of teacher research.

The book is divided into three main sections. The first section examines the background and framework for our story, including a description in chapter 1, Getting Started on Inquiry, of the teacher education program at Trinity and of the more personal grounds from which my own ideas and practices in teacher education arose. I encouraged students to write personally, and I modeled this in my own writing. Chapter 2, From Resistance to Excitement, describes and interprets the problems that the interns faced in getting started on their projects, and how we overcame obstacles as individuals and as a group.

The second section honors the work of the intern teachers in our program by devoting a chapter to each of their research projects in their entirety. Five intern papers appear, constituting chapters 3 through 7. The reader also examines the proposals each student wrote for the papers; they are included in the Appendices. Each of the students' papers stands on its own as a substantive piece of work, as well as a model for the type of study and perspective that students of teaching might take when examining the school during their preservice experiences.

The third section pulls out lessons from the students' work on their projects and in the program in order to inform a wider audience about what we learned during this process. Chapter 8, Foundations of Learning From Inquiry, examines in more detail the relationships and experiences that the five scholar-teachers and I shared during the internship. Our relationships and experiences together stand as foundational considerations from which to better understand the deeper learning that went on among us. Chapter 9, Considerations for Defining Problems for Study and Identifying Emerging Research Methodologies in Inquiry, looks closely at the very substance of the interns' research activities, what they chose to focus on and why, and it addresses several methodological issues in research. Chapter 10, Learning From Inquiry, discusses how the interns' studies and their own reflections on their work and experiences in the internship contributed to their understanding of the theory and practice that undergirded their growing conceptions of teaching. Chapter 11, Emerging Lessons From the Experience of Conducting Inquiry, examines lessons we learned from our experience that should challenge teacher educators and students of teaching as they consider their work together.

Several works about teacher research adopt an approach that more closely resembles a "how-to" guide, showing the steps taken in setting up a program and making a case for those steps. This book does not do this. Instead, we show what we did and interpret the consequences of those actions. The reader might glean from a close reading of this text a conceptual model for the implementation of an inquiry component in a teacher education program. We don't intend for you to treat the book this way. We would rather draw you into our world, introduce you to the ideas, passions, conflicts, and resolutions that governed our experiences. Then, we would have you interpret, imagine, and gain what you will as you consider the opportunities, possibilities, and pitfalls for teacher research in your own programs and experiences.

ACKNOWLEDGMENTS

Many important parties deserve special recognition here for helping to make this work possible. Of course, the co-authors of this text, the intern teachers whose works and words and stories appear here—Jennifer Pierson, Chelsea Caivano, Shawn Stanley, Sherry Hughes, and Heidi Anderson—gave full measure to the project, working hard to see it through while commitments to teaching, school, and family competed. They are outstanding colleagues and teachers and scholars. Dr. Laura Van Zandt and I taught the Pedagogics course and guided the interns' research together. She agreed to give the project a try; she became and will always be an outstanding and trusted colleague. My own family gave much to the process, including giving me up for long periods of time. Sons Mitchell and Samuel kept me centered on what is important in life by loving me as dad and dad only. My wife Chris supported and encouraged me as we worked through problems with the project. She, too, loved me regardless of what anybody else thought, and this was important to me.

To those early believers, teachers and students who knew or sensed the value of what we were trying to do with inquiry, and the direction it could take to benefit them in the short and long runs, thank you for your vision and support. To all the teachers, students, mentors, and interns who participated in this first round of inquiry projects as participants and as researchers, thank you for your hard work and bravery in opening up your classrooms and lives. As a result, you have opened up the schools to deeper conversations about education and teaching practice. This is no small feat.

Distinguished colleagues John Moore, Tom Sergiovanni, Bill Fish, and Angela Breidenstein generously volunteered their time and expertise to early readings and reviews of the manuscript. John Moore, Chairperson of the Education Department at Trinity University, made the core of the writing effort possible with a generous departmental grant. He believed in the depth and worth of the project from the very beginning. Tom Sergiovanni made an early commitment by being the first to read the initial draft. It meant a great deal to me for him to like it, to suggest direction, and to agree to write the Foreword. The coauthors worked hard on final drafts, getting them in shape for public review. Graduate assistant Justin Kuravackal provided a discerning, honest eye on late readings of the text. The reviewers from Lawrence Erlbaum, John C. Stansell of Texas A & M University, Susan E Noffke of the University of Illinois, and H. James McLaughlin of the University of Georgia, gave excellent guidance throughout the writing process, and helped us to sharpen our ideas, presentation, and prose. Editor Naomi Silverman and Assistant Editor Linda Henigin gave the book a chance and supported our work with helpful comments and professional guidance. As a first-time author, I really appreciated their vision for the volume and their positive attitude. Outstanding office support came from Debra Phelps, who transcribed all of the intern teachers' interviews. Sonia Mircles, Departmental Secretary, helped me with millions of details too numerous and too complex to name here. Thank you all for your support and effort.

—*Thomas S. Poetter*

Part I

Background and Framework for the Story

1

Getting Started on Inquiry

ভ ◆ ৪৩

DREAMS

I dreamed for years about becoming a teacher educator. My dreams mani-
fested themselves in actions of preparation—going to college, studying to
become a teacher and then teaching high school English, coaching baseball
and basketball, pursuing graduate work in education, supervising student
teachers, and landing a job as a teacher educator at Trinity University.
During my preparatory experiences in teacher education, I asked prospective teachers, friends, relatives, and colleagues involved in various teacher
education programs if they felt as though they had been adequately prepared
for teaching through their studies and field experiences. I often met answers
from them that point to the perceived malaise in the field that has been
written about extensively and pointedly (Kramer, 1991).

Prospective teachers often feel distanced from the demands of quality
practice in their future classrooms and from the lives of their future students
when they study educational theory and methods at the university. They
sometimes feel displaced from educational theory and the exciting prospects
of educational change when they confront the realities of school in their
interactions with teachers who serve as their supervisors in field practicums.
Prospective teachers sometimes feel displaced in their work toward a
teaching certificate and a professional career, often lacking the experiences
that might help them make connections with ideas and practices and people
that will serve as firm foundations for a long and successful and productive
career as a teacher.

Student teaching as an 8- to 16-week practicum experience just doesn't
seem able—mostly because of deficiencies in time and in curricular continuity in most contexts—to move students past the survival mode. Students
may learn how to survive the everyday rigors of the classroom in their
student teaching experience, but this doesn't mean that they have truly
learned to teach or learned to think about teaching or even started down

the right pathways toward these lifelong goals of thought and action. So many student teachers are just starting to feel comfortable in the classroom when their 10 weeks are up and they have to return to the university for more methods courses or for graduation. I recall my own 8-week student teaching stint, and feeling that I had survived it but that somehow there must be so much more. So many get through the short experience of student teaching but need more time to hone much needed skills in curriculum development, lesson delivery, and classroom management before they confront the oftentimes harsh realities of full-time teaching during their first full year in the field, let alone come to terms with what education truly is and who they want to be as a teacher.

Now I don't profess to have found the panacea for this well-documented problem to be imbedded in the complex world of prospective teacher inquiry, nor do I believe that those who worked toward their degree and their teaching licenses under my care this past year necessarily got it right because of anything I did. Trinity University already had in place a substantive clinical component in its Fifth-Year Master of Arts in Teaching Program (MAT). Anticipating the changes that had been forecast and that occurred since the Holmes Group began meeting and making recommendations for reform in teacher education (Goodlad, 1994; The Holmes Group Report, 1986), Trinity has made cutting-edge program changes to better educate teachers and better serve the eight partner schools in the community—four elementary and four secondary—that offer field placements for interns.

Fifth-year interns take a 4-year baccalaureate degree in their chosen discipline; complete a core of education classes and practica that serve as introductions to the profession and to life in schools during their undergraduate preparation; then spend a fifth-year internship (beginning the second day after undergraduate graduation exercises with summer courses on curriculum and teaching) working in their school placement full-time for eight months of an academic year as an unpaid member of the partner school's faculty under the direction of a mentor teacher who also receives a dual appointment as a clinical member of the Trinity faculty (unpaid). The program is designed and implemented by practitioners in the field and by clinical faculty members from Trinity. The program strives for shared purposes and the participation of many voices and stakeholders. The practicum truly becomes an internship, that is, more than student teaching in that interns become a part of the faculty and the school culture for an extended period of time and take on many more substantive roles in their experience. Interns, as valued and contributing members of the school's social and cultural fabric, get the opportunity to move past the survival mode and truly teach during their teacher education experience.

What has happened for interns and for the schools they serve has been remarkable in terms of taking steps toward getting teacher education right. Mentor teachers treat interns as teaching partners from day one. Interns develop a collegial, familial cohort that acts as a resource and support system for the internship and for further professional development and social support after they move into full-time paid positions in schools, often in the school systems where they served their internship. Interns live their class-room lives and their university coursework together for an academic year; they immerse themselves in the lives of the schools, their students, and their mentors. We see the positive results in excellent teachers who stay in the field. This ought to be the summative measure of any program, and what makes faculty members like me justify their vocational existences.

The partner schools and the mentor teachers benefit, too. They hone and shape shared purposes with Trinity for conducting their primary mission of educating their own student populations. Intern–Mentor teams bring added enthusiasm and dynamic ideas to the faculties, students, and school cultures with which they interact. Mentors and other teachers gain status and professional development opportunities from working with interns and Trinity. Mentors often comment on how mentoring makes them feel as though they are making a difference in the profession beyond themselves and beyond their own students' lives by shaping the persons and practices in teaching for the next generation. Reform initiatives taken up by schools are supported and enhanced by interns and faculty from Trinity. Many benefit and many excel from the collaborative efforts that dominate the way we function as and are as partners together.

But this rosy (and for the most part accurate) picture does not tell the whole story. It does not point to the potential gaps that can and do form and exist in a program of this sort. Having graduated five cohorts of fifth-year graduates by the spring of 1995, Trinity and its partner schools set them-selves on a path toward excellence in teacher education and toward shaping school reform initiatives. But the move toward excellence is a journey that continues and evolves, even past the point of thinking that you've got it down. When I began interviewing for the position of University Liaison to the high school in the spring of 1994, Trinity Education department chair Dr. John Moore made it clear to me that he hoped I could help to fill a gap in the secondary part of the program. This gap, in his opinion, was consti-tuted by a seeming lack of continuity and depth in the academic component for the internship.

Dr. Moore hoped that I, along with my new colleague Dr. Laura Van Zandt, also a new PhD and charged to work with the middle school interns, mentors, and site, could reshape the Pedagogics Curriculum to better meet the needs of students in the field. We took the challenge with great zest, and Dr. Van Zandt and I began reviewing what had been done in the past in the course and discussing what we thought we might do in the fall of 1994. The course, called Pedagogics, supposedly served the purpose of connecting thought about teaching with experience in the field. Our discussions began in early summer of 1994 and were cordial. We agreed to many things, including a focus for the course and a syllabus, which I counted as a marvelous achievement because we had never met each other in person and conducted all of our discussions over the phone and through the mail.

We decided that the Pedagogics course would have several layers, all designed to meet the challenge of helping to connect the interns' academic efforts in the study of teaching with their everyday experiences in the field. For the Pedagogics class, we decided to mix readings about, and case studies of, topics such as classroom management, curriculum development, and multicultural education (Silverman, Welty, & Lyon, 1991; Wasserman, 1993); with presentations on models of teaching (Joyce & Weil, 1992); discussions led by interns on self-selected topics; and interns' individual, self-selected qualitative research projects (Poetter, 1996; Poetter & Van Zandt, 1996).

Instead of consisting of academic exercises disconnected from experience and practice in classrooms, the Pedagogics course activities connect the study of teaching and learning with the doing of teaching and learning in the field. Interns, by becoming reflective inquirers in their own classrooms and schools, construct their own knowledge of teaching. They tap not only the wealth of existing research about teaching and their topic for study, but also make their own way by informing their growing conceptions of teaching and learning in practice while sharing this journey with others through their reflective research on practice (Gitlin & Bullough, 1995).

We suggested that the interns focus their qualitative research projects on some aspect of teaching or learning important for their growing conceptualizations and practices of teaching. Their data collection activities could take place in their own classrooms or in classrooms where they hoped to observe some activity of interest to them. We encouraged action research projects in the classic sense, or "research undertaken by practitioners in order that they may improve their practices" (Corey cited in Ross, 1987, p. 132). Action research projects conducted by preservice teachers on their own practice have the potential for helping students move toward viewing teaching as both a theoretical and practical endeavor that can be understood and improved. Action research can promote "the role of teachers as theory makers because of their intimate knowledge of the inner workings of the classroom, leading to teachers taking on new roles as the driving forces for change in the schools" (Fleischer, 1995, p. 15). We also encouraged qualitative case studies of schooling depicting scenes and practices outside interns' own classrooms so that those who selected this route could more clearly appreciate and understand the complexities of teaching, learning, and schooling, and as a result of reporting findings from their disciplined studies of scenes, share their new knowledge with their colleagues in the form of a final paper due at the end of the first semester (Eisner, 1985).

We prepared the interns for doing fieldwork by holding seminars on qualitative research, as well as teaching methods for gathering data including observing, interviewing, and collecting artifacts. We asked them to adopt a posture in the classrooms as participant–observer, noting their interactions with students, materials, and ideas in their daily journals. We thought that their journals could be a place to vent feelings and frustrations about teaching, all substantive data with which to interpret their experiences, as well as a place to keep more formal observations of classroom scenes. Interns wrote a proposal for their studies early in the semester (see appendices) and we counseled them about defining their problems and topics for study as well as on shaping their research activities to best fit the demands of the school and university classrooms. We spent parts of class meetings discussing their progress in data collection and addressed the scary issue of writing it up. We met individually with interns throughout the term as needed as they worked in the field as prospective teacher inquirers.

We truly believed conducting fieldwork that focused on interns' own teaching, their own students' learning, and their own classrooms and schools would enhance interns' deeper conceptions of teaching and school life. We believed that interns would see things by doing disciplined inquiry in the field that they wouldn't see if they were *only* teaching. We believed that interns could become more than technicians of teaching, more than builders of databases of activities and lessons (Johnston, 1994).

Instead, interns could become reflective, thoughtful learners empowered to shape and change their complex classrooms and schools and enhance the learning lives of students because they know and understand them better as a result of their own disciplined inquiry. We believed they could share their findings and insights with others in a meaningful way through their writing and presentations. We believed that a culture of inquiry could become contagious, fostering a new path for teacher action, improvement, and communication among interns, mentors, and school staff.

The research endeavor was not designed to produce a new cadre of professional educational researchers. Yes, we think that teachers can and must become inquirers of teaching practice, knowledge-absorbing and knowledge-producing human beings. But we did not have in mind that research would somehow replace the focus of the program on quality teaching practice in classrooms. The project was meant to bridge the gaps between theory and practice and to provide a new way for viewing the necessary marriage between study and practice.

The experiences, results, and lessons from our cumulative endeavors on this journey to become more reflective teachers, as interns, mentors, and as first-year teacher educators, are the foci of this volume. This book is about what happens when prospective teachers are asked to conduct their own inquiries about teaching and learning. This book doesn't simply list the drawbacks and potential benefits of prospective teacher inquiry; it encounters and tells about them, and the people who experience them in the context of a teacher education experience. Our story is certainly not an uncommon one; it is filled with clashes of personality and purpose, and with the victories of learning and reconciliation. It is a particular story that needs to be told, for it points to learnings and lessons about teacher education and teaching and inquiry that can't be gotten out of textbooks.

HOPES

I want this volume to accomplish several things. First, I want this book to be accessible and interesting for people interested in teaching, inquiry, and schools. When I set out to write my dissertation, a study of a women's intercollegiate volleyball team and its experience of the curriculum (Goodlad, 1979; Poetter, 1994b), I decided at the beginning that I would attempt to write the text as informally in language and as story-like as I could. The first chapter of the dissertation told the story of my seemingly fruitless, but ultimately successful attempts to gain access to the field for my study. The first chapter became, and remained, the best chapter of the document (Poetter, 1994b, 1995).

However, my committee chair—and my most respected mentor, colleague, and friend in the field—urged me to resist my own inclination to write the entire text in a narrative form, and I agreed with him, somewhat begrudgingly, in that the purpose of my writing was to produce a dissertation and not a book or a novel. As a result, the text lost the spark and interpretive flavor of the first chapter, and I remember being asked by other members of my committee during the dissertation defense, "Why did you decide to switch from the narrative mode to the analytic mode when your first chapter story had been so very strong?" I glanced nervously at my committee chair, and then responded to the group with all due confidence, "Because this is a dissertation, and not a book." Make no mistake; the text you are reading is a book and not a dissertation, and although there are some important sections of analyses here with exposition, of course, I spend most of my time and effort telling the story. You may analyze, synthesize, and take away what you will.

The deeper conversation here in terms of methodology and interpretation, I suppose then, is about hermeneutical stance: I take the interpretivist's stance here as inquirer and writer. My goals are to interpret my own life as experienced in this context, as well as the lives of those students and contexts with which I intimately interacted as teacher and fellow inquirer (Smith, 1993). I write in context, and share my subjective interactions and interpretations with other subjects and with you. I bring my own subjective realities and predispositions to this book, and I outline a few of these in the pages to come. I hope to understand myself, others, and experiences better through the acts of inquiring and writing. The meaning I make here can be judged on the basis of whether the text connects with the reader, reveals aspects of other and self previously covered, reveals and dispels mysteries, and opens up more questions and avenues for inquiry.

Brunner (1994) helped clarify the interpretivist's position in her work *Inquiry and Reflection: Framing Narrative Practice in Education* by reminding interpretivist researchers and writers that: "When we include stories gathered from research settings or classroom settings in our texts, . . . we have an obligation to preserve the dignity of that storyteller. . . . And as people bring their stories to us, they can only hope we understand them; when we interpret a story, we are interpreting a life" (p. 67).

My goal is to tell accurately and sensitively the stories and lives of the coauthors as well as my own. I don't claim to know their minds and lives and hearts as some sort of all-knowing third party. I know that although we have different purposes, expectations, and perceptions, we discovered much in common in our experiences. The interns agreed that my story connects to theirs with integrity because they have read and commented on this work. This volume is an intense dialogue of sorts, for the respondents judged if it accurately portrays their realities.

This work represents, then, a step toward *collaborative resonance*, that is, the type of relationship between the worlds of practice and theory wherein an intensification of the collaboration of school and university learning communities produces the opportunity for students of teaching to tap the "resources needed to learn from and reform teaching throughout their careers" (Cochran-Smith, 1994, p. 149). Prospective teachers' stories are worth hearing and can tell us much. To this end, you hear and read the voices of the interns; I not only interpret their voices, but I also included their voices in the text, both in their reflections on their research gathered in interviews, as well as their own writing located in their own research reports. Their accounts are potentially empowering, liberalizing interpretations of life and experience inside schools that stand in collaborative unison with me and the program, as well as in their own right.

Second, I want to inform beginning and novice teacher educators about the wacky turns and important nooks and crannies in the real-life experience of living out this calling as teacher educator. Mine is only one story, and set in a particular place and time, but I believe that we can learn from "the particular," especially if the story connects with some deeper sensibilities. Every first-time experience is different and I don't expect the prospective, new, or veteran teacher educator who decides to read this book to have the same experiences, or even to connect with or understand the importance of each one of my experiences. I do expect that he or she might confront similar issues or situations reflectively in action or in the future (Schon, 1983). I expect that he or she might gain an understanding of the complexities of teacher research in a teacher education program and how it can impact the collaborative lives of those engaged deeply in it. If this book connects and spurs thought, reflection, and possibly action in the reader, as well as in the lives of the authors, then this effort will have accomplished much.

I suppose, in retrospect, that it is a bit risky to take this bent and to subsequently admit mistakes and pinpoint where others may have gone wrong, too. Academic types tend to pursue success by reporting about success. I'm not altogether above this approach, but I happen to think that our failures and mistakes have something to teach us as well. Although I by no means consider myself a failure—in fact, I think our first year together in the program turned out quite well—I did make mistakes. I don't want to write a whiny book about only all the silly and mean things I dished out and encountered, although some of that might show up here, and I tried not to complain too much. It is from this honest looking at self and other, though, that we might approach understanding.

Third, I want this volume to serve as a living, evolving example of how much we can learn from conducting inquiry on our practice. The prospective teachers (successful, practicing teachers in the field now) who participated in the fifth-year program this past year and whose lives, research, and writing appear here as central parts of the text are living examples of how much growth, introspection, and reflection can affect the development of self as teacher. In turn, their learning has inspired me to continue on with my own inquiry and lifelong learning agenda. I grew leaps and bounds from my interactions with them and from this effort.

The interns' unflagging attempts at helping me to see the point, get it right, adjust, negotiate, and shape experiences so that these shifts or transformations, in turn, foster improvement in teaching and in understanding the complexities of school culture, teachers, students, and curriculum constitute the dialectic of teaching in which I am so fond of participating. Their work as inquirers in the field during their intern teaching experience has much to teach us. I hope that you enjoy looking at their work, their lives, and their thoughtful reflections as much as I have. Students are a key to understanding what we as mentors and teacher educators are doing. Funny that we spend little time listening to their voices in typical educational research attempts or in school reform efforts. I won't commit this mistake. I intend to listen to them and present them here to you as honestly as I can (Erickson & Shultz, 1992; Goodlad, 1979; Soohoo, 1993).

Fourth, I address the movement of teacher inquiry in the field of teacher education by showing an example of how inquiry as a learning tool is working in the field. I intend for this book to delineate some of the paths toward connecting the study of theory in education with the practice of teaching. I firmly believe that one of the responsibilities that teacher educators have, among many, is to help our prospective teachers to become inquirers and generators of knowledge (Boomer, 1987; Hollingsworth & Sockett, 1994; Rudduck, 1985). It is no longer okay, or even reasonable, to make attempts at educating teachers without asking prospective teachers to learn and to inquire about teaching in their coursework on teaching and in their practice of teaching.

We have a moral responsibility as teacher educators, teachers, students, and citizens, given the changing nature of knowledge in the world both in type and in quantity, to help our teachers understand and generate knowledge in order to empower them as human beings and as professionals. To fill our teachers with the supposed knowledge of teaching without asking them to reflect on practice, or study their practices or school cultures, is to treat them as mechanics of teaching and not as artists or craftspersons of teaching. The empty container approach to filling up future practitioners with recipes for good teaching will continue the stagnation of our schools' classrooms: We can ill afford more generations of teachers and students who cannot understand information, use it, or generate knowledge. We have little hope of seeing our communities and schools become stronger without good teachers and good citizens. Therefore, prospective teachers must interact intimately in the process of defining self, teaching, and school if we are to have a quality cadre of teachers and administrators in our nation's schools. One way to start down this path is to encourage a culture of inquiry among teachers.

By extension, students of tomorrow must be able to both inquire and know so that they can become civilized members of our democracy and participate in its institutions and economy. Our prospective teachers must become lifelong learners and be inspired to affect their own students with the passion of lifelong learning (Overly, 1979). Inquiry is one direction toward these lofty goals. To ask questions; to talk to people, students, teachers, and parents; to observe; to reflect; and to write—these are the things we are asking our interns to do in their field experience and for a major portion of their coursework. I hope they continue to inquire as teachers, keep a continuous journal of their experiences, meet in groups to study and solve school problems, and shape new agendas as they define themselves through experiences in schools. I hope their own students will inquire in their future classes. So much depends on movement in this direction (Teitelbaum & Britzman, 1991).

What we are seeking to do by introducing an inquiry component in this teacher education program is to help students of teaching build their own theories of teaching and practice that will begin and guide their long careers as reflective teachers. This step, past seeing a teacher education program as "training" for a mechanical career in teaching, requires that students of teaching consider an alternative epistemology that places their "knowing-in-action" as the primary source for their knowledge and ability in teaching (Schon, 1983). To maintain the dominant "trickle down" view of the relationship between theory and practice, wherein academics dictate the current state of theory and practice to teachers in the field, is to continue to devalue the potential for teachers themselves to generate knowledge about teaching, learning, and schooling and to share that knowledge in public forums (Cochran-Smith & Lytle, 1990; Hollingsworth, 1990; Hollingsworth & Sockett, 1994; Rudduck, 1985).

REALITIES

So what am I really doing here and who am I, anyway? In order for you to have some inkling of where I'm coming from, I think we have to go back to sixth grade, at least. I know that's pretty far back. But come along with me just for a moment to sixth grade and to Bunker Hill School in St. Marys, Ohio.

The year would be 1974 (dating me too young for many current teacher educators and too old for most students of teaching—a veritable "no person's land" in terms of voice, but I will continue on), in rural America, a small city with agriculture and industry and church and school at its base, with a good heart and tradition. Things seem to stay the same; change is slow. St. Marys is in the middle of the nation's breadbasket, where farmers, machinists, nurses, teachers, lawyers, doctors, and homemakers have equal footing most of the time and at least stand on the same ground. Astronaut Neil Armstrong lived in St. Marys and went to school there for 3 years of his childhood before settling with his family in Wapakoneta, just down the road. He went to the moon, remember? No small step. The county went for Kennedy in 1960, but mostly for Republicans before and since. The town is mostly White. It supports its schools and teachers and sometimes reveres them both. The kids are smart and often dream of college.

Bunker Hill had six grades, one class each, and a morning and afternoon kindergarten (the school was shut down in the late 1970s for one year and then reopened later as a full-day kindergarten for the whole city). Things have been done the same ways here for years and the teachers don't change much. They stay on or pass away. Students sit in desks in rows and learn to read and write and play on the playground. The changes in seasons and the passing of years are welcomed and appreciated. Tackle football on gravel, space launch watches in the basement, wiffle ball, filmstrips, marbles, Halloween masks, Pilgrim hats, Santa suits, continuous-flow water fountains, recess, chocolate Easter bunnies, and rough green wide-ruled paper and fat pencils marked the passing of years in the senses and memory. Several other things stick out in my mind, such as learning to read in Miss Conner's first-grade class, and chipping my tooth running from first to second base when Rick Langhorn jumped up for a ball and then landed on my head. Ouch! And Sonny Glinden tearing his forearm open climbing over the school's jagged fence top after a ball, and then not even crying as his arm lay limp at his side. Hitting second grade and being able to ride my bike to school. Big time. Some pain, but not much, and lots of joy (Poetter, 1994a).

Yes, childhood was good to me. And Bunker Hill was good to me. Then came Mr. Andrews, and the world opened up the wider possibilities of goodness and learning. Mr. Andrews became my sixth-grade teacher in 1974. Mr. Andrews tried so many new things as a teacher. He gave us chances that had rarely been presented before. He taught us photography and we took pictures and developed them in school. We created and wrote scripts for movies in groups, shot the films, and showed them as part of our coursework. We formed teams for street hockey, touch football, and wiffle ball games after school, the first elementary intramurals in town. We did science projects where we decided on a topic and then researched the problem. Wait! Go back! There it is!!!

School had come alive in that science experience in sixth grade with Mr. Andrews. He, like all of my best teachers before, asked me to decide for myself what to look at and then gave me the tools and the guidance to shape questions, study, and report the results of my own work. How novel—the seeds of inquiry had been planted in me and in us as a class. I had become an inquirer and I had fun doing the project. Mr. Andrews and others believed that we had something to learn and something to say. He did not just take it on himself to fill us up with facts. He let us find and create knowledge on our own. Learning became very exciting when I had the chance to inquire about a problem or a subject. I must admit, however, that I had few teachers after Mr. Andrews who encouraged open inquiry, all the way through graduate school! I determined, however, despite the seeming gaps, to be a learner and teacher who inquired and encouraged inquiry.

It's hard to estimate just how strongly these conceptions of self and knowledge and learning can take hold of us. I can't separate myself from the memories of sixth grade and their positive value for shaping who I am. I think who I have become as a teacher and person is a good thing, and I owe so much of that to those who have encouraged me to think and study on my own, from my parents to teachers all the way through. These foundations are the roots of the thoughts and actions that played out this past year in my first attempt at educating teachers. I never told my students the story of Mr. Andrews, and I wish I had. What I did tell them about my passion for inquiry actually resides several steps removed from sixth grade and Mr. Andrews, but it is no less related and governing for me.

I told them of my dissertation study, and its rather out-of-the-ordinary focus on students' perceptions of their educational experiences as members of an intercollegiate women's volleyball team (Poetter, 1994b). This was not a study of volleyball, per se, but a study of the meaning that students make of their educational and curricular experiences in a particular context. Some have called for more inquiry in the area of student perceptions of curriculum including Goodlad (1979) and Erickson and Shultz (1992). I followed their calls and built the dissertation and my learning from them and on my own hopes of studying further how and what it is that students take away and make from curricular experiences. Therefore, by extension, I wanted the interns as students of teaching to study their own experience and I wanted to participate in that study as well, interpreting their stories of conducting inquiry and becoming teachers along the way.

Also, when making the case for inquiry in one of our first meetings together last fall, I told our interns about the influence on my life and thinking of Elliot Eisner (1985) and his book *The Educational Imagination*. Eisner's arguments for encouraging connoisseurship and criticism among students in teaching and curriculum-making activities profoundly influenced me as a student and scholar. His theoretical framework for understanding educational phenomena and for conducting inquiry shaped my perceptions of what I had been doing and been hoping to do in my attempts at inquiry. I have at times held Eisner close like some estranged but purposeful wanderer might somehow clutch Salinger's (1951) *Catcher in the Rye*. It may be time in the near future to move past this, but for now Eisner's work connects with, and continues to inspire me in the direction of advocating inquiry as a way of being for me and for my students.

I hoped to understand things such as educational scenes, events, lessons, papers, and people by appreciating their qualities as an educational connoisseur and interpreting them as an educational critic. The leap to educational critic comes when one reveals the perceptions of things experienced in educational scenes. Eisner (1985) states it better when he noted the distinction between educational connoisseurship and educational criticism:

> The major distinction between connoisseurship and criticism is this: connoisseurship is the art of appreciation, criticism is the art of disclosure. Connoisseurship is a private act; it consists of recognizing and appreciating the qualities of a particular, but it does not require either a public judgment or a public description of those qualities. . . . Criticism is the art of disclosing the qualities of events or objects that connoisseurship perceives. Criticism is the public side of connoisseurship. One can be a connoisseur without the skills of criticism, but one cannot be a critic without the skills of connoisseurship. (pp. 221–223)

Eisner's book opens the world up to prospective teachers seeking to understand themselves and the field better by studying teaching and learning and curriculum-making in particular classroom scenes, and actually empowers them by including in his book the work of his own students as connoisseurs and critics of educational scenes! His students model the type of work and intellectual growth that can come from the experience of inquiry. When I first saw these chapters of student writing, I knew that someday students in my classes would do high quality work, and that their writing would inform the field of teacher education by serving as examples of inquiry-in-action (See especially Porro, 1985). I knew that my students would be empowered by understanding and interpreting the qualities of the things they saw and experienced as prospective teachers. Their experiences might affect a new way of being, and foster a lifetime of inquiry into practice and context that would inform their teaching and learning as teachers.

I came on strong with the interns last fall. Having just completed what turned out to be a life-changing experience, writing a dissertation, I felt compelled to encourage others to find their eyes, ears, hearts, minds, and voices through inquiry. Although I did not fight my committee chair to the end for the opportunity to tell my own complete story in my dissertation (knowing his graciousness and care, he was probably leaving room for me to grow into the discipline of telling a story in a more narrative frame), I found the confidence and the ability in my experience as a fledgling scholar and writer and as teacher, nevertheless, to spur interest and action in the interns. I didn't expect interns to do a dissertation, or to be prolific and profound writers, or to become professional educational researchers, but I knew they could approach what Eisner's students had done and could grow immensely from the experience. They could begin to find their own voices for shaping their own and others' practice throughout their teaching careers. So, I plowed ahead with plans to help our students shape qualitative research projects for their first semester of the internship while they worked in school and in the Pedagogics class. This setup has always been inevitable, as you and my students now well know, and the context was right for its implementation. At least we thought it was.

Notable others have made attempts at implementing inquiry components in teacher preparation programs, as well as at describing and interpreting them. The use of teacher research in teacher education is not a new phenomenon, though it has been little studied or understood until most recently. The tradition of teacher research as a component in teacher education emerged from two sources: (a) Social psychologist Kurt Lewin (1948), whose groundbreaking work in the 1940s with groups of school teachers and others was designed "to find ways to involve social actors with researchers through group decision making and elaborate problem-solving procedures as ways of implementing social and cultural changes" (Hollingsworth & Sockett, 1994, p. 3); and (b) John Dewey, whose life and work, in part, emphasized "the importance of teachers' reflecting on their practices and integrating their observations into their emerging theories of teaching and learning" (Cochran-Smith & Lytle, 1990, p. 4).

In the 1950s, Stephen Corey (1953) and colleagues at Teachers College, Columbia University, began action research projects with teachers out of the Lewin tradition under the assumption that teachers would use the results of their own investigations to bring about social reconstruction (Hollingsworth & Sockett, 1994). Hilda Taba's intergroup education projects engaged schools in a form of action research out of the Deweyan tradition "in the belief that not only could such involvement improve teachers' own practices, but that research findings would then pragmatically contribute to general theoretical knowledge" (Hollingsworth & Sockett, 1994, p. 3–4).

By the late 1950s, teacher research had found its way into teacher education programs (Beckman, 1957; Perrodin, 1959), but any momentum gained for the use of teacher research in preservice teacher education quietly faded. Hollingsworth and Sockett (1994) attributed the lack of staying power for the movement toward teacher research to two problems: the judgment of the output of teacher projects on conventional research criteria and the controlled participation demanded by Lewin's social model, which many teachers resisted. As well, a post-Sputnik conventional wisdom focused attention and resources on "discipline-based curriculum programs and (a) government sponsored research, development, and dissemination model of educational innovation" (Hollingsworth & Sockett, p. 4). Research and practice were again viewed by discipline-based academics and educational researchers as separate entities, and their high profile, expensive interventions bypassed and overshadowed the agendas of progressive reformers (p. 4).

By the late 1960s and 1970s, an energy for collaborative teacher research that focused on teacher professionalization emerged from Britain in the work of Lawrence Stenhouse and John Elliott (Cochran-Smith & Lytle, 1990). The goal of the Center for Applied Research in Education at the University of East Anglia, founded by Stenhouse and his colleagues, was to "demystify and democratize research, which was seen as failing to contribute effectively to the growth of professional understanding and to the improvement of professional practice" (Stenhouse, cited in Cochran-Smith & Lytle, 1990, p. 3). Stenhouse and colleagues "encouraged teachers to become intimately involved in the research process. They believed that through their own research, teachers could strengthen their judgment and improve their classroom practices" (p. 3). Stenhouse claimed that research was the route to teacher emancipation, and that "researchers [should] justify themselves to practitioners, not practitioners to researchers" (p. 4).

This influential movement in teacher research took root and flourished in Britain and in the United States, for example, in the work of Patricia Carini and her teacher colleagues at the Prospect Center and School in Bennington, Vermont, and of Vito Perrone and teachers for the North Dakota Study Group on Evaluation (Cochran-Smith & Lytle, 1990). Both movements empowered teachers and moved the field toward sound conceptualizations of teacher-based theory, knowledge, and practical action. But the use and implications of teacher research for teacher education remained mostly untapped through the 1970s. Donald Schon's *The Reflective Practitioner* (1983) proved itself a source around which educators in the United States could rally, moving the profound innovation of the epistemological position of knowing-in-action to an honored and legitimate status in many camps (Hollingsworth & Sockett, 1994). Throughout the 1980s and 1990s, more articles, books, and programs of teacher research came into being and flourished (Cochran-Smith & Lytle, 1993; Fleischer, 1995; Goswami & Stillman, 1987; Hollingsworth, 1994).

By the early 1980s, teacher educators and their accounts of the use of teacher research in teacher preparation programs began to spring up. Gitlin and Teitelbaum (1983) wrote one of the earliest, most lucid, and persuasive explanations of the use of "mini-ethnography" with student teachers. They proposed and reported out about the use of ethnographic inquiry by preservice teachers as part of their undergraduate teacher training experiences, and specifically about its use during the student-teaching practicum by their own students. Their argument stands opposed to the "apprenticeship perspective"—dominant in most teacher-training programs and lamented by the likes of Dewey—that is focused on giving "teachers in training working command of the necessary tools of their profession; control of the techniques of class instruction and management; and skill and proficiency in the work of teaching" (Dewey, cited in Gitlin & Teitelbaum, 1983, p. 226).

An apprenticeship approach to teacher education as the focus, although necessary in teacher preparation programs to some degree, tends to foster a primary concern for "facilitating present school conditions" and for carrying out "currently held explicit and implicit goals" (Gitlin & Teitelbaum, 1983, p. 226). As is often the result in the apprenticeship mode, the goals of the university and of the school are divorced in terms of the relationship between theory and practice. In contrast to the widening gaps between theory and practice in educational programs that foster mechanical approaches and distance prospective teachers from mindful practice, the use of qualitative research by prospective teachers is:

> One strategy that allows for a linkage of theory and practice. Students consider hypotheses as they apply to observations of actual practice and utilize these observations of practice to formulate hypotheses. They systematically view school practice at the same time that . . . they are becoming more aware of the range of educational aims and of educational research. Conducting small-scale, modified ethnographies of their own can enable these future teachers to become sensitive to the process of schooling in a far more fruitful way than is usually the case in teacher education programs. (Gitlin & Teitelbaum, 1983, p. 226)

Gitlin and Teitelbaum (1983) continued, and expressed the specific processes of the inquiry experience and how those processes may potentially help connect prospective teachers' growing conceptions of educational theory with classroom practice:

By encouraging prospective teachers to 1) systematically observe school and classroom practice; 2) "step back" from these observations and "utilize" their university instruction and other sources of relevant knowledge to consider why particular schooling practices occur and their educational (and ethical) implications; and 3) present this study in a coherent written form so that it can be read and discussed by others at the university and in the schools; "doing ethnography" enables these students in teacher education programs to more concretely and directly link theory and practice. Through such an experience it is hoped that these future teachers will become more acutely sensitive to the fact that even the most mundane classroom activities (the practice that they observe) reflect particular educational and political commitments and perspectives (the theory that they learn at the university and elsewhere), and vice versa. The intent is to impress upon the student the need to become more than a mere "technician" as a teacher and to develop a more reflective perspective toward classroom teaching. (p. 230)

I responded to Gitlin and Teitelbaum's (1983) stirring, concluding call by seeking ways to implement inquiry projects in our teacher education program:

We need to provide strategies by which our student teachers can take a more active role in "extraordinarily re-experiencing the ordinary," (Shor, 1980) in making visible the widespread and powerful "hidden dimensions" of schooling and their relationship to the present socio-cultural system, and in becoming the kind of reflective, questioning, investigative and flexible teachers that a viable democratic culture demands. (p. 233)

Gitlin and teaching partner Bullough (1995) recently published *Becoming a Student of Teaching*, which more extensively lays out the philosophical and practical frameworks for prospective teacher inquiry in their work with students at the University of Utah. Whereas Gitlin's earlier work with Teitelbaum (1983) downplays the possibility of students' writing for publication and achieving voice with a wider audience beyond the self and school context, *Becoming a Student of Teaching* actually includes several writings of prospective teachers and an exposition about their lives and growth as teachers in connecting theory and practice through inquiry. Our work here also focuses on the use of qualitative research in a variety of forms (namely action research and qualitative criticism), but it is different from *Becoming a Student of Teaching* in its primary foci on the interns' written reports and their perceptions of the experience of conducting inquiry. These foci comprise the center of this work, as opposed to Gitlin and Bullough's focus on an explication of different qualitative methodologies for use in a teacher education program.

Other contemporary scholars laid out their approaches to inquiry in teacher education. Rudduck (1985) skillfully called for a research-based teacher education that pushes the fledgling teacher "to lay a foundation for lifelong professionalism . . . the capacity of a teacher to continue to develop his or her art as a teacher" (p. 288). By making their work public, teachers can affect an "opening up of the established research tradition and the democratization of the research community" (p. 282). Furthermore, by making a commitment to teacher research, teachers gain: (a) "a way of structuring a familiar situation that allows the teacher to explore it in depth, gain new insights, set new goals and achieve new levels of competence and confidence" (p. 283); and (b) "a sense of professional excitement that can draw attention back to the professional core of schooling—the mutuality of teaching and learning as an interactive process" (p. 283). These personal takeaways from joining the researcher's and practitioner's perspective together have the potential for transforming the teacher and the profession of teaching by allowing for further understanding of the teacher's art.

Cochran-Smith (1994) extended Rudduck's focus on the primarily personal affects of teacher research. The power of teacher research, she said, "can only be regarded in terms of its value as a vehicle to help student teachers develop a stance—that is, a way of positioning themselves as prospective teachers (and eventually across the professional lifespan) in relation to (a) knowledge (i.e., their positions as generators as well as users of knowledge for and about teaching), (b) agency, (i.e., their positions as activists and agents for school and social change), and (c) collaboration (i.e., their positions as professional colleagues in relation to other teachers, to administrators, and policymakers, and to their own students)" (pp. 151–152). She clarified that "what it means for new teachers to use research as a basis for teaching, then, is a question that can only be answered in particular local contexts" (p. 152). It is my hope that this text illuminates how knowledge, agency, and collaboration were affected by the use of teacher research in context.

Zeichner and Gore (1995) reached past the personal or developmental uses of teacher research in teacher education, past Cochran-Smith's notion of "agency," in stressing a critical approach to reflective practice and research that focuses on "the social and the political context of schooling and the assessment of classroom actions for their ability to contribute toward greater equity, social justice, and humane conditions in schooling and society" (Beyer, cited in Zeichner & Gore, 1995, p. 16). They said that teacher research should take on a critical approach that is social reconstructionist because, according to their experience, "the 'critical' is embedded in the very essence of the student teacher's classroom reality. The problem is one of helping student teachers develop the dispositions and capabilities to see and act upon the connections between the classroom and the social and political contexts in which it is embedded" (p. 20). They lamented that, in most attempts in the United States, "reflection is often encouraged as an end in itself and as a purely individual activity unconnected to any democratic educational and/or political project" (p. 16).

The framework that best fits my conception of the use of teacher research in teacher education, and the one that has operated in this local context for this project, rests more closely with the personal approach than with the critical approach, although we address issues of race, class, gender, equity, social justice, and humanity in our work with intern researchers in our teacher education curriculum in a variety of ways including readings, debriefings, participation in school reform initiatives, and classroom discussions. Although several of the interns' chapters here deal directly with critical issues and the research component is an excellent avenue for revealing the embedded "critical," the worth of their research work does not depend on focusing on the critical. More important for this curricular component are the potential connections drawn by the intern between educational theory and research and classroom practice and the increased understanding of the self as teacher and professional.

FUTURES

I ran the higher education job-search gauntlet in the spring of 1994, had my dissertation in hand and wanted to get back to full-time teaching, this time at the college level. I didn't have much choice, anyway, because wife Chris gave me 3 years to complete the doctoral coursework and writing; then I had to go back to work. That was the deal, we had agreed to it, and so, it got done. So many doctoral students never complete the dissertation, I know; I am fortunate to have had both external and internal motivations working in my life. Besides, young Mitchell was on the way and we thought he needed a working daddy.

I missed teaching while I pursued graduate work, though I worked as a student teaching supervisor for my doctoral alma mater and stayed connected with students and teaching as a result. But I felt eager to get out there; nothing I ever did as a supervisor gave me that good feeling of fatigue like teaching a great lesson all day. It just wasn't "full-time-ish" enough. I knew that my pathway into academia would be through the field of teacher education. I didn't feel relegated to teacher education, but instead felt called to follow the path into it. No delusions about landing a position on the first crack as a teacher of curriculum in a graduate program ever creeped into my head. Besides, I didn't want to be distanced from schools and teachers. The gatekeeper for positions on faculties of education is teacher education. That is a fact. So I went there, not unwillingly and, in fact, probably intending to stay. I view work in teacher education as a calling, a most rewarding venture.

About 80 applications passed in and out of my little "application factory" back home in Indiana to prospective employers all over the United States. Three schools called and all offered me jobs after interviews. Some called this great, "three-for-three." I knew, however, that it was "3-for-80." I took the job at Trinity because I believed in what it was doing in its fifth-year program, educating teachers over a 5-year timeframe and focusing on an extensive field component during a year-long internship. The quality of students and the beauty of the campus and city didn't hurt either. I felt up to the adventure after sitting in an office studying and writing for 3 years (I had pulled a similar 3-year stint, although more lonely than the doctorate, toward my master's degree at Princeton Theological Seminary), and Chris was impressed by the city and the job. We had made the transition in our lives from Buckeyes to Hoosiers with little trauma. From Hoosiers to Tigers? Why not?

All this aside, the determining factor for Trinity, as opposed to the other two jobs offered, had to be the insistence of the faculty and the students that I meet with students and mentor teachers and spend time with them during the interview process. The two other schools I interviewed with, both in session at the time of the interviews, never introduced me to one student or one school teacher, even when I insisted that they do so. Also, during my interview with Trinity, I had closed-door meetings with students, meetings planned by the search committee before I ever made my wishes for meeting students known to them. Also, I was introduced to several key mentors from our Alliance schools who gave me insights concerning the job ahead.

Were the other schools embarrassed by their students? Were they reluc-tant to leave me alone with them, scared of what they might say or tell? Did the faculty in charge of the interviews just not want to put the time in for recruiting students and teachers for me to meet? I'll never know, nor do I care to know now, but I learned how much responsibility and talent the Trinity students have because I got to know them during my short visit. I wanted to work with them, and have never lost sight of this experience in my interactions with them since. They deserve my best efforts, my care, and understanding at all times. They are good, they are inspiring, and they are committed to becoming and staying great teachers in the field.

I signed a contract and began planning our move to Texas in August. Chris and I sold the house in Indiana, I defended my dissertation, had the baby (she did that), graduated, stayed up with a crying Mitchell night after night (Chris did most of that, too), took care of Mitchell when Chris went back to work (I did that), packed the house, moved, and did a lot of other stuff in between. I don't think we ever experienced a more hectic time in our lives. Friends continued to warn us about stress throughout, and how the things we were experiencing together ranked up there in some other PhD's top 10 list of marriage-breakers—getting and using a higher degree, finding and starting a new job, having and raising a baby, selling and buying a house, and moving. But Chris and I and Mitchell stayed together, and found excitement in our trials and new experiences together. After all, we were healthy and didn't want for much. Yes, this was fun.

As I mentioned earlier, Dr. Van Zandt and I had been communicating about the new class, but we hadn't heard much about starting dates for the interns' clinical assignments in the schools, or when orientation started, or when school started. In all honesty, I was mostly trying to keep my life together, at home and on the road. When I pulled out of our Indiana driveway on August 1 with my father-in-law (thank goodness we had the sense to have Mitchell and Chris fly down the next week—sorry if I disrupted your growing pioneer image of the family), and drove a U-Haul truck packed to the gills with our junk, in all honesty making it through the 3-day trip became job one. I pulled several scary stunts while driving the 30-foot truck with our car trailing at the back, such as pulling a U-turn on a two-way road, getting stuck and then backing and rocking my way out (heaven only knows how), and nearly scraping every restaurant, hotel, and gas station sign along our path for 1,000 miles and more. Despite all this, my father-in-law and I, although he continued to spend time wondering why his daughter married someone with so little common sense, remained friends (I think I provide good comic relief in his life), and, yes, we made it and students were there to greet us. Wouldn't you know?

Our meeting and talking and unpacking together dumped me into a new reality very quickly. These new interns wanted to know who I was, what to expect, and if I had any answers. "When do we start? What do we do?", they asked. I could only reply, "I don't know, I'll check it out." This began a year-long adventure of trying to find out the basic answers to the most basic questions: What? When? Where? Why? How? It rained all day as we unpacked the truck and grew tired together. I felt as though I knew these several new interns rather well after that first day of moving. The joy ride didn't last very long.

The first day of orientation for teachers began early the next week. All interns and clinical faculty were expected to be on hand to participate in the program from the very beginning of school. Dr. Van Zandt and I decided that we would start our classes for interns early, before the official opening of classes (scheduled for approximately 2 weeks after the opening of the local schools), so that we could introduce the interns to the research project and get them started on their journal writing in the crucial opening days of school when so many things would happen to them. We wanted interns to have a chance to record these once-in-a-lifetime events so that they could serve as building blocks for coming up with a topic and for starting their database of observations and reflections, in general. We thought we were doing them a favor by starting early.

We met with a firestorm of controversy with these four early seminars, scheduled to meet twice a week for 2 weeks before the university officially opened for class meetings. We had permission from the department chair to go ahead with our early meetings. He said, "Why are you asking me? You're the professors." We appreciated the support and freedom from the very beginning; in fact, these were crucial factors, ultimately, that helped make us successful in our work the first year. But the support and freedom didn't mean that we wouldn't meet opposition, which we did, from both our interns and their mentors.

The interns argued that the meetings overwhelmed them at the beginning, that time was too short for just trying to get used to the time demands and rigors of the school day even without the seminars. Their understanding of the program and what it was about, in total, was challenged by the very notion of inquiry and a substantive academic component. They argued that the research component would take away from the real focus of the program on the clinical, on the practical, and on the doing of teaching. They felt shocked, angered, and betrayed by the meetings, the research requirement, and by us. They were surprised, and so were we.

The mentors, though not overtly so at the beginning, were overwhelmed as well. Here was a new component they had no hand in shaping that would substantively alter their interactions with their interns and colleagues. They felt underprepared, nervous, and unsure about what we were trying to do. Some didn't value any academic component at all in the program and would rather have seen us chuck the coursework altogether and simply make learning to teach a training exercise, an apprenticeship. I am fundamentally opposed to this position because it fosters mimicry, even modeling, as a major tool for teacher training. This is the opposite of teacher education, wherein a person experiences teaching, but defines the self and school culture on his or her own terms and pace, beyond the modeling of even outstanding practice. My viewpoints ruffled others, and who was I anyway? Just some kid with comparitively little teaching experience, trying to change everything all at once. Bad rap?

I suppose that Dr. Van Zandt and I didn't expect our charges and our colleagues to react this way. We assumed that we were to make the syllabus for the coursework and that our students would trust us and do what we wanted them to do because these things would enhance their teaching and professional development. After all, we trusted and respected our college teachers and did what we were asked to do, whether we agreed that it was valuable, I guess, in the spirit of compliance or maybe in fear of a bad grade or disappointing the teacher and hurting our chances for achievement. Our approach wasn't very democratic, nor very sensitive, but that's the way we were raised and the way we lived our lives in school; we did not encounter a similar attitude in our students or teacher colleagues.

Of course, this scenario of resistance is so often the case for beginning teachers, as our interns soon found out, when their own students sometimes balked at doing what they wanted them to do. We, like them, had to adjust our thinking to understand our students and their teachers while still holding our philosophical grounds. This book is in part the story of our transformations and stultifications in thought and practice given this cultural milieu of resistance, misunderstanding, and reconciliation. Chapter 2 lays out the journey we took together during the year through the recesses of resistance and the heights of excitement and expectation, especially as these points related to the inquiry projects our students conducted and to all of us as human beings, inquirers, teachers, students, and teacher educators growing in our lives and work together.

2

From Resistance to Excitement[*]

૮ક ◆ ৪০

NARRATIVE SKETCH

"Stories function as arguments in which we learn something essentially human by understanding an actual life or community as lived." (Connelly & Clandinin, 1990, p. 8)

The year-long internship in teaching program consists of 6 hours of summer coursework; 6 hours of Pedagogics and 6 hours of Clinical Practice in the fall; 3 hours of School Leadership in Education and 9 hours of Clinical Practice in the spring. The fall and spring semesters' clinical components require a full-time placement with a mentor teacher in a public school classroom. The fall serves as an introductory and transitional experience to full-time teaching in the spring. The Pedagogics class and the clinical classroom placement represent an opportunity to help interns build the bridges between theory and practice necessary for a successful full-time teaching experience and, by extension, a long professional career in teaching.

During the interview process for the job, I took pleasure in listening to the interns' and mentors' stories and tried out my ideas on them. Understanding that without a university liaison in place during the past academic year, the curriculum for the fall Pedagogics class had become disjointed, I tested the waters at an interview luncheon, saying, "Someday I want to have interns and mentors do qualitative research projects as a means for helping interns make connections between theory, research, and practice in education." Positive feedback followed from the interns and mentors present. But they must have thought, "He surely won't follow through. It's too early to worry. He may not even get the job."

But, as you know, I did get the job, and Dr. Van Zandt and I soon began planning to implement an inquiry component for the Pedagogics class in the

*Thank you to the Editors of *Teaching Education* who graciously allowed the authors to use the previously published article "From Resistance to Excitement in a Teacher Education Program: Becoming Qualitative Researchers and Reflective Practitioners," which first appeared in the Fall/Winter issue, 1996, as the springboard for chapter 2, "From Resistance to Excitement."

fall. We shared an initial draft of our course outline with members of the education faculty in the summer. Our colleagues said that we were going in the right direction; our plan looked good.

Laura and I assumed that our interns and mentor teachers would go along with our new syllabus and focus on cases and qualitative research without question. After all, we were the professors, and we assumed that all parties shared the goal our department chair had for us and the program as a whole, that is, shoring up the academic component of the program. In Laura's case, the middle school interns and their mentors wholeheartedly accepted the challenge of the inquiry projects. In a sense then, Laura becomes less of a player in this story, though she acted as Sherry Hughes' supervisor, whose story is included here. But, in my case, the high school interns and mentors did not accept the challenge at the beginning. In retrospect, I have never been so wrong, or found myself so completely in the dark in terms of not anticipating potential problems.

I had not sought input from school colleagues regarding how they thought a research component would or would not work, and what it might look like and meant for the fifth-year experience in toto. The grounds for change were my own convictions and comments made after an interview luncheon with interns and mentors who weren't even around anymore—not the stuff of a negotiated, meaningful curriculum in this or any case.

Resistance to the qualitative research component by interns and mentors—buoyed by feelings of terror, anger, and disillusionment—marked the first weeks of our time working with the cohort during August and some very important points thereafter. Interns and their mentors thought that we were unfairly changing the program by requiring a component that would, according to their sensibilities, shift the focus from immersion in clinical practice to immersion in research. Our most vocal interns and mentors let us know how upset they were. The mentors wondered, now that they were being heard, if I could be shipped back to Indiana. After all, the mentors held the program together for an entire academic year while the university searched for a person to act as liaison. They had voice and they did not intend to lose it.

The title of this chapter comes from a discussion I had with intern Chelsea Caivano in November. I asked her, "How do the interns perceive the research project now that it is well underway?" She said, "It's been like two stages, from resistance at the beginning, to excitement about doing the project. I think everyone is excited about it now."

WITH REGARD TO METHOD

Because our first meeting of the school year focused on establishing a methodology for doing qualitative research of teaching and learning in schools, I informed the interns that I would model good form by performing my own qualitative inquiry during the first semester. I proposed to study my own, as well as their perceptions of doing a qualitative research project as a major component of the course and internship. I intended for this study and my writing to model a disciplined, reflective inquiry that could be shared with interns and mentors.

I received intern consent to collect data having to do with their perceptions of conducting the research project. Interns permitted my access to: (a) intern journal entries; (b) interview transcripts from informal discussions with individual interns or intern groups, and from taped, open-ended interviews with individual interns; and (c) intern artifacts such as lesson plans, observation notes, and student work. I also kept a running journal, just as interns did as part of their coursework assignment, which included observation notes from my experiences in the field, as well as reflections on my experience of conducting the inquiry.

I attempted to render the scene, to relate the qualities of it, and to interpret those qualities and their importance for this teacher education context (Eisner, 1985). Of course, certain risks come with writing up one's own backyard scene (Glesne & Peshkin, 1992), but the risks are outweighed by how an honest rendering of the scene might act as a stimulus for shared understanding and knowledge among participants and those interested in the notion of reflective teacher education and how teacher research is connected to reflective practice.

It was difficult to choose the authors and the papers that share this text with me (I chose 5 of 13). I often wished I didn't have to choose—each research endeavor and each paper among the cohort of students involved in the internship had something special and unique to offer and was worthy of being chosen for this endeavor. The fact that these students wrote sound studies wasn't the only subjective ground I used to choose them as respondents and participants for this final write-up. Others wrote good papers, too, and maybe even better ones, and weren't selected.

In general, I think the group here represents the range in reaction to the research project from extensive resistance, for instance on the part of Jennifer, to utter commitment, for instance on the part of Shawn. Their work looks at teaching and curriculum, at students and schooling, from varying perspectives and purposes. Heidi paints a picture of classroom scenes where females may not be getting the kind of instruction and attention they deserve. Chelsea tells about the struggles of curriculum-making from the ground up and shows herself in action as a teacher, testing her own ideas and practices with students. And Sherry examines the "at-risk" student and his or her perceptions of teachers and good teaching. You may notice that all of the respondents are women. Eleven of the 14 cohort members were women. I had no bias against the men in our group, nor any bias for the women for that matter. I do know that all of their voices are strong and that

their experiences have taught me much about teaching and teacher education. I hope the same holds for you as reader as you venture on from here.

RESISTANCE

I hate this [bleep]-ing program. If I had wanted to be a scholar, I would have gone on
to get my PhD. I entered the MAT program because I wanted to spend this year
becoming the best teacher I can be. Now all of that has changed and I am totally
unprepared. Nice of the new profs to show up the week school starts to dump all of
this on us. I can't believe they are changing the entire program, everything I expected,
after we've already begun. (Jennifer, journal)

Frankly, I don't care about spending my days in the library. I would like to focus on
being the best teacher I can be, not a scholar. (Heidi, journal)

Intern and mentor resistance to the project took hold in several specific,
initial conceptions of how a research component would fundamentally
change the structure and meaning of the internship. The way the interns
and their mentors saw it, the project would take time away from what they
considered to be the most meaningful activity of the year—building a
teaching repertoire by practicing in classrooms. The mentors vocalized their
concerns in front and behind the scenes, arguing that the research component would take the focus off the "how"s of teaching. The fact is that Laura
and I also believe that the primary strength of the program lies in the
foundation of a clinical component; the twist from our perspective, however,
is that the program's overall strength depends on a strong academic component to complement the clinical. Learning about teaching and learning
to teach ought to be inextricably intertwined.

Interns and mentors peppered me with questions, disagreements, and
problems at the beginning of the fall term. But my answers carried little
weight as the interns struggled. A lack of time pressed them, squeezing them
tighter with their growing perceptions that the project loomed larger than
life. An underlying conception that teaching doesn't have to do with
scholarship, or research, or inquiry festered at the surface of our early
interactions. Little sense of intellectual curiosity pervaded the talk or writing
of the interns in the early days of the term.

After asking what the "theory part" should be about on the case study proposal, Bert
asked in all seriousness, "Does this mean I'll have to go to the library?" I saw Lynn
going into the library yesterday as I was leaving, and she said with a twist, "I'm going
to the library on *my day off.*" Instead of love and passion for learning, these teachers
may pass on to their students a feeling of oppression that comes with books and
reading. At least that's what they are passing to me. (Poetter, journal)

At the time of the interns' initial reactions to the project, I did not fully
appreciate all that they had been through in forming their conceptions of

the program. I felt disappointed that they weren't excited about the possibilities of doing their own research. So I set out to convince them that the research component fit the program better than they initially thought it did and was better than what had been done in the past. I hadn't taken into account how powerful their previous experiences were, how committed and prepared they were for the program, and how they had been psyching themselves up for what would have been a stressful and challenging year anyway, even without the research component in the class.

Three significant "turns," (Schon, 1983) or momentous events of the first term, mark the transition toward excitement about the research component. These turns give a picture of my attempts to convince everyone that a research component constituted "the right thing to do."

THE FIRST TURN: A PUPPET SHOW

After hearing initial rumblings about the project in the field, Laura and I decided that we had to put the research component into perspective. No, we weren't training students for lives as university researchers. No, we weren't expecting a thesis or dissertation. No, we didn't want the students to sacrifice the quality of their clinical experience for the case study, or vice versa. But we did want them to acquire new perspectives, and sometimes this requires a novel approach:

> I wrote, "Taking risks—Change . . . What it isn't and What it is" and "This is a dramatization" on the chalkboard. I opened by dropping to one knee. I pretended to faint. There I was, flat on my back with my eyes closed, prone, and at the mercy of the class. "Dr. Poetter? Dr. Poetter?" Dr. Van Zandt pleaded for me to awaken (she was part of the dramatization). She shook me, and I muttered, "It wasn't supposed to be like this . . . It wasn't supposed to be like this." Laughter followed. A good sign. (Poetter, journal)

We put the interns' fear of the project into perspective by drawing a comparison between the introductory chapter to my dissertation, which resembled what we thought the interns might do for their final reports in terms of length (about 20 pages), and my full dissertation (a 350-page tome). At one point, Laura was throwing the piles of my dissertation draft manuscripts at me like they were live snakes (more laughter followed when I broke character to protest her indiscriminate handling of the text. She, too, got a little carried away.) I kicked the texts away in fear, as if they could harm me if allowed too close. The interns didn't need to have piles of data, write a book, or handle live snakes to do the case study research project well. We could see the realizations on their faces; they could handle it.

As we took our bows, I felt as though we had connected with the interns and with this job. We had made new friends and allies, and we had gained some respect. We were willing to take risks, and to stand up for our ideas, and to make a case. The project didn't have to be a monster. (Poetter, Journal)

Heidi and Jennifer wrote that the dramatization helped ease their fears and clarified the direction and purpose of the project.

Thank you so much for the class meeting today. You really helped to clear things up for me regarding the case study. I feel more confident about myself. It is a great honor to have you two be so supportive and confident of our abilities. (Heidi, journal)

Today was a sweet day. I feel so much better about the program now. I'm sorry I overreacted. Apparently most of the big 20-page paper is going to come from our journal, so that's a relief. (Jennifer, journal)

The energy from that class period lasted a long time. It also helped build a bridge of trust between us and the interns. The success of that event made it possible for all to continue together in a spirit of active cooperation, though pockets of resistance among interns still remained.

And yet even though a sense of goodwill emerged from this event, I realized that I had resisted truly hearing the interns, that I had instead chosen to argue with them, to persuade them. In so doing, I had breached the grounds for implementing successful, deep-rooted change in a school setting. Fullan and Miles (1992) warned against "misunderstanding resistance" (p. 748), and said that a fearfulness of change and a reluctance to buy-in should be "framed as natural responses to transition, not misunderstood as 'resistance'" (p. 748). Initially, at least, I was the resistant one, pushing my own perspectives on others, and not being sensitive and open to how this change could potentially alter our interns' and mentors' experiences in school.

You see, I had it all worked out in my head. But even when others see the initial merits of the change, they may have difficulty in the transition because they don't share similar perceptions for the need for change or the potential value of the change. Fullan and Miles (1992) used Peter Morris' insights to describe the problem:

When those who have the power to manipulate changes act as if they have only to explain, and when their explanations are not at once accepted, shrug off opposition as ignorance or prejudice, they express a profound contempt for the meaning of lives other than their own. For the reformers have already assimilated these changes to their purposes, and worked out a reformulation which makes sense to them, perhaps through months or years of analysis and debate. *If they deny others the chance to do the same, they treat them as puppets dangling by the threads of their own conceptions.* (p. 749, italics added)

As puppeteer, I imposed my own set of stage directions on the experience and the parties involved. When my puppets then took on life and balked, I initially resisted the possibility of revising the assignment or dropping it all together. But how can one ask others to pour themselves into a substantive task such as a research project and not allow them at least to shape the scene? Could or would they ever take ownership of this project? Do I simply have the right to make them do what I ask them to do because of the authority long inherent to my position as professor? Is the response, "Get to work, this will be good for you," adequate, appropriate, or possible in this day and age? Does this position fit my purposes and style as teacher anyway?

After all, there were several alternative routes that we could have taken as professors at this point. We could have chucked the whole thing and designed a skills course and would have made many initial friends that way. We could have made our case for the research component and asked the group and members to decide if they wanted to participate in it. Maybe we could have offered to guide those who wanted to try it, and give an alternative course of study to those who chose not to try. We could have adjusted the assignments for the journals to reflect a more systematic viewing of action in the classroom, without guiding the students toward a traditional research focus of defining the problem and data collection procedures. Still, we could have left our first attempt, then, more open-ended, still guiding students toward a reflective activity but taking off that research edge. Maybe we could have shortened the paper (from an expected 20 pages) and our expectations for interns to interact intimately with data from the field across an extended period of time (about 10 weeks as it turned out, to say 2 or 4 weeks, for instance). There were alternatives and these and many more ran through our minds. But we decided to hold our positions—for better or worse—out of conviction and pride. In retrospect, some other option than holding firm might have made a better choice—I'm not sure.

But struggling and thinking this way helped me to recognize the need to help the interns come to terms with the project by helping them see beyond the requirement of doing the project. I would help them realize that they would be in charge of determining what it would look like and how it would help them grow as a new teacher, all this despite the reality that they hadn't chosen to get involved with it in the first place. This tension was real in all of us. The silly skit helped set the stage for getting started on the project and for seeing value in it. But the puppet show didn't solve anything; in fact, even more crucial, bitter battles would take place at later points in the semester. It wasn't long after this that I was back at odds with individuals and groups regarding the focus of the program. I sat in the hot seat answering the question, "Are we educating teachers or researchers?" My passionate frenzy for making a case for the research component extended into my working relationships with the mentors. Our problems with each other and the change came to a crescendo in late September.

THE SECOND TURN: TAKING THE GLOVES OFF

Traditionally, mentors have two meetings on the university campus each semester. The meetings are designed to provide professional development opportunities in mentoring, mainly the opportunity for mentors to debrief about their current mentoring experiences. The mentors seemed ready and excited for the meeting in late September after working with their interns for 6 weeks. It was time to meet and debrief and get some things straight with each other and with me. I tossed and turned in bed the night before, however, nervous for the day to turn out all right. I suspected that the meeting could get tense, with mentors pushing for justification and clarification of the project and program's direction.

The mentors confirmed my nervous predictions early in the meeting. I met in a small group with "new" mentors in order to clarify and support their early experiences, and "veteran" mentors met in a small group to discuss their concerns. When the groups rejoined to report out their discussions, the veteran mentors launched a list of questions and observations, reading from a long, computer generated list they had brainstormed in their short meeting. The list included the following:

> Are interns stretched, and not focusing their time and energy in the right places?
> Interns need to focus on the *how* to be a teacher!
> So what is the focus of the program? Clinical practice or academics?

I wish I could report that I came up with some clever way of addressing their concerns, perceived misconceptions, and disagreements that fostered camaraderie and understanding through the use of humor and interesting, reasoned, purposeful discourse. But I just jumped in and started arguing, clarifying positions and rationales in order to stake some ground. Sometimes you have to just throw yourself into the fray, no holds barred. That goes for both parties. Otherwise, ground will not be shared, university and school purposes will continue to be separate, or we won't understand the reasons behind those separate purposes. We can share purposes and ground and effectively educate students and teachers together. This became our first and most important chance to do so. My, how that spring interview luncheon filled with hope and goodwill seemed so long ago and far away.

I contended that there must be a balancing of and a shared commitment for both clinical practice and academic experiences among all of us in this program. The performance of inquiry projects in classrooms gives interns a unique opportunity to utilize the coursework component to inform practice. As I have stated earlier, the research project allows the intern to weave reading in the field with disciplined looking at practice. The two foci—the academic and the clinical—ought not to be mutually exclusive.

Granted, allowing time for the type of work that we want interns to do for their projects requires some flexibility and planning during the school day. In an environment where teachers already feel pressed for time, it is difficult to make the necessary adjustments for doing research. And the adjustments needed for successful completion of the course and project sometimes pressed the mentors' established methods for interacting with interns. Mentors had to prioritize seeing how activities and events during the school day fit their interns' research as well as holding off interns' immersion in the teaching activities of their classes until a balanced schedule for teaching and observing could be negotiated. These are not small steps or adjustments to be taken lightly.

This process of adjusting became a source of conflict and tension for experienced mentors. As mentioned earlier, many mentors wondered if there should even be a coursework component in the internship; not many had a conception of meaningful coursework in education, let alone a positive conception of research in education. Saddled with memories of mindless "cut and paste" or abstract theory courses that seemed disconnected from teaching experience, many teachers don't see the worth of doing coursework in education at all, especially when an apprenticeship experience could serve as a replacement. But the current alternative of teacher inquiry transcends the limitations of these two castaway poles of mindless or too mindful coursework by placing the student on the scene as an active participant charged with drawing out the connections between educational theory and practice.

I'm not so sure, in retrospect, that we solved any specific problems at this meeting. But I am convinced that we came to several understandings that set the tone for mutual growth throughout the year. I think we agreed that we could talk reasonably (sometimes not) and passionately about the issue most important to us: the implementation of curriculum for the enhancement of students' and prospective teachers' learning. I learned that teachers must be heard, included, and valued for their tremendous knowledge and resources. I knew this before, but didn't operationalize it as a result of my eagerness to do my own thing well and of my ignorance in anticipating the potential problems in this situation. I exhibited a tendency to defend instead of examine my positions and ideas. I would have to grow more secure and open in this regard in order to make true progress with the interns and the mentors. Also, teachers learned that I was at least capable and needed some room to cut my own path in this job—and that this might include a syllabus with assignments that looked a little different.

I also wish I could conclude at this point that the angst and goodwill poured out during this mentor meeting signaled the end to the resistance for the inquiry project. But the most important event of the semester left itself to be played out the very next week, on a day that will go down in my own personal history, as well as the program's, as Black Thursday. I suspect that these turns are connected, but doubt if I will ever know for sure how or why.

THE THIRD TURN: BLACK THURSDAY

The Thursday evening class with interns on October 6 started out innocently enough. We spent an hour hearing a presentation by local principals about evaluation and professional conduct. Good stuff. Afterward, we met as a group to debrief. Part of my agenda called for interns to voice their concerns and ideas regarding their research projects. I hoped that we all might gain some insight about what people were doing in the field. I wanted to help anyone with specific problems collecting data. I felt confident following the previous week's meeting with mentors, but the interns did not share this energy. We never got to the rest of the agenda.

I began the meeting by asking Bert to tell us how things were going with his project as well as any special problems he was encountering, if any. Bert dragged on that he was having a hard time finding information about his topic, and that he hadn't even had time to get the information that was available. I cut him off and moved on to Louise. She complained that she didn't want to start on the case because it would take away from her time with the students. She was just getting to know her students, was now taking on more responsibility in the classroom, and didn't want to give all this up. This is what she wanted from the program, so she wasn't going to start working on her case study.

Heidi echoed Louise. She just couldn't see herself devoting time to the case study now, and she didn't want to do it at all, anyway. She said that she could intellectualize the value of the project, but she couldn't say that she wanted to do it or that it fit what she thinks the experience should be about. She had been having trouble with her observations, and she felt as though she hadn't been in her own class forever. She believed that the project was taking her away from the experience that she was paying for, the one she signed up for, and the one for which she had been preparing for several years.

Then Jennifer said that things were going so badly for her she decided, along with her mentors, that she ought to leave the classroom completely in order to do the data collection for her study and get it out of the way so that she could get back to what she was truly there for, teaching. I nearly flipped. I tried to keep myself together, so I moved on to Chelsea. The echo continued. The circle seemed to be closing in around me. "I don't want to do this research; I want to teach." Then Lynn, then Jamie, and then Sam, who chimed in, "I don't want to be a researcher. I want to teach."

I had to say something, I thought. In retrospect, maybe I should have said nothing. I know that nothing I said was effective, but Jennifer's decision to pull out of class to handle research tasks did not quite match what I had in mind in terms of weaving together the clinical with the research component, so I felt as though I had to address this and some other details they mentioned. Finally, Sam, wisely said, "This is not productive," and I brokenheartedly agreed. I let them go under the worst of circumstances; they would just "grin and bear it," they said. I made a last plea for a piece of their collective hearts to connect with the spirit of the project, what I felt they knew was its value, but I got no response. I felt as though all had been lost after the meeting. Thankfully, I was wrong.

Several interns followed me to my office after class. There they apologized for jumping on the negative bandwagon. I thanked them for coming up and staying late with me, but also stressed my hope that they wouldn't abandon ship so early next time. Jamie said, "We saw you crashing and burning, but we didn't want to go down with you. We don't want the intern group to splinter, so it is hard to take sides sometimes." I replied that there was a fine line between preservation of group culture and watching a person drown, but that I could live with the fine line as long as the group stayed together and was productive. I really did understand, although it hurt.

Interns had mixed reactions to the meeting. On the one hand, interns took great pains to reconcile with me and with each other, hoping that we could get back on track together individually and as a group.

I am shocked at some people's reactions to this project. I can't believe the self-centeredness of some people who only want to do what they want to do. We paid for our undergraduate courses and I bet they cannot say they did what they wanted then. What we did then was trust the professors to give us the best college education possible. We did not question them like I see us questioning now. (Kyle, journal)

I don't disagree with the research paper assignment or think that too much is being asked of us. Regardless, I popped off and complained. In retrospect, I realize that no one anticipated what happened last night, and no one left feeling comfortable with what happened. No one left feeling like they had expressed what they wanted to say in the way they wanted to say it. I know I look back on my "contributions" to the discussion and am embarrassed and frustrated. (Sam, journal)

I was so upset after the meeting because I realized how upset Dr. Poetter was. Everyone had completely attacked him and his "baby"—this program, and this just kills me. He is *my teacher*. How would we like it if our students did to us what we did to him? I can't imagine. (Lynn, journal)

On the other hand, interns criticized how I handled the event. Of course, they had hoped that I would be more supportive and less defensive.

We just got back from class. It turned out to be one big bitch and cry session. I really wish Dr. Poetter wouldn't ask how we are doing if he's not prepared to deal with our answers. Next time he asks how I'm doing, I think I'll just say, "Fine, thank you, how are you?" (Jennifer, journal)

> It appears more and more as if we interns have to take care of ourselves. I really hope
> that no one wants to "clear things up" regarding last Thursday with Poetter. What's
> to clear up? Dr. Poetter asked for our opinions (we thought) and we gave them. No
> one asked for the assignment to be changed. (Louise, journal)

> Heidi was concerned that things had been left hanging and she regretted what happened
> last Thursday. She also said that she wished that I would have been more supportive. I
> added that the discussion put me on the defensive. She understood how I could have
> perceived it all that way. She perceives this experience in her own internship and with
> the class as a roller coaster, with so many highs and lows. I assured her that there was
> no way that I would let her or us reach another low this low. (Poetter, journal)

I wish I had kept my mouth shut, or consoled the interns and engaged
them in discussion that would have helped solve their problems. If only I
could have found some objective distance for myself at that moment, but I
couldn't. I felt the discussion getting dangerously close to the topic of
dropping the research component altogether. If it went that far, I would have
to take one of those dramatic last stands. One never wants an educational
scene to come to that. I certainly didn't. So I had a hand in making the scene
less than productive, at least according to Sam, but at least the scene wasn't
destroyed. I am glad for that.

In fact, by mid-November the interns helped shape my perspective of this
event as an important turn in the term. Before class one early November
evening, Jamie said he was looking forward to the next debriefing meeting.
Somehow the subject of Black Thursday came up, and the meaning it had
for him became apparent. It was a watershed moment, as important as any
positive event, cathartically pushing us ahead toward the business of doing
our research projects and coming to terms with who each other really is, a
human being with feelings and foibles.

Although the group has not really spoken about Black Thursday openly
with me (there has been no attempt to "clear things up"), we have joked
about it subtly. On several occasions, the group has agreed that no matter
how bad some event seemed, it couldn't be as bad as Black Thursday.
Sometimes events that seem so negative and devastating can bring individuals and groups to understand each other better and to new shared ground.
People build histories together through tough times. These momentous turns
sometimes make for stronger ties, stronger commitments, stronger experiences. These moments give people perspective about what is important—respecting others' ideas and opinions, even when they are in disagreement, and
maintaining a personal, human relationship in the midst of these struggles.

EXCITEMENT

Although not all parties felt totally comfortable with what was happening,
most settled in to the inquiry task and began reflecting on new perspectives

of teaching and learning. A picture dominated by positive feelings and experiences that interns and I were having together and with the mentor teachers became a more focused image. Some even became excited about the internship and its components fitting together.

Funny. The weeks following Black Thursday proved to be the best of the semester. Students found themselves establishing confidence in the classroom. They talked more openly about their research projects and made progress in their work. Some began to see the connections between their fieldwork and teaching practice. I began to see signs of excitement about the whole internship experience, including both the clinical component and the research component, in my interactions with the interns. I saw the biggest turnaround in Heidi, whose next low seemed far distant on the internship roller coaster.

Heidi's words stirred an enthusiasm and excitement for teaching and learning that I hadn't felt all term. Her and others' manifestations of excitement for the internship at this point in the course made the pain of the early going well worth it.

> I met with Heidi in the library in order to help her start sorting out her data for her study on gender in the classroom. It was a great meeting for several reasons. First, she had requested the meeting, and not because she was under duress. She simply wanted help in the initial stages of making sense out of what she had done so far in her project. Second, I felt as though I was able to give her some good guidance. I encouraged her to ask her respondent to interpret the scene first, before she spilled her interpretation in the interview. Third, I asked her if the project had helped her make any connections to her teaching experience or to her developing conceptions of teaching. She said that the research she has done has made her reconsider and adjust everything she does in the classroom to ensure that she approaches students justly and equitably with regard to gender. That was the highest testimony of positive effect that anyone had given regarding the research project in terms of connecting the project to reflective practice. This was truly a high-water mark. (Poetter, journal)

Heidi's entire picture of the classroom scene and the internship changed. Although she may have been formerly aware of the potentially dangerous effects of not paying attention to issues surrounding gender in classrooms and schools, her sensibilities about the planning, delivery, and evaluation of curriculum now take into account the perspective of gender. Her reflective study of this area made her a better teacher; she now focuses on deeper, complex issues that surround instructional decisions in her practice. Also, in her interactions with others concerning her research, she is educating herself as well as her intern and mentor colleagues. In fact, her final portfolio presentation to the entire group of graduating interns and faculty focused on the theme of "inclusion," and in it she looked in part at the lack of inclusion of girls in the math curriculum. Her interactive presentation engaged us all in the wider discussion of several crucial issues for teaching. Isn't this what it's all about? Exciting!

These first two chapters lay the groundwork for the reader's general understanding of the scene and what went on there. The next five chapters consist of the interns' research projects. The body of this book is dedicated to the writings of these prospective teachers who found a level of excitement and insight through their inquiry projects and teaching experiences and who wrote outstanding reports of their research. Each piece of writing is different from the other, and each student had a different group of perceptions regarding her project and its impact on the subsequent views she holds about teaching and research. Their own words and research speak to you here, as well as in the concluding chapters, where I expound on their works and stories and pull out lessons we learned from the scene as well as for the field of teacher education and inquiry.

Part II

Prospective Teachers' Research

3

A Case Study of the Use of Manipulatives and Technology in High School Mathematics

ෆ ♦ හ

Jennifer Pierson

INTRODUCTION

Like many mathematics teachers, I was always one of the "good" math students in elementary and high school. I understood most of the work after the first explanation. I genuinely liked all of the rules my teachers presented in the traditional lecture format. Mathematics was simple to me: There are a lot of very specific rules that cannot ever be broken and, if you follow these rules, you will get the right answer, always. I liked that. It wasn't like my English or history courses, where different interpretations were possible. There was always a right answer in math class. I took notes during class lecture and worked through all of my drill and practice homework with zeal.

I owned a scientific calculator when I was in high school, which I used for my homework, but I was not encouraged or oftentimes even allowed to use it in class. No one I knew in high school owned a graphing calculator. They could be bought, but were expensive and there didn't seem to be any point in purchasing one because you couldn't use it for your schoolwork. When I graduated from high school, I had never even held a graphing calculator and would have had no idea what to do if someone had given me one.

I don't remember doing any mathematics projects, papers, or presentations in high school other than a tessellation drawing for extra credit in geometry. I don't remember ever using any type of manipulatives in high school, either. There were no algebra tiles, no geoboards, no integer chips, no paddy paper, nor origami. My Algebra II teacher had some neat models of conics, but she always held them up to show us. My Geometry teacher held up pencils to represent lines, and sheets of paper became planes, but we never got to "play" with the models ourselves. All of the work we did for math class was pencil-and-paper calculations. The only tools I can remember using are a compass and a protractor, and I dreaded those geometric constructions.

Being creative in a mathematics class usually involved drawing a nice illustration for a word problem. But even so, I loved math. I was good at it. It was comfortingly straightforward. And I liked the challenge of a difficult problem, something I could figure out on my own with a little free time, some determination, and my handy set of math rules. I took a math course each year, and finished with Advanced Placement Calculus my senior year of high school. In 1990, I graduated, going on to college to study mathematics with the hope that I would be teaching it to other high school students one day.

Throughout my undergraduate and graduate studies of educational theory and practice, I learned about the mounting changes in mathematics education. The media brought forth report after report stating how standardized test scores were declining and U.S. students were falling behind their international counterparts in all subject areas, but especially in mathematics. I learned that I had gone to school during what was commonly referred to as the "back-to-basics" era in American public schools, but that yet another new education reform movement was coming.

THE CALL FOR CHANGE

In 1990, President George Bush and the governors of the 50 states met to discuss the future of American education. As a result of this meeting, six goals to be achieved by the year 2000 were established. The fourth goal states that "U.S. students will be first in the world in science and mathematics achievement" (Berenbeim, 1993, p. 6).

In the past 5 years, mathematics teachers have been barraged with publications dictating how they should change their teaching practices in order to meet the Goals 2000. The fundamental text is the National Council of Teachers of Mathematics (NCTM, 1989) *Curriculum and Evaluation Standards for School Mathematics*, commonly referred to as the *Standards*. Other important texts include *Everybody Counts: A Report to the Nation on the Future of Mathematics Education* (National Research Council, 1989); *Improving Math and Science Teaching: A Report on the Secretary's Second Conference on Mathematics and Science* (U.S. Department of Education, 1993); *Counting on You: Actions Supporting Mathematics Teaching Standards* (Mathematical Sciences Education Board and National Research Council,

1991); *Teaching and Learning Mathematics in the 1990s: 1990 Yearbook, Reshaping School Mathematics: A Philosophy and Framework for Curriculum* (Cooney, 1990); *Professional Standards for Teaching Mathematics* (NCTM, 1991); *Results from the Fourth Mathematics Assessment of the National Assessment of Educational Progress* (Lindquist, 1989); *Calculators in Mathematics Education: 1992 Yearbook*; the list goes on.

Hoping to prepare myself for a successful career in mathematics education, I began to read all the new recommended mathematics education books, papers, reports, and pamphlets I could get my hands on. According to the U.S. Department of Education (1993), if we hope to achieve the Goals 2000, "we must radically change what goes on in our classrooms—both what we teach and how we teach it" (U.S. Department of Education, 1993, p. v). In order to begin teaching in this new era of mathematics education, I needed to understand what specific expectations would be placed on me.

The Mathematical Sciences Education Board and the National Research Council (1991) explained that "this special focus [of the Goals 2000] on mathematics and science education reflects a growing awareness of their direct impact on the quality of the nation's work force—its ability to function well in an increasingly technological workplace, the ability of business and industry to compete effectively in the international marketplace, and the ability of each of us to carry out our roles as worker and citizen in a world increasingly shaped by mathematics, science, and technology" (Mathematics Sciences Education Board and National Research Council, 1991, p. 3).

"Teachers of mathematics are leading a nationwide effort to bring about a complete redesign of school and college university mathematics programs. By means of an unprecedented series of publications, they have set new and more demanding standards for what our students must learn about mathematics and for what the teachers themselves must accomplish as professionals in the classroom" (Mathematics Sciences Education Board and National Research Council, 1991, p. 1). According to the NCTM (1989), the high school mathematics curriculum should shift from one "dominated by memorization of isolated facts and procedures and by proficiency with paper-and-pencil skills to one that emphasizes conceptual understandings, multiple representations and connections, mathematical modeling, and mathematical problem solving" and "a variety of instructional methods should be used in classrooms in order to cultivate students' abilities to investigate, to make sense of, and to construct meanings from new situations; to make and provide arguments for conjectures and to use a flexible set of strategies to solve problems" (NCTM, 1989, p. 125).

Two of the "Underlying Assumptions" cited by the NCTM (1989) are that "scientific calculators with graphing capabilities will be available to all students at all times" and that "a computer will be available at all times for demonstration purposes, and all students will have access to computers for individual and group work" (p. 124).

Just reading through the titles of all the recommended literature is enough to give a teacher a headache. And yet, after having read many of these texts myself, it seems necessary that teachers not only read and understand these texts, but practice the advocated changes in order for the United States to have any hopes of meeting the Goals 2000. Whereas many of these texts contain minor variations in the instructional methods they recommend for teachers, they unanimously support the development of higher order thinking and problem-solving skills and the inclusion of real-world applications and mathematics models in the new curriculum. It is no longer acceptable for mathematics teachers to disseminate information for the majority of a class period in the traditional lecture format by giving students the basic rules and then assigning a lot of drill and practice problems. Most educators agree that the goals can be achieved through the inclusion of appropriate use of technology and hands-on mathematics investigations by students within the new curriculum.

THE DILEMMA

In August 1994, I began my year-long high school teaching internship. I was excited to be working with Mr. Baker, my mentor teacher in mathematics with 28 years of teaching experience. At an inservice at the beginning of the year, I received a copy of the new curriculum guide, a document outlining curriculum changes for our school district. I was pleased to find that two other teachers from the school were on the committee and that the changes seemed to follow the *Standards* almost exactly.

I had been worried that my internship placement would be in a school still advocating the "back-to-basics" approach to mathematics. I knew that all of the goals, standards, and recommendations I studied in college were made at the national level. In a system where each school district adopts its own textbooks, develops its own curriculum, and hires its own teachers, it seems hard to believe that participating in a nationwide change in mathematics education could be possible. But in examining our district's high school mathematics curriculum guide, it seemed that the national call for change had indeed reached and been accepted at the local level. The goals were there in black and white and each mathematics teacher in the district would have a copy.

The first five goals for teaching in math, as presented in the *District Mathematics Curriculum Guide* (1994) are:

1) Teaching for all students to understand and succeed, including concept and skill mastery, especially using manipulatives in the concrete-connecting-symbolic learning sequence; 2) Teaching that promotes wide-range problem solving skills and higher order thinking capabilities in students; 3) Teaching for motivational, functional use of learning on interesting, real-world problems and applications in real-world settings; 4) Teaching that

involves the learner actively, such as within simulations, projects, learning/task groups, multiple lesson formats, etc.; and 5) Teaching that utilizes, integrates and adapts math teaching and problem solving to the latest technologies. (p. 1)

The recommended instructional strategies included "developing the skills within real-world problems and applications using technology and concrete materials for concept development" (p. 2). I thought to myself, "This is great. I know all about this stuff. It will be difficult since I do not have any experience with it; I went through school in what is now being derogatorily called the old 'sit and get' method. But, I'm ready to learn how to make these changes. I want to make them. I believe that this really is a better way of teaching mathematics. Just show me the way."

But when I began team teaching with Mr. John Baker and doing my classroom observations with other members of the mathematics faculty, what I found surprised me. Even my mentor teacher, with 28 years of teaching experience and a firm belief in the goals, who tries to live up to the *Standards*, falls short. Even more surprising to me, of the 23 teachers of mathematics at the school, more than half do not even come close to the goals. At the beginning of the 1993–1994 school year, the school switched to a block schedule with 90-minute class periods that meet every other day and some mathematics teachers are still using the entire class period for lecture. This increases the pain of "sit and get"; it borders on torture.

So why is this happening? What is creating the disparity between the recommended pedagogy and the actual classroom practice? Why are the pedagogical and curricular changes, which are being called for at both the local and national levels, not being met? If all of the research and literature is correct and the use of manipulatives and technology is so fundamental, why do some teachers choose to use them and others do not? For those classes and teachers that do use them, is their use meaningful? Does use of these tools promote and facilitate understanding or are these tools just seen by teachers and students as neat toys? Are secondary mathematics teachers really using manipulatives and technology or are the algebra tiles and graphing calculators sitting in a closet somewhere collecting dust?

METHODOLOGY

When asked to choose a topic for my graduate research, I thought this project would provide me with the perfect opportunity to investigate the disparity between theory and practice with respect to the use of manipulatives and technology in classrooms. I would reread the important literature, survey members of the faculty, keep a personal journal of my experiences with my own mentor teacher, and observe different mathematics classes, looking in particular at the use or nonuse of technology and manipulatives.

For the purpose of this chapter, I use the term *technology* to refer to the use of electronic resources in secondary mathematics classrooms. These might include calculators (both scientific and graphing), computer software and networks, video cameras, televisions, and LCD displays, which project images from a calculator or computer onto a larger viewing screen for the entire class to view. These tools allow students to conduct extended investigations of two- and three-dimensional graphs that used to be too time consuming or curriculum inappropriate for the secondary mathematics classroom.

The term *manipulative* refers to any hands-on, concrete item used by students with the direction of the teacher to obtain a better understanding of a mathematical concept. These might include some of the newer, commercial items offered by education suppliers such as algebra tiles, geoboards, and paddy paper. They might also include more commonplace objects such as rulers, thermometers, construction paper, tape, and string. Within my working definition, ordinary pencils and paper might even be considered manipulatives if they were used by the students to represent physically a mathematics concept such as the intersection of a line segment and a plane or parallel lines in a plane. Again, the key is that students have concrete objects to manipulate in order to explore the ramifications of a mathematical concept. Thus, they are able to see and feel the math themselves.

In September, I began observing different members of the mathematics faculty, looking for their use or nonuse of manipulatives and technology with their classes. I kept a record of my impressions in an observation journal. When I finished my research, I had conducted 10 observations of seven different mathematics teachers, covering a wide variety of the mathematics courses. Each observation lasted between 45 and 90 minutes. The names of the teachers have been changed here to maintain the respondents' anonymity. When notes from the observation journal are used in the text they are cited as (*Observation journal*, page).

In an effort to gain an overall feeling about the attitudes of the mathematics faculty toward the use of manipulatives and technology, I conducted a survey. This survey was distributed to the 18 members of the mathematics faculty as well as to 5 other special education and school-within-a-school teachers who also conduct mathematics courses on campus. The surveys were delivered personally when possible, so that I could better explain the survey's purpose to respondents and respond to any preliminary questions or concerns, all with the hope of getting a good return. The survey contained 11 questions on the use of manipulatives and technology, ranging from general feelings, to perceived advantages and disadvantages, to training, to implementation and classroom experience, and then five additional demographic questions at the end. There was also space provided for any additional remarks the respondents might have. Fourteen of the 23 surveys were returned, expressing a wide variety of opinions. Hopefully, these views are representative of those found at the school. When commentary from these surveys is used in the paper it is cited as (*Manipulatives and Technology Survey*, Respondent #).

The remainder of my research data comes from a personal journal that I have been keeping over the course of my internship. Entries from this source are cited as (*Personal journal*, page).

A FIRST LOOK

In examining my data, I identified three very different types of reactions by mathematics teachers toward manipulatives and/or technology. I think that by examining these three types of reactions, it may be possible to reach some conclusions about the disparity between theory and practice in teaching and in the classroom.

Type 1: Mr. Hamilton

I saw Mr. Hamilton work in two different lower level math classes. In one, Mr. Hamilton begins class with a short, 15- to 30-minute lecture involving the basic rules for the day's topic during which the students are to take notes. Then, Mr. Hamilton leaves the students to work at their own pace on drill and practice worksheets for the remainder of the 90-minute period. During this time, he circulates through the room helping students with their work on an individual basis (*Observation journal*, p. 57).

In the other class, Mr. Hamilton spends a greater portion of the class period lecturing on the new material, giving definitions and other notes as well as several example problems. On the occasion of my observation, he lectured for more than 60 minutes of the 90-minute class period (*Observation journal*, p. 65). After 40 minutes of lecture, it was obvious that the class was "getting bored, tired, and disinterested" (*Observation journal*, p. 63). Mr. Hamilton seemed aware of this and added some humor to the lecture by using one of his students in an example of inductive versus deductive reasoning: "If Jerry kisses five girls and all five girls throw up, then Jerry makes girls sick" (*Observation journal*, p. 64). It was a cute example, everyone laughed, and it seemed to bring the students' attention back to the lecture.

But wouldn't it have been better for Mr. Hamilton to break up the monotony of the lecture time with some hands-on manipulative work? The additional 40 minutes of class time each period produced by the block schedule has not pushed Mr. Hamilton to change his teaching strategies, as teachers and administrators had hoped some of the more traditional teachers would. If there is any time left at the end of Mr. Hamilton's lecture, the students may use the rest of the period to start working on their assignment.

Mr. Hamilton's is one mathematics course that is especially conducive to the use of manipulatives. The school has some good software packages available that provide opportunities for the use of technology in this course as well. Ms. Taylor, who teaches the same subject as Mr. Hamilton, sometimes takes her students to the math computer lab to use one of the programs applicable to the course of study. Her students perform individual guided investigations using the computer. Then, the information they should have discovered on their own is summarized in a brief discussion/lecture at the end of class before the assignment is given (*Observation journal*, pp. 32–34).

While I was observing Mr. Hamilton, he allowed his students to use calculators in class if they had their own. However, he did not encourage their use, nor did he offer to provide students with the school-owned calculators available for in-class use. In one class I observed, which had 19 students, there were a few scientific calculators, but no graphing calculators (*Observation journal*, p. 56). In the other class, which had 18 students, two students had graphing calculators out on their desks during the lecture (*Observation journal*, p. 60). Mr. Hamilton did mention the use of calculators once, saying that a calculator might make some of the work more simple. But here, the only use of calculators he was encouraging involved basic addition, subtraction, multiplication, and division to speed up the calculation process (*Observation journal*, p. 63).

On one occasion during my observation, Mr. Hamilton missed a prime opportunity to use manipulatives. One of the students asked him to go over a problem from the previous night's homework assignment on concave and convex polygons. The question in the textbook shows several figures, some of which are concave and some of which are convex, and asks the students to explain what the result would be if a rubber band were stretched around each shape. The objective of the question is to demonstrate that the rubber band would have the same shape as the convex objects, but not the same shape as the concave ones because they have sides that "cut into" the figure that the rubber band would not conform to.

The students did not understand the question. I thought that this situation constituted a perfect opportunity to get out some physical objects, manipulatives of concave and convex shapes and some rubber bands, and have the students try a few themselves. Instead, Mr. Hamilton drew the figures from the textbook on the chalkboard and then drew a line representing the rubber band around them (*Observation journal*, p. 63). Not only does Mr. Hamilton not create lesson plans that incorporate manipulatives and technology to involve the students in the learning process, he seems to avoid or overlook their use when the situation presents an opportunity.

Other members of the faculty supported this Type 1 position in their commentary on the *Manipulatives and Technology Survey*. Respondent 1 stated "Manipulatives are often time consuming and counter productive" and "Care must be taken to ensure basic skills are understood before tools are used." Respondent 10 wrote "I believe that there is a place for technology and manipulatives, but it should not be the whole emphasis. Basic fundamentals with paper and pencil should still be taught." And Respondent 13 most directly supported the Type 1 teaching example, stating "It [technology and manipulatives] is keeping the students from learning the basics in the lower level classes" and that he or she does not use any manipulatives or technology with any of his or her classes. Respondent 7 agreed: "I believe that in upper level classes technology is of benefit to the student. I do not like to use calculators for lower classes just for addition and other simple operations. I feel we still need to use our brain and not be so lazy."

Mr. Hamilton and these other teachers belong to a group representing the Type 1 reaction to manipulatives and technology. These teachers seem oblivious to the possibility of using manipulatives and technology or in some instances they go so far as to avoid the use of such tools in their own classrooms. They do not provide calculators and computers, which are available to all math students by teacher request, nor do they encourage students to use their own even if they have them. They also miss opportunities to use manipulatives as they present themselves in their lessons.

This absence of change in teaching strategies has many potential causes. It may come from a lack of training or materials. Because this call for change has only been heard about for the past 5 years, many of the practical instruction-based ideas have not yet reached teachers at the local level; there are not many people capable of training other teachers yet and it is pointless for teachers to try to incorporate technology and manipulatives that they themselves do not understand in hopes that the students will. Survey Respondent 9 addresses this point, writing, "I think a lot of math teachers have not invested their time on manipulatives or technology training. . . . Many teachers are not willing to give themselves the opportunity to try new things. . . . Progress is very slow toward implementing manipulatives and technology" (*Manipulatives and Technology Survey*).

Also, school districts cannot afford to purchase a lot of manipulatives and technology all at once, no matter how desperately they are needed. Many of the surveyed teachers felt this need for materials, saying they would like more computers (modern/Pentium), more calculators (scientific and graphing), individual sets of algebra tiles for the students, a set of clear 3-D models, scissors, balances or scales, markers, compasses, protractors, remediation software, and spreadsheet software (*Manipulatives and Technology Survey*, Respondents 1, 2, 3, 5, 9, 10, 11).

But the lack of change may also come in part from tradition. Type 1 mathematics teachers probably learned mathematics the same way they are teaching it today. Therefore, they feel that because they were successful, this is a valid method of instruction. This is true, but couldn't the use of manipulatives and technology make that instruction even better? And finally, according to the *Manipulatives and Technology Survey*, there seems to be an underlying sentiment by many teachers that these tools hinder if not destroy the student's ability to learn the basics. Even though recent research has shown that if these tools are used properly this is not the case, it does not make these teachers more willing to bring them into their classrooms.

Type 2: Ms. Dobbs

Ms. Dobbs uses technology on a daily basis. However, she typically does not help her students make connections between their work with the technology and the mathematical concepts behind it. Thus, her students will be very technologically skilled when they complete the course, but I do not know if they will know why they are using the technology or if they will be capable of making an independent decision on how to use their technology skills when presented with a new, real-world situation rather than the typical drill and practice problems assigned for class.

When I observed Ms. Dobbs' class, there were 17 students present, each had a graphing calculator out on his or her desk. At the beginning of class, she asked if everyone had his or her calculator. They all did. "Good, because you'll need it for your quiz today" (*Observation journal*, p. 14). Obviously, Ms. Dobbs requires each student to have his or her own calculator for class and home use. This is a far cry from Mr. Hamilton's classes.

To begin the day's lesson, the class learned how to delete a program from the calculator's memory and then how to transfer existing programs from one calculator to another using the link-up cables. Ms. Dobbs demonstrated this procedure using an overhead LCD projection device and a big poster of the calculator's keyboard that is hanging on a bulletin board in the front of the room. She taught the keystrokes and went through the entire process, step by step, with the students. Afterward, Ms. Dobbs "gave one student the program from her calculator and then the students got it from each other," practicing the file transfer procedure using the cables Ms. Dobbs provided (*Observation journal*, p. 14).

Once all of the students had the program in their personal calculators, Ms. Dobbs explained that this program would be used to locate the real roots of polynomial functions. She "had everyone put in the same function and then they went through the process of using the program together, step by step. She used the LCD display to demonstrate" (*Observation journal*, p. 14). There were a lot of student questions during the first example, but most of them centered on how to use the program. They were "technical difficulties" rather than questions about the mathematics concepts.

I commented in my observation journal, "Where is the theory? Do these students really understand what is going on? Do they really know what the calculator is doing in a mathematical sense? Or do they just know how to use the calculator?" (p. 15). In retrospect, I think the latter is more true. After working several examples together, Ms. Dobbs has the students "clear their desks of everything except the calculator and a pencil. She says, 'You may, you must, use your calculator'" (*Observation journal*, p. 15).

Before taking their quiz, one student asked, "How can you tell how many roots there are?" Ms. Dobbs did a quick review on cubics and how they have either one or three real roots. "This leads to a lecture on how you have to know what you are doing and why. She (Ms. Dobbs) said she loves the program because it is so much easier than what she had to do in school, but you still have to understand the material" (*Observation journal*, p. 15). It was a nice speech. I believe it is very appropriate that students be made to realize that the calculator is only a tool. But, in this case, I don't think the students really did understand the material. Maybe Ms. Dobbs is not making the connections explicitly enough for them. The students like the program because it makes their work much easier. But the entire class period was spent on how to use the calculator and this program, not on why the students should use it, when its use is appropriate, or how it works in a mathematical sense. Before handing out the quiz, Ms. Dobbs "asked what the location principle is. No one knew" (*Observation journal*, p. 16).

Other mathematics teachers at school seem to be having similar problems using manipulatives. The students gain proficiency in using a tool, such as algebra tiles or integer chips very easily, but they rarely make the connection between their use of manipulatives and the symbolic work they should advance to later. Therefore, they cannot multiply expressions or solve simple equations correctly without the concrete tool.

Several other mathematics teachers expressed this concern as well (*Manipulatives and Technology Survey*). Respondent 2 commented, "Sometimes students rely too much on manipulatives and find it difficult to apply concepts to real-world situations." Respondent 4 supported this statement saying that "some students can't make the connection when asked to do the problem with pencil and paper." Respondent 8 agreed: "Many kids I know who have used algebra tiles don't make the connections between the concrete experience and the abstract concepts" and later stated "student overdependence on calculators" as one of the major drawbacks of using the tools. "Students have a lack of 'common sense' in judging their answers, not really knowing when or when not to reach for their calculator to solve a problem."

The purpose of bringing manipulatives and technology into the classroom is to provide a concrete model for students so that they understand that the mathematics really does work, that there is a reason behind what they are doing, and that mathematics is not just abstract theory that educators make them study as a form of torture. But the manipulatives and technology are only meant to be tools; the student must eventually make the move away from concrete objects to symbolic manipulation and understand what he or she is doing at that level as well.

Without this connection between the concrete and the abstract, there will never be any higher order thinking. Our students will be in the same place they have historically been: They can manipulate a problem to obtain the correct answer, but they don't know why; and they can work particular types of problems, but they cannot address new situations. Without knowing why, that is, understanding the concept, our students will never be able to transfer their skill to use in real-world situations. Sadly, their mathematics skills will only be used in a math classroom. And, maybe even worse than before, we have given them a crutch, a calculator or some algebra tiles, which they are now dependent on to complete their work.

An exaggerated example of this would be the student who does not realize that the total bill for a piece of gum and a licorice stick that cost 5 cents and 2 cents respectively can be found by adding 5 and 2 together. And, once this connection is explained to them, they still need to count on their fingers to get an answer, never getting past the concrete stage to be able to perform the work mentally without constant teacher prompts. However, one teacher countered the concern of the tool becoming a crutch, saying that although it is a valid concern, "It is better to go through life in a wheelchair than to stay bedridden" (*Manipulatives and Technology Survey*, Respondent 3).

Unlike Type 1 teachers, Type 2 teachers are making a valiant effort to change. They are bringing manipulatives and technology into their classrooms and putting these tools into the hands of their students. However, they are not living up to the spirit of the goals. These teachers are not promoting higher order thinking. And without higher order thinking skills, our students will never be first in the world in science and mathematics achievement, no matter how well they can use a graphing calculator and algebra tiles. The distressing thought is, these Type 2 teachers may not even realize that they are not fulfilling the goals.

Type 3: Ms. Sims and Mr. Baker

The Type 3 teacher is closest to meeting the Standards. These teachers try to incorporate the use of manipulatives and technology into their classrooms as often as possible, yet in a meaningful way. Ms. Sims and Mr. Baker are two examples of the Type 3 teacher.

So far this school year, Ms. Sims has used a wide variety of manipulatives and technology including algebra tiles, integer chips, rulers, tape measures, 1-inch square tiles representing area, giant number lines taped to the floor with students acting as points on the line, estimation of M&Ms in a jar, spheres, prisms, and cubes as models of volume, probability by the random drawing of different items from a bag, and calculators, both scientific and graphing.

On one of the days I observed Ms. Sims teach, she was working with her students on simplifying algebraic expressions involving multiplication and addition using algebra tiles. Each student had his or her own set of tiles and

Ms. Sims had a set of transparent tiles that she used on the overhead projector for demonstration purposes. The class had obviously been using the tiles for several weeks and many of the students had already moved on to the purely symbolic form of simplifying algebraic expressions. Others were being encouraged by Ms. Sims to sketch the tiles on the paper, rather than physically manipulate them. This, she explained to me, is the first step away from the concrete toward the abstract. The next step is to complete the work without the sketches. Most students make the transition from concrete to abstract on their own, because it is ultimately faster and simpler, but many students have to be pushed to put down the tiles and try the work without them (*Observation journal*, p. 45). Ms. Sims encourages students to make the transition as soon as they are capable of it. Here we see how one teacher has successfully overcome some of the Type 2 teaching difficulties.

Mr. Baker's (my mentor teacher) and my classes have used rulers, tape measures, scissors, stacks of cups, miras, celsius thermometers, 3-D coordinate system models, and a TI-82 overhead projection device (almost daily) this year (*Personal journal*). Our classes use graphing calculators regularly and every student is required to have one of his or her own. However, if a student cannot afford one, Mr. Baker makes arrangements to loan the student a calculator for the duration of the school year.

In planning our lessons, Mr. Baker and I always try to include some kind of hands-on activity, whether it be manipulatives or a graphing calculator exploration. However, this is not always easy to do. The use of the tools does not seem to fit in as easily as the literature suggests it should, nor are the connections between the concrete and the abstract always readily apparent. The comment is often made that the constructivist movement started in mathematics; thus, mathematics lessons should be easy to teach with tangible things so students can construct his or her own knowledge. But, it is hard to find concrete hands-on-type activities to explain some mathematical concepts such as exponential functions or geometric sequences and series.

At this point, we usually incorporate a graphing calculator exploration rather than a manipulative one. This change from a primary use of manipulatives to technology seems to take place somewhere in the upper levels of the curriculum; the lower level courses seem more conducive to manipulative use whereas the upper level classes are more technological. However, at all levels of high school mathematics, it is possible for teachers to involve their students actively in the mathematics so they have control of a visible representation of their work and shared ownership of the learning process.

Both Ms. Sims and Mr. Baker have expressed their desire to do more with manipulatives and technology because they believe their use does help students learn better. Still, there is room for improvement in our use of these tools, which will come with time and experience. Also, as more activities are developed and published, there will be less of a daily struggle to develop lesson plans that meet the *Standards*. Thus, even though these two teachers can be considered among the best in regards to technology and manipulatives use, there are still some changes to be made if we are to achieve the Goals 2000.

The Others

We have looked at three types of teacher reactions to manipulatives and technology, represented by four members of the mathematics faculty. If my classroom observations and the results from the returned surveys are any indication, the other 19 members of the faculty who teach mathematics fall somewhere among the three types. Some, like Mr. Hamilton, are resisting change for one reason or another. Others have begun the transition but are still relying heavily on the traditional lecture format. Still others, like Ms. Dobbs, are excited about change and moving forward, but have not quite achieved the full potential of using manipulatives and technology. Then, there are the few, like Ms. Taylor, Ms. Sims, and Mr. Baker who are closest to achieving the goals. These last few teachers set an example for others to follow and hopefully someday to surpass.

THE MATH CLOSET

Although it may seem a little out of place in the greater scheme of this chapter, I believe the math closet is an important part of the issue of using manipulatives and technology at school.

Each department at the school has a storage area of some kind. For the mathematics department, it is a big closet. Only 3 of the 18 members of the mathematics faculty have a key to this closet, so access to the closet is somewhat of a commodity. The closet is full. The shelves are stacked high with boxes of stuff, most of which are not labeled. Who knows what's inside? My mentor and I borrow the key from one of those three special people from time to time to scrounge around inside the math closet for something we need.

To me the math closet is like a treasure chest. There are so many things there that could be used: scissors, compasses, geometer templates, old calculators, rulers, and so forth. It's incredible. I would love to spend a day digging through all of it. But very few people seem to go in there. Do they not know it's there? Surely they must. Maybe they do not know what great stuff is in there. Or maybe they do not want to bother one of the special people to unlock the door for them. It seems so wasteful to me, when teachers are obviously longing for more materials (*Manipulatives and Technology Survey*). All of those tools are just sitting there collecting dust. Students should be using them, especially today, amidst the call for change. Therefore, as a basic part of our movement toward the Goals 2000, each mathematics teacher should be given his or her own key to the math closet and a list of materials available there.

CONCLUSION

None of the teachers described here are bad teachers. They all know the content of their curriculum backward and forward. They care deeply about the education of their students. They have good rapport with their students. The keyholders are not trying to hoard all of the goodies in the math closet. But most teachers, including Type 3 teachers and myself, are simply not living up to the goals and standards, and things need to change.

As previously discussed, there are many reasons for the slow or sometimes nonexistent move away from traditional paper and pencil, drill and practice, "sit and get" lecture style instruction to a more active, cooperative learning, alternative assessment type of environment: tradition; a belief in the basics; a lack of a personal teaching model to follow; the absence of training; a need for new, better, or additional materials; a need for more class time to teach with these tools or more professional development time to learn how; or, a lack of creativity, the originality to come up with new and different lesson plans that incorporate all of these tools in a meaningful way. Each of these reasons is a valid one and each exists at the high school. Thus, if we are going to meet the Goals 2000, these issues must soon be addressed.

4

Teaching Future Members of the Fourth Estate

Chelsea Caivano

> Burke said there were Three Estates in Parliament; but, in the Reporters' Gallery yonder, there sat a Fourth Estate more important far than they all.
>
> —*Thomas Carlyle*

Teaching, to some degree, is an autocratic structure. Each teacher is king or queen of his or her classroom, and as monarchs they are allowed to establish their own sets of rules. They expect their subjects to follow their laws lest they be punished—hopefully not by beheading but by time-outs and referral slips. There is also, however, a system of checks and balances in teaching. Educators must follow the state and local curricula, they must use assigned textbooks, and they cannot deviate too far from the administration's expectations and policies without recourse.

The journalism discipline at times lends itself to such an arrangement. Although the state has compiled and published a skeletal outline for journalism curriculum that governs what areas and topics should be taught, and whereas our school district has adopted a fairly thorough textbook and teacher's guide for use in its introductory journalism classes, little other direction is available for instructors. Individual journalism teachers are left to put together their own curriculum, resulting in an autonomous structure with minimal continuity between schools and among teachers.

This lack of a specific journalism curriculum is particularly detrimental to first-year teachers. A typical journalism teacher serves as both publication adviser and instructor of at least four different sections of the discipline:

yearbook production, newspaper production, photojournalism, and introductory journalism. Because the deadlines and production output demands
are often overwhelming, it is easy to see how natural and common it is for
a journalism teacher to focus his or her energies on the production classes
while virtually ignoring the beginning journalism students. Yet, it is in this
introductory course where the future reporters, editors, and designers
receive their initial training. If the journalism students do not effectively
learn the basics, do not hone their writing skills, and do not, at the very
least, become interested in the field of journalism, there may not be a
qualified yearbook or newspaper staff the following year.

I was not aware of the underdeveloped journalism curriculum until I
began my internship. When I first met with my mentor Mr. Fletcher, I asked
him what he usually covers with the beginning journalism students. He gave
me the course outline that he hands out to students on the first day of class.
I was disappointed to see that the syllabus was no more than the verbatim
outline of sections and chapters from the textbook. As we discussed our
expectations for the school year, I again asked about the journalism class
and inquired if he ever taught outside of and beyond the textbook.

Mr. Fletcher admitted that he hadn't really ever gotten involved much
with the beginning journalism students. Last year his intern had taken over
the class almost entirely, allowing him time to concentrate on the yearbook
and newspaper. Although this arrangement may have worked well then, I
initially felt overwhelmed by the thought of suddenly pulling together a
year's worth of activities, readings, and projects. Within a few weeks, I
realized how difficult creating a curriculum can be with few guidelines and
little collaboration with other educators and professional journalists. It was
at this point I decided to focus my research paper on the development of a
journalism curriculum from the perspectives of a first-year teacher.

In addition to recording and reflecting on my own experiences in the
classroom, I read more than 2 dozen articles written by both journalism teachers
and professional journalists. Although not all of the literature directly dealt
with high school journalism, I found the articles written about collegiate-level
journalism programs to be very applicable and helpful to my research. Further,
I set up interviews with two local first-year journalism teachers. My interview
with Liz Logan, a former intern teacher, was extremely insightful and fruitful.
In contrast, Cathy Ferrell, a teacher at a nearby suburban high school, denied
an interview because she said she wasn't yet sure of her curriculum and wasn't
ready to share it with anyone else. Whether she was afraid to share her
curriculum or was uneasy about being observed by a stranger or simply didn't
have enough time to meet with me, her refusal proves a point: Journalism
teachers do not have to and are not accustomed to working together. Because
each school typically hires only one journalism teacher, he or she is allowed
to, and almost forced to, work independently, rarely leaving the boundaries
of the classroom or the grounds of the school.

> "A teacher affects eternity; he can never tell where his influence stops."
>
> —Henry Brooks Adams

On the first day of school, Mr. Fletcher and I asked our beginning journalism students, "What is journalism?" Their answers ranged from the obvious ("The name of this class") to the profound ("How we communicate with the masses and record history for the future"). I was interested in their initial perceptions of the course because journalism is an anomaly. Journalism is classified as fine arts, yet it is often located in the old vocational building. It's a training ground for professionals, yet it is often taught by unqualified educators with little or no journalism experience. It's the largest and most pervading industry in the world, yet it traditionally receives meager school funding.

Regardless of the definition or classification of journalism, though, it is the course that shapes the minds of future journalists. A study by Forrester for the American Society of Newspaper Editors' Committee on Education "found that nearly 70 percent of the respondents claimed to have been influenced in a media career choice by a high school journalism experience" (Dvorak, 1990, p. 37). The same article quotes the results of two American College Testing studies, which claim that students who had newspaper or yearbook staff experience in high school were four times more likely to select communications as a college major than were those with no publications experience. Moreover, students who had both high school publications experience and a journalism course were 10 times more likely to select journalism as a college major or as a career choice as those who had neither experience.

Not all of our current high school journalism students, however, intend on entering the field of journalism as a college major or a career. When we asked our students why they were taking journalism, only 3 of 18 students said they actually wanted to take journalism, offering reasons such as "I write in a journal at home and wanted to see what the class is like" and "I like to learn why some people act or react to things that happen in everyday life." Only one person in the class said he is considering a journalism major and/or career. "I've always thought I could express myself better through a pen than with my voice," Lucas said.

If only 3 of 18 students wanted to take journalism, how did the other 15 get enrolled? Simply put, the counselors assigned them by default to the journalism elective. According to a study conducted by the Freedom Forum, "Far too many educators and administrators rank journalism with metal shop, rather than Shakespeare. At worst, it's viewed as a dumping ground for hard-to-handle students" (Hernandez, 1994, p. 14). My mentor's experiences concurred with the study: "I've walked into the counsel-

ing office three times and heard them say, 'Oh, just stick them in journalism.'" Likewise, Ms. Logan defined her journalism classes: "In two words:
dumping ground." Many of our students were placed into our class because
nothing else was open.

It was easy for me to become frustrated at the beginning of the year when
I realized that my students didn't want to learn how to write a news story. I
expected them to be intrinsically motivated by a love for journalism. I
wondered how I could teach a journalism course when only one student
planned on becoming a journalist. I worried about excluding the other 17
students if I taught toward Lucas' goal of becoming a professional. I wondered if I should change the angle of the class, teaching to the 17 but risking
letting Lucas leave high school underprepared for a college journalism
curriculum. I found guidance in a textbook:

> The authors believe there is no subject that needs understanding more than journal-
> ism. The mass media today wield an enormous influence over daily life in this country.
> While they do not mold men's minds in the fashion once suspected, they do provide
> the information upon which persons in a democratic society can base their decisions,
> both in the polling place and the marketplace. (Ferguson & Patten, 1993, p. 2)

Instead of educating my students to become journalists, I decided to
educate them to become discerning consumers of news. I would still teach
the basics of newswriting and editing as the state curriculum guidelines
dictate, but this passage gave me comfort that I need not be disappointed if
my students did not become award-winning writers. Instead, they needed
to understand how journalists create what appears on their televisions and
in their newspapers and how this information affects their lives. I would
educate them to be "media savvy." This approach would include all 18
students. Lucas would get the professional training he desires, and the others
would learn about the news industry and its impact on American society.
My hope was that during the course of the year some victims of the dumping
ground would be won over and develop a passion for driving on the
information highway.

Journalism is not only a dumping ground for students, but also a dumping
ground for teachers. Article after article I read claimed that journalism
teachers and advisers are unqualified in the very subject they are teaching.
Schaub (1993) said, "Research indicates that most newspaper and yearbook
advisers throughout the country have had little or no training in journalism"
(p. 56) and Hernandez (1994) said, "Fewer than one third hold state
certificates to teach journalism, and no state requires a certificate to advise
a publication" (p. 14).

Even if the teacher has been certified in the discipline and has journalism
teaching experience, he or she may not be qualified to teach such an
ever-changing subject, according to some soldiers in the ongoing war

between professional journalists and journalism educators. Stein (1993a) warned, "Journalism students whose [teachers] have been out of the news business for more than five years will not be ready for newspaper jobs" (p. 38).

On the other hand, some professional journalists are not effective teachers. A practicing journalist "may do the course more harm than good, dabbling as he often does, in dribble, personal inclinations, unsystematic and illogical development of points, personal anecdote, [and] his newspaper's policy" (Merrill, 1978, p. 60). Ms. Ferrell, the teacher who declined an interview, was a professional in town for several years before jumping the fence to education. Although very knowledgeable in journalistic theory and practice, she lacks skills in classroom management and lesson planning. Since September she has been placed on probation, and apparently will not teach at the same high school next year.

> Professional journalists are viewed by many people as rude, arrogant, uncaring people who think only about "getting the story." Increasingly, people object to intrusive behavior by journalists—for example, shoving a microphone into the face of someone whose house has just burned down and demanding, "How do you feel?" (Ferguson & Patten, 1993, p. 25)

Educators, on the other hand, are ideally the opposite. They are supposed to be encouraging and supportive mentors who care more about the people than the product. So who should teach journalism—the professional or the professor?

I believe the teacher should be both. Mr. Fletcher has neither a journalism degree nor any professional experience beyond a brief stint at an advertising firm. He and I frequently contradicted each other in class when discussing the "real world" with the students. I certainly would not nominate myself for a Pulitzer, but I have worked for a newspaper, two magazines, a book publishing company, and an advertising department. Through my experiences I have seen what is and is not acceptable in journalism, and I can read the textbook with a critical eye and share my observations with my students. I know, for example, that the PageMaker publishing program, which we currently use to lay out both the newspaper and yearbook, has virtually become obsolete. Although most high school journalism students are still using PageMaker, four of my five journalism jobs use Quark XPress. Likewise, counting headlines is an old-fashioned skill that is no longer necessary with desktop publishing. However, Mr. Fletcher insisted on spending two class periods teaching the technique.

Stein (1993a) claimed that rapidly changing technology is not the problem: "Anyone can sit down at a terminal, a leaf desk, a Macintosh or pagination station and learn it enough to be useful after some training. It's absolutely not brain surgery" (p. 38). However, being out of touch with revolutionary journalism changes can be. At the annual convention of the Association for Education in Journalism and Mass Communication (AEJMC), a delegation of newspaper executives and journalism professors joined together to discuss journalism education: "The rationale for the conference is that j-schools are not keeping pace with the powerful changes taking place among newspapers and their readers. . . . Journalism education needs a sweeping overhaul" (Stein, 1993b, p. 12). From their general discussion and breakout sessions, the delegates wrote the following recommendations for revamping journalism education: (a) Use state-of-the-art equipment and software; (b) put more emphasis on critical thinking and pay more attention to human values and less to technology; and (c) change the present journalism curriculum to include a variety of information to give students "a better sense of reality" (p. 13). This so-called reality would include teaching journalism students to become multilingual and encouraging inner-city internships and cross-cultural experiences. Moreover, the industry wants a student to "emerge with some idea of how the world works" (p. 13). He or she should know how to:

> Turn on a computer, find area codes in the phone book, hail a cab in the city, ask delicate questions without offending someone, and comb his hair before standing in front of 500 people with a Nikon in his hand. [He or she should] know about Watergate, the importance of Omaha Beach in World War II, how Congressional districts are set up, and why names must be spelled correctly. (Stein, 1993b, p. 13)

At the convention there was across-the-board agreement that newspapers and journalism education programs are too far apart. The danger in not changing journalism education is that the curriculum will become an anachronism. Educators need to keep abreast of the current trends of journalism. Ms. Logan subscribes to *American Journalism Review* magazine and says, "You absolutely, positively have to keep up with what the professionals are doing. The beauty of journalism is that it is not and cannot be limited to a specific curriculum or textbook. As news and events change daily, so does journalism class." At the time of the interview, Ms. Logan's class had just finished a two-week unit on the media coverage of the O. J. Simpson trial, an idea she certainly did not pull out of the teacher's manual.

"In youth men are apt to write more wisely than they really know or feel; and the remainder of life may be idly spent in realizing and convincing themselves of the wisdom which they uttered long ago."

—*Nathaniel Hawthorne*

As I was conducting my research, I wanted to know if the current journalism curriculum met the needs of the students from the perspective of a college journalism professor. I asked my college adviser what her incoming freshmen lacked in terms of journalistic knowledge or skills.

"Writing," Dr. Zachary said tersely. "Journalism is not about computers or cameras. Journalism is nothing more than a process of creating something and re-creating it. You write and edit, write and rewrite." In fact, writing is the one skill so basic to journalism that anyone who doesn't have it or is unwilling to work to acquire it will never become a successful journalist. But writing is not, as some people believe, an inherent talent that some have and some do not. There is no formula to learn good writing, but through trial and error and through reflection on constructive criticism, I believe every one of my students can learn to write effectively. Joe Murray says journalism is not five Ws and an H, but rather is five Ws and an R: "That's writing, writing, writing, writing, writing, and rewriting" (Ferguson & Patten, 1993, p. 84).

When I visited Ms. Logan's classroom, she was beginning the most important unit of the curriculum: newswriting. On the board she had written three steps to becoming a better writer:

1. Read—read the newspaper, read the magazines, read what the professionals are doing.
2. Practice—write, *write*, *Write!*
3. Evaluate—read my comments [on your articles] and ask yourself, "What could I have done better?"

Ms. Logan said she didn't have any set curriculum on how to teach newswriting other than having the students write as much as possible.

Journalistic writing has always been easy for me. Because I don't remember how I was taught to write a news story, I was unsure how to teach my students. At first I tried telling the students all the rules of journalistic style, such as "Be objective, use direct quotes, use third person, and keep your opinions for the editorial pages." The students' first set of articles were a direct reflection of how effective my teaching strategy was—they were horrible. Stumped, I spent the next class period meeting individually with students, critiquing their stories and offering suggestions. "Journalism class seems to be getting more fruitful for the kids. Today I wandered around giving each of them help. I think the one-to-one approach has enabled them to see where they are missing the boat and where their strengths are" (*Journal*, p. 21). We continued this procedure over the next 2 months, working with students one at a time as they composed their articles in class. Whereas before I thought it would be more productive to have the students write their articles as homework, I soon began to see how beneficial it was for the unsure writers to ask us questions as they are creating, not after they are finished.

McKeen and Bleske (1992) suggested that, when working one-on-one, editors should "allow student writers to speak first, commenting and critiquing the story. Then the editor responds to the writer's comments and vice versa" (p. 82). They further suggested that the writer should do more than half of the talking. At first I found this approach frustrating, because I wanted to simply tell the student where his or her article lacks clarity or is biased. With time, however, I began to see the advantages.

Most of my students seemed uncomfortable with my silence, and would begin rambling in order to fill the gap in conversation. Soon their babbling developed into a self-conducted brainstorm, in which they answered their own questions. I have seen the most improvement in Jason, a freshman whose favorite phrase used to be, "This is too hard." During the first month of newswriting, Jason would frequently become frustrated when I refused to rewrite his lead or tell him what his next quotation should be. Although some may think my teaching style isn't really teaching, I believe Jason has learned more through this strategy than if I had spoon-fed him the answers. His writing has improved as have his self-confidence and speaking ability.

> "The first law for the historian is that he shall never dare utter an untruth. The second is that they shall suppress nothing that is true. Moreover, there shall be no suspicion of partiality in his writing, or of malice."
>
> —Cicero

The panelists at the aforementioned AEJMC Convention (Stein, 1993) further suggested that the journalism curriculum should put more emphasis on critical thinking and pay more attention to human values. They concluded that teaching basic ethics is a must. But just how ethics should be covered is a dilemma, as John C. Merrill (1978) points out in his question, "Do we teach ethics—or do we teach *about* ethics?" (p. 59)

In late September, we began a 2-week unit covering both journalism ethics and communication law. Only one of the six class days, however, was devoted to ethics. The other five class meetings were focused on libel law, invasion of privacy, and applicable court cases. During the 1 day when ethics were discussed, the majority of the 87-minute period was spent reading the Society of Professional Journalists' Code of Ethics, a lofty piece of rhetoric that seemed to go over the students' heads. When I suggested that the class might need a real-world example in order to make these ethics more tangible, Mr. Fletcher said the kids could answer one or two of the scenarios at the end of the chapter. The students were asked to assume they are the editors of the school newspaper. An editorial is planned criticizing the football coach for pressuring the parents of the students he coaches into buying kitchen appliances from him. The class discussed whether they would publish the piece and why.

Although the exercise was not completely devoid of worth (it did, after all, employ critical thinking skills), it was silly and certainly not "real world." My attitude toward the unit worsened when we gave them a test and the end of the 2 weeks.

The test asked them to list and explain six elements of ethical journalism and explain what happened in the Hazelwood case. Complete regurgitation—absolutely no critical thinking. Yes, it's important for the kids to know the elements of ethics, but will they be able to apply them, use them? If they do become journalists and find themselves in an awkward situation, will they be able to handle it ethically? Or will they just know that they were once tested on something having to do with ethics in high school? (*Journal*, pp. 55–56)

Only 2 weeks later my questions became an unpleasant reality. Dylan took journalism last year and now is a member of our newspaper staff. At the beginning of the school year, Dylan approached us requesting to write the editorial pages. We decided that Dylan could write responses to the published letters to the editor. We didn't receive any letters to the editor for the first issue, and when the October issue deadlines came with still nary a letter, Dylan became frustrated. He persuaded a member of the class to write a letter about the tardy policy. The letter filled only half the allotted space, though, so Dylan asked the same person to write a second letter, this time signing it under a pseudonym.

Perhaps Mr. Fletcher and I are too trustful of our students, or perhaps it was just an oversight, but we didn't check to see if the authors of the letters were actual students. Both letters, one signed Jack Sundmin and the other signed Stan Tracy (the pseudonym), and Dylan's response ran in the October issue. A week later another newspaper student came to me and said the letters were a joke, that Stan Tracy doesn't exist and Jack wrote both letters at Dylan's request.

That afternoon we sat down with Dylan and discussed the ethics and potential legal problems of what he did—soliciting letters and knowingly running them under false pretenses. I told him that the credibility of the paper had been damaged by his lack of forethought.

He really didn't get it. Mr. Fletcher reminded Dylan that he learned this last year in journalism. He even tested Dylan over the ethics of journalism and editorial policies, he said. But testing these kids does not ensure their understanding of the material. Dylan was faced with a situation where he needed to apply one of the codes of ethics we just tested this year's journalism students on, and he couldn't do it. The challenge now is to come up with another way of driving those ethics home and making them very real to the students. (*Journal*, pp. 67–68)

Merrill (1978) said, "We should do both—*teach* ethics and teach *about* ethics, and certainly in the final analysis, we *must* leave with the students final decisions—but these certainly can be influenced by the instructor and the total class experience" (p. 59). He encouraged teachers to try to instill ethical standards and principals in students, and he warned against simply presenting ethical problem cases without resolving them in class discussion. In addition, Merrill suggested breaking down the professional–educational barrier by inviting a practicing journalist into class to discuss ethics:

> Many visiting journalists can add an interesting and valuable dimension to the class
> if they can show how in daily journalism the theoretical problems are actually met,
> wrestled with, and solved. It is always good when a person, involved in a real ethical
> situation, explains the situation and takes the students step by step through to a
> solution. (p. 60)

Of course, if the teacher is currently involved in the professional realm of journalism, inviting another professional journalist may be unnecessary. Furthermore, the outside professional may do more harm than good, particularly if he or she has not given serious thought to ethics or cannot communicate logically and effectively.

In retrospect, I believe we did our students a great disservice by dedicating so little class time to ethics. Dylan (who, incidentally, earned an A in both semesters of journalism) and his ethical blunder demonstrates how ineffectual the lesson plan was. The revision includes many more real-life examples for class discussion and resolution. Moreover, I want to have the students analyze the Society's Code of Ethics, which was written in 1987, critique its strengths and its weaknesses, and create a code that they feel is superior and perhaps more applicable today.

"A teacher who can arouse a feeling for one single good action, for one single good poem, accomplishes more than he who fills our memory with rows on rows of natural objects with name and form."

—*Johann Wolfgang von Goethe*

Although the original purpose of this research project was to examine and create a journalism curriculum, I've come to the conclusion that I cannot simply compile a year's worth of activities and assignments and file them away for next year's students. I've learned that the nature of my discipline will not allow such advanced planning. As technology changes, as newspapers evolve, and as events continue to happen on a daily basis, so will my curriculum change. At the beginning of the year, I saw journalism curriculum as teacher-based and teacher-directed. I have since seen how the needs of the students govern what I teach, when I teach it, and how I will teach it. Whereas this year's class has enjoyed McKeen and Bleske's silent coaching strategy, next year's students may have different needs. Although I plan to analyze the media coverage of the O. J. Simpson trial with my students next semester, such a unit is a one-time experience. Journalism is a fast-paced, ever-changing field with scores of facets and subdivisions. I cannot limit such a field to a set curriculum.

I have also come to the conclusion that teaching methods, to some extent, don't matter. It wasn't necessarily the method that enabled the students to improve their writing abilities—it was the atmosphere in which they were writing and being critiqued. Had I ruthlessly criticized their writing as I had been criticized when I wrote professionally, they would have been reluctant to express themselves in their writing. I didn't have to relax my academic standards; I had to rethink how I would have preferred to have been treated when I first began my journalism career. I've adopted Mills' (1994) theory:

> It's not the method, but the quality of the relationship you establish with students that fosters learning. If you create a warm, loving classroom setting where emotional needs are recognized and accepted as part of school life, students feel free to step into the light and learn. If you pay attention to each one, letting all of them know they matter to you . . . they feel less need to resist learning. (p. 68)

Finally, I have learned that enthusiasm is, indeed, contagious. When I first told my students about the rush of writing, about typing fast and hard with sweaty palms and pounding heart as you watch thoughts appear and realize you are, finally, a journalist, their eyes lit up with excitement and anticipation. My only hope is that each of them experiences that thrill before leaving my classroom next May.

5

Student–Teacher Connections

os ✦ ဆ

Shawn Stanley

Connections between teachers and students occur everyday in the classroom. These connections are often the first steps toward a growing, meaningful relationship between students and teachers. These relationships are
formed over a period of time and are vital for maintaining the healthy,
positive influence that a teacher has with students.

In this chapter, I discuss these connections, the roles of teachers and
students in making these connections, and the ramifications of these
connections. I proceed under the assumption that teachers ultimately want
to connect with their students' lives. This assumption is made based on the
fact that teaching involves a close contact with students in helping them
gain knowledge and skills at school. Positive teacher–student relationships
are associated with positive attitudes toward school, increased academic
achievement, and more positive behavior (Medina, 1990).

Teachers have an enormous influence on students. Teachers see students
every day, in school and at activities outside of school. Because of their status
and position, teachers have a rare opportunity to make a positive impact on
their students. In today's society, especially, students often do not have
positive role models outside of school. Teachers can take on this role and
fulfill this need for the students. Because of the teacher's duty and responsibility to do what it takes to increase student learning and achievement, he
or she cannot overlook the potential roles that he or she may be in a prime
position to fill.

Students need personal support as well as academic support, and the
teacher needs to recognize what each student is dealing with in and out of
the classroom to effectively provide this support. These positive connections
increase student learning (Medina, 1990). Drugs, the breakdown of the
family unit, gangs, and violence are some of the many stresses that students

today must face. To combat these, teachers have a duty to reach out to their students and make positive connections with the students. Not only does making connections enhance students' academic achievement, it also improves students' social development.

Every single student has something inside of him or her that is positive. The positive aspect about one student may be more difficult to find than in another student, but it exists. Teachers need to find these aspects and recognize them. In order to do this, teachers need to listen to the students. Each student has a prize within him or her. Like a box of Cracker Jacks, there is always a prize within the student, although one might have to dig to the bottom of the box to find it.

> Somehow educators have forgotten the important connection between teachers and students. We listen to outside experts to inform us, and, consequently, we overlook the treasure in our very own backyards: our students. Student perceptions are valuable to our practice because they are authentic sources; they personally experience our classrooms firsthand. As teachers, we need to find ways to continually seek out these silent voices because they can teach us so much about learning and learners. (SooHoo, 1993, p. 390)

METHOD

To learn more about the connections between students and teachers, I wanted to find out what students felt was important in their learning. I wanted to see what made them enjoy school, what helped them to learn, and how they felt about their teachers as far as professional roles, and how, if at all, this flowed into personal roles. I shadowed three different high school students for one full day observing their interactions with their teachers as well as the teachers' interactions with the whole class. I then met with the students and interviewed them about different situations that occurred during the day. I chose these students because I felt they would completely and openly answer my questions. They represented different grade levels so that I would see a broader range of situations. I also conducted a review of current literature on the topic of student–teacher relationships.

Following are two scenes that I observed as I followed two of my students, Carol and Samantha.

> Carol walked into her Russian class where clumps of students were standing and talking together about their day. The tardy bell rang and the teacher went from group to group trying to get them all in their seats. As they went through the homework, most of the class had fallen asleep. One girl was using the file cabinet next to her desk as a pillow as the others buried their heads into their arms on their desks. One student who was awake interrupted to ask to use the bathroom. Two other boys were snickering back and forth. None of these actions were acknowledged by the teacher.

Samantha was sitting at her desk in a different Russian class with two other students clustered around her. They were working on a poster on a topic of their choice that was related in some way to the material they were studying. The scissors were cutting, markers were writing, and glue was spurting as the students discussed how they were going to present their topic to the class in Russian. Every once in a while, another student would come by to inspect and comment on what this group was doing. The teacher was also roaming the room, offering ideas and commenting on the students' work.

Students often experience school in a negative way. The following section explains how some students normally experience school—the boredom, the requirements, the rigid structure, and the uncaring atmosphere. The need exists for actions that will make school a positive, meaningful experience for students.

"NORMAL" SCHOOL VERSUS "CONNECTING" SCHOOL

First, school is often boring to students, and students sometimes have a hard time staying awake. Carol especially expressed this with regard to her Russian class. Nearly half of the class fell asleep during the lesson, which consisted of a video, audio tape exercise, and checking the previous homework. There were no opportunities for the students to move around and participate interactively in the lesson, and there were no discussions or creative projects that would let the students explore and make decisions in the classroom. This is "normal" school.

Samantha, on the other hand, had a project she was working on in Russian class. She was in a group cutting, coloring, planning, and discussing with the members of the poster team about how they were going to present their work to the class. She was not bored during this class, but instead, actively participated in her learning. This is "connecting" school.

Second, some students who are taking required classes do not want to be in these normal classes. They sometimes disrupt the class for all the other students. This problem brings up issues of class management and making a class appealing. No student has the right to hinder another in learning. Teachers need to control this by making the class interactive, interesting, and fun, so that students do not dread the class. Although teachers cannot always control school requirements, the responsibility to connect with their students still exists, and could ultimately help the situation by making a dreaded class fun and exciting.

Third, students felt school was rigid and petty because of its rules and structure. They were not allowed to express their feelings and felt they could just not be themselves. Carol expressed this feeling about another class where during class discussions she was cut off and her opinion deemed wrong by the teacher. She felt uncomfortable opening up and revealing her ideas and opinions because they were stomped on by the teacher. Samantha expressed her dislike of rules that are petty and are there just to have rules, according to her perception. These rules make school very rigid and when they are not truly meaningful or not enforced consistently, they become petty.

Fourth, students sometimes experience a lack of caring from teachers. Several students have complained to me about a teacher who openly has said to them on several occasions, "I do not care about you." This teacher has openly said that she does not care about the students personally but cares only that they do what she wants them to do in her classroom. The importance of socially connecting with the students is devalued by this teacher. The students dread this class and are intimidated by the teacher. In Carol's Personal Health class, the opposite was true. She felt cared for not only in the academic setting but also in the personal setting:

Personal Health class:

Q: What makes this teacher a good teacher?

Carol
A: She wanted to know about you. She takes time to sit and talk with you. She knows everything about you. She is caring. She wants to know how you are doing every day.

STUDENTS' NEEDS

Juhasz (1989) conducted a study on the influences that different people have on the lives of students. Students said the following about teachers:

My teacher says I am capable.
My teacher helps me learn more about life.
My teacher teaches me morals, discipline, good & bad, not to steal, fight, or lie.
My teacher makes me feel good. (pp. 588–590)

This study points to different issues than the ones policymakers feel are critical in today's schools. Class size, funding, or lack of parent support do not make the students' list of concerns. The students are often more concerned with the social aspects of school than the academic or political aspects. These social needs must be met before successful cognitive development can occur.

Students expect caring in relationships with faculty, and these expectations are frequently not met. Students want to be stimulated and pushed to learn. They want what they are being taught to have meaning and to be relevant to them. They want to be cared for and treated with understanding, and they want to feel secure and free enough to be able to be themselves at school. Students want school to be personal. They need to be able to relate to teachers on a personal level and to relate to the academics on a level that is relevant to them. "Students should not be expected to seek out learning experiences that are associated with boring, uninteresting, and dislikable teachers who provide punishing experiences" (Frymier, 1994, p. 103).

How true this is. And it is human! Teachers react in the same way. They take papers to grade or books to read during school meetings or presentations that may be less than exciting. Should we expect different behavior from our students? I think if teachers dread sitting through a boring presentation at an in-service event, we should expect the same reaction from students in our boring classes. I do think there is a time to endure situations such as these, but if this is not necessary, then let the students enjoy class. Having caring teachers, smaller classes with a sense of family, and active, hands-on learning activities are necessary factors for creating a learning environment where students care enough to learn.

David participated in his Personal Health class. It is evident how his needs are being met:

> David walked into his Personal Health class with a football. Today was his day to do his presentation to the class on football and the role it plays in his life. The teacher read a children's book to them to illustrate a topic they were discussing and not a single person fell asleep. They did a creative, art-type project to enforce what they learned from the story. Later, the class went outside to do some of the student presentations. One was on basketball in the gym and David's took place on the football field. The whole class got to learn a football play taught by David.

David loved this class. He was never bored and got to do meaningful activities that were interactive and fun, and got to present something that was very relevant in his life to the entire class.

WHAT TEACHERS CAN DO TO CONNECT WITH STUDENTS

How can we connect with students? There are some beginning qualities that can be fulfilled by teachers to start the process of connecting and relating to students. Some of these qualities were expressed by the students that I shadowed in school:

Q: What do you like about your teacher?

Carol
A: When they are caring, personal, encouraging, supportive.

David
A: When they are interesting, personal.

Samantha
A: When they are patient; know what they are doing; get students ready
for the future; have and enforce reasonable rules; are nice; have a sense
of humor; are genuine; are a friend in class and outside as well; take
time to help. (Student interviews)

First, and most important, teachers must know their students in order to
meet their needs. Students' needs vary with the increasingly diverse populations that schools serve today. In order to serve the changing age, racial,
ethnic, and socioeconomic diversity in the multicultural demographics of
school, teachers must get to know their students, learn about their backgrounds, and take into consideration where the students are in their lives.
Interest survey-type activities can help teachers learn about their students.
"We must remember that part of our job is that of bridge builders. We build
bridges to connect what students already know to what we want them to
know" (Thomas, 1993, p. 236). We must learn what the students already
know and relate this to the knowledge we want them to gain. If teachers
can make student tasks relate to what the students already know or have
experienced, they will be much more motivated to learn.

Next, in order to learn about students, what they need, what they like,
and so on, we must listen to them. They have so much to say and desire
desperately to be heard. "If we as teachers and administrators are to
understand and work with adolescents, perhaps we should begin listening
to the adolescent voices" (Smith & Johnson, 1993, p. 18). It takes time and
patience to listen to students, and a desire to understand and grasp the clues
that will help teachers and students connect. I have a student with whom I
worked closely in a counseling format who was talking about how he liked
spending time with me because, "She lets me talk and really listens to me"
(Journal notes).

Students so badly wish to be heard. They have opinions and feelings just
bursting out of them as they go through such a time of change during
adolescence. They need to express these thoughts to explore their validity
and also in order to understand the views of others as they express themselves. This process helps students learn to function with all different types
of people in society.

Teachers can begin connecting with students by showing that they care
about them. One definition of caring states that it "involves engrossment

in the other—feeling as nearly as possible what the other feels—and then acting as though in one's own behalf, but on behalf of the other" (Stinson, 1993, p. 234). Teachers' caring in school involves receptivity of the student, relatedness of material to the student's life, and responsiveness to the student.

The receptivity aspect of caring occurs when listening is incorporated into the classroom; then the students can express themselves and be heard by the teacher. Relatedness of material can be accomplished when teachers share with students on topics that interest them, or relate class material to experiences or activities that students can understand or relate to. Students are more motivated, can form their own way of understanding in their own minds, and are much more willing to "have fun" with what teachers are doing instead of being bored. This keeps students active in their learning. Also, there is always a response to an individual in caring *for* someone. Caring *about* someone does not require a response. Teachers must take care to respond to students so that they feel cared for. Otherwise, the students do not feel the care that they need.

Students also need support. They are often involved in many outside-of-school activities such as band, sports, academic teams, work, and so forth. They feel supported when they see teachers outside of school cheering them on or shopping at their place of work, on purpose. Students glow when teachers ask them about their other activities or congratulate them on an achievement. Often, parents do not come to activities and support their children. This role can easily be fulfilled by caring, active, involved teachers.

Trust is crucial in connecting with students. Students must feel comfortable with teachers in order to feel safe and be willing to deal with uncertainty and doubts and feelings of precariousness as they grow. As with support, trust may not be an aspect of the student's home life. Trust needs to be encouraged by teachers so that the student may feel secure in their classrooms. This makes the classroom an inviting, safe place. When all of these needs—their needs for receptivity, relatedness, responsiveness, support, and trust—are being met for students, the teacher has then taken on different roles within the role of teacher.

ROLES TEACHERS ADOPT TO MEET STUDENTS' NEEDS

Teachers can fulfill several different roles including friend, parent, and of course, instructor. Students explain how teachers take on the role of friend:

- "She's real understanding and patient. She helps with personal problems as well as problems in the class."
- ". . . likes to talk with us, listens to what we have to say."
- "Strict but more of a friend." (Stinson, 1993, p. 223)

Students respond well to the role of friend because friends are a very important aspect of their lives as they are growing up and learning social skills. Students like to call teachers whom they admire and look up to "friend" because it makes them feel good that this older person in a place of authority and power cares about them enough to listen to their personal problems and interact with them. The role of friend is great for students, but they need even more than just a friendship with teachers. The parental role adds more to the relationship, yet still allows a friendship to exist.

The parental role is filled when the teacher responds to the emotional needs of the students by caring for, trusting, and supporting students. The teacher pushes the students to learn and teaches them morals and acceptable behavior. This may be a role that doesn't excite students as much as the friend role, but the desire and need for this role definitely exists.

Next, of course, teachers fulfill an instructional role. This role ultimately is filled by teachers' meaningful, exciting, interactive lessons. The students want relevance and entertainment in their classroom experience. The teacher can implement these in the instructor role as he or she plans and delivers lessons and classroom procedures that are conducive to the students' desires, as well as to the curriculum standards that must be fulfilled.

Students do not just want a friend as a teacher. They want a friend, parent, and teacher all rolled into one. It is natural for many teachers to take on these roles in their positions of influence. Establishing connections does not mean just becoming a student's friend; it also involves taking on the roles of parent and instructor.

THE SPLIT

So far I have discussed aspects of connections and relationships between students and teachers and shown a need for connections based on the assumption that teachers should ultimately desire to know and be close to their students. As teachers make these initial connections with their students, there comes a point where there is a decision to be made by the students. Care, trust, and support encourage connections, but having these things in place does not necessarily ensure that strong relationships will actually be formed between student and teacher. Whether students want teachers to, teachers can make some connections with students. Students, however, ultimately decide whether to let teachers completely into their lives. We cannot have a relationship with students without their consent. They have control as to whether they will let teachers into their lives, or if they will choose to keep teachers out and at a distance.

Teachers can easily fit into the role of significant other and can have a strong impact on the lives of students. "The significant other is someone who is important to us, whose opinion we desire, value, and respect" (Juhasz,

1989, p. 581). Many aspects are taken into consideration in a student's perceptions of significance including time, place, and situation as well as individual needs, attributes, values, and attitudes. Each student is different but each has needs that should not be overlooked. Teacher feedback to the students as a significant other has the greatest effect on the student's self-esteem, self-worth, and self-confidence.

Because the student has a considerable amount of control in this process of connecting and relating with the teacher, it seems only logical to see what students need and like the most from teachers and use these data as an idea source for our methods and mannerisms in the schools. There are certain qualities and aspects that make connections between teachers and students turn into relationships. These differ from the previous qualities such as caring, trusting, and supporting in that the student cannot keep teachers from acting these qualities out in their everyday classroom or cocurricular interactions. Teachers can listen and care and support students all they want without the consent of the student.

The next ideas on how to connect with students are different from the previous ones in that the students have the decision as to how these aspects will affect them. Students may choose to go with the teacher's effort to make school meaningful and exciting, or they may choose to reject these efforts.

ENCOURAGING THE FORMATION OF RELATIONSHIPS

Teachers can take some crucial actions in the classroom that can cultivate connections with students who may not be as accepting as others. There are some aspects of teaching and teachers that students respond well to in the classroom environment that can help the teacher make connections.

First, students are more receptive to an egalitarian classroom. "Teachers they most admired worked with them on 'ground level' wanting to discover along with the students what is important. They were 'co-learners' and would be willing 'to get off the pedestal' " (Ruenzel, 1994, p. 32). Students respond much better to this type of classroom leadership atmosphere than they do to a dictatorship. There is a difference between stuffing students' brains with knowledge from above, and getting beside a student, nudging, probing, and pushing the whole way, but being stable and available to meet the needs of the students as they experience and learn new concepts.

Hand-in-hand with placing the self on an equal level goes the idea of letting students make choices in the class. By letting go of some of the power, the teacher gives up tight control and becomes more of a partner with the students, helping students make decisions on various class activities. This can be done in several arenas including forming rules, creating seating arrangements, making bulletin boards, and designing curriculum. The students love to have a say in their environment and it also helps in their individual learning as well as building class continuity. "Students could accentuate what they wanted to study in an environment conducive to their diverse capabilities" (Smith & Johnson, 1993, p. 28).

Next, students need to learn concepts and ideas as they relate to their lives. Students respond well when teachers try "to illustrate concepts with examples from rented videos, CNN, and TV commercials" (Elder, 1994, p. 570). Relevant activities let students form ways of thinking that fit them best and that help them remember. As a result of experiencing material that relates to their lives, students enjoy what they are learning and see the relevance of school to real life. Making class relevant is a helpful way to develop a classroom environment that is enjoyable, where learning is both interesting and entertaining. A relevant environment has been proven to help students like what they are doing and in turn, increase learning.

Students love interesting, challenging, weird, strange ideas and concepts and the opportunity to explore them. They also like to be free to discover things on their own. The following example shows how a math lesson can be developed to fit this description:

> I am teaching a Geometry lesson on the Mobius Strip. This concept involves a strip of paper, twisted once with both ends connected to form a loop. It is physical, tangible, and perplexing. Along with this, I am structuring the class with meaningful, open-ended questions that students should consider and a list of goals they will need to work on during their discovery time. This will give students the freedom to explore as they work and will not require a strict structure which might make the lesson no fun, but I will provide enough structure to keep the students from going wild. (Journal notes)

Providing interesting, fun problems that make students think critically and questioning them about how they come up with solutions shows students that you care about how they are thinking. Students should not just regurgitate information back to teachers but should have to use this information in meaningful ways. Teachers can relate the material to something the students have experience in and that attracts them. This will increase student learning and will encourage positive attitudes toward school.

The way teachers question students has much to do with increasing the enjoyment in student learning. Dichotomous questions can keep discussions on the surface and prevent thinking in-depth. Using open-ended questions allows students to learn, discover, and explore openly and freely and lets them delve deeper into topics of discussion. The teacher needs to let go of total control by not doing all the talking. We should be silent sometimes and let the students explore and discover on their own. We must interact meaningfully with the students and be silent when needed.

Establishing meaningful personal contact between the students and teachers encourages connections as well. At the beginning of the school year, teachers take the time to get to know their students. Students let teachers into their lives and may do so even more as the year progresses. It seems only fair, especially if teachers are truly stepping "off the pedestal," that teachers would let students know them as well. Students often do not see teachers as real human beings but as "the big mean people who won't let you make up work when you're absent and can't remember your name the first week of school" (SooHoo, 1993, p. 392). Students like to see that teachers have spouses and kids, second jobs, boyfriends, apartments to move into, private problems, and their own homework. It makes the teacher more real to the students, more human. To see that teachers really are human and deal sometimes with the same issues that students deal with is educational in itself. Teachers have a life outside of school, and bringing that into the classroom can be both intellectually stimulating as well as emotionally fulfilling for the students.

Students have been trained to be entertained or not pay attention as a result of the media and video games. If a teacher is liked by the students, he or she has won a big battle. Learning can occur when a student does not like the teacher, but it is more difficult on all parties involved when the teacher is trying to get the students to achieve certain goals and the students are fighting this effort or completely hating the experience and/or the teacher. This situation does not help educators as they try to make school positive.

Maybe it boils down to the following statements of what teachers can do to keep connecting with students and to encourage the growth of these connections into relationships.

- Believe in them.
- Challenge them academically.
- Encourage them to extend themselves to peers and teachers.
- Become partners in learning with them.
- Appreciate and respond to individual differences.
- Always boost students' self-image, self-esteem, and self-confidence through praise, understanding, and trust. (Flores, 1991, p. 59)

WHEN STUDENTS DO NOT LET TEACHERS INTO THEIR LIVES

Sometimes students choose not to let teachers into their lives.

Brett was one of the volleyball students that I coached. I was getting to know the players and they were getting used to me and all was going well. As the season progressed, Brett was very open with me and we talked and joked together before and after practice and after games. One day, out of nowhere, she closed up. She acted as if she didn't want to talk to me. I asked her if everything was going all right and she said yes. From then on, she was never the same fun-loving, open student but quiet and reserved toward me. I could not get back in. She had shut me out and I did not know why. (Journal notes)

The hard reality is that situations like this one are bound to happen, but we cannot give up our efforts to connect and to relate with students. We cannot cut off our support for a student when he or she rejects us; instead, we need to keep trying for the little connections in hopes that someday we may fulfill the right need for the student or that the student reaches a point inside himself or herself that allows us to come in. If we just shut the door, however, we will never get in. One never knows what lies in the minds of students, but teachers do have control over the fact that students' needs will be addressed by the teacher as best as can be done with the access the student has given. This actually makes the closed or open door of connecting with student needs through our many roles and actions as teachers more of a revolving door that is ever turning, with the teacher hoping, waiting for the chance to jump into the opening when given the opportunity.

OTHER ASPECTS THAT TEACHERS MUST CONSIDER FOR CONNECTING WITH STUDENTS

When teachers have established connections or are continuing the effort to connect, there are some obstacles and boundaries that teachers must be aware of. Teachers have the potential of having a great impact on students. Not only do they influence students in their lessons or daily classroom activities, but students gain or lose from teachers' mannerisms. "Students absorbed as much from teachers 'off-the-cuff' remarks and idiosyncrasies as they did from the 'official' curriculum" (Ruenzel, 1994, p. 35). Teachers are in such a position that they become a role model for all of their students. Especially when students do not have positive role models at home, teachers may end up fulfilling this need for students.

There is a concern to be addressed in our actions to bond with students. "All educators are expected to conduct themselves in a professional manner" (Wishnietsky & Felder, 1989, p. 79). Teachers need to be aware of the relationships or connections they are making and the direction they are taking. The focus must be kept on positive and healthy connections. Boundaries still exist and must be upheld in order to stay within the confines of professionalism. This is very important as teachers deal with fragile students who have real needs. Teachers are in a sensitive position; sometimes the possibility of total disaster exists when lines of professionalism are crossed.

Teachers may encounter other obstacles as they pursue connecting with their students. "The structure of teaching in public schools can keep teachers from being able to show they care. They are expected to respond to children in a detached way rather than as parents would" (Stinson, 1993, p. 233). We have already established the possibility of taking on some parental-type roles, making the structure in some schools a hindrance to the connecting process. This is something to be aware of so that teachers can try to stay out of this structure and develop their own structure that is conducive to students. After all, isn't that a duty of teachers in the first place? "Large classes, alienated and disruptive students, and bureaucratic pressures can keep teachers from being able to respond to the many needs—both personal and academic—of students" (Stinson, 1993, p. 233).

As hard as it seems in classrooms sometimes, teachers must constantly try to crush these barriers between students and teachers. "Human interaction is the single most important ingredient in education and schooling practices should be devised to enhance rather than suppress interaction" (Medina, 1990, p. 15). Teachers not only have the position to interact but can take it a step further and relate and connect to the students. This is what the students are concerned about. We have to start with the students' basic needs before we can expect academic achievement from them.

THOUGHTS ON THE "PERFECT TEACHER"

Now that we have laid this all out, the question may arise, "How can I be this parent–teacher–friend type with all of my students?" Obviously, teachers cannot fulfill all students' needs or be everything to everyone. It takes time, patience, and constant effort. Teachers are by no means perfect. They sometimes make mistakes and lose their composure. However, if the students are confident in the teacher's ultimate devotion to them, they will work with him or her and forgive when necessary. If students trust their teachers, students will trust that teachers will be there for them even in the worst of situations. If students can see teachers' efforts, students will respect teachers for that. Students need to see teachers' foibles. It is more valuable for a student to see a less-than-perfect teacher rather than a perfect, nonhuman-type teacher instructing them only through lessons. This makes teachers more real and more human. When teachers admit to these faults and try hard to fix them, the student gains respect for the teacher and can even sometimes relate to teachers' difficulties as well.

REFLECTIONS/CONCLUSIONS

"Positive relationships between teachers and students cultivate positive attitudes toward education in general, as well as towards specific learning tasks" (Frymier, 1994, p. 103). A student's positive attitude may be reflected onto the teacher as well, thus creating a positive classroom environment conducive to higher academic achievement. Connections between student and teacher sometimes help meet the goals of the curriculum.

One study provided support for the notion that ". . . teachers whose actions are thought to be friendly and loving toward their students more likely had students who acted similarly toward them" (Necessary & Parish, 1993, p. 62). We are humans teaching humans and should not overlook this. Connections are valuable in relation to classroom behavior and can be a great help in classroom management.

These connections also fulfill the personal needs of teachers. I think teachers usually desire to be liked by their students just as any human wishes to be liked by others. When the connections between students and teachers are made, they can make the teacher feel fulfilled as well. This puts the teachers on a direct line of affecting future generations. This can be very rewarding as teachers pursue acts of purpose and contribute to the greater society.

So what does all this mean for teachers? Students have definite needs. Teachers are in a position to fulfill these needs. If connecting with students really does help students, then it is the duty of educators based on their status and position to make the effort to reach the students in order to build positive attitudes about school and learning. This not only is beneficial for the students, but also for the teachers; the resultant possibility is that school will be a positive, meaningful experience for all.

6

A Study of Teachers and Their Relationships with At-Risk Students

cs ◆ so

Sherry Hughes

Even before the school year began, fellow teachers, administrators, and friends began to warn me of the "situation I had gotten myself into." The situation was my choice to spend my year-long internship in middle school.

The middle school is an inner-city school. The school population is predominately Hispanic, with only 5% African-American and 5% Anglo students. Over 95% of the students are currently participating in free or reduced lunch programs. Therefore, as an inner-city school, its reputation preceded it. The mere mention of the name to anyone in the teaching profession drew looks of compassion and "better you than me" comments:

- "If you are there, then you will see it all."
- "The students are dumb, violent, lazy, gang members, drug users, and unteachable."
- "Students can be flat out mean. . . . You have to be more like a prison warden than a teacher."

From the beginning of the school year, I realized that the students who walk the halls each day are not your "typical" young adolescents. However, they aren't mean, but rather young individuals leading tough lives. Many of the students come from broken homes, where they often lack the basic needs of food, shelter, and clothing. Although I had spent approximately 90 hours at the middle school as an undergraduate, I knew that the only good working knowledge I possessed of middle school was my own personal junior high experience. Having attended a junior high in a middle to upper class neighborhood, I knew that the similarities between the two schools would

83

be limited. Therefore, in order to be successful with these students, I would have to understand their needs and discover what works and what does not work.

But something about these students made them special. These students had so much "personality" (often referred to as "attitude"). I had to know what helped them succeed in one classroom and not another. I began to consider the notion that these unique students needed unique teachers. The recognition of this need for unique teachers led me to this study describing what types of teachers work best in a school with an inordinately large population of at-risk students.

With a significant rise in the number of at-risk students in our school system (Stevens & Price, 1992), the increased need for teachers who can work well with these students is evident. The focus of my study is to assist in my learning process of becoming a teacher, and also to provide future interns, student teachers, and current faculty with a base knowledge regarding at-risk students. Through this research, I hope to help teachers evaluate and effectively adapt their own personality and teaching style to better suit students at schools with large populations of at-risk students.

My essential question is, "Do at-risk students benefit from certain types of teaching styles?" I based my research on the following questions:

1. Are there certain similarities in teaching styles among teachers who are most successful with at-risk students? If so, what are these similarities?
2. Do distinct differences exist between the personalities of teachers who work effectively with at-risk students and those who do not?
3. If my findings from Questions 1 and 2 suggest differences, then how can teachers adapt their own teaching style and personality to best meet the needs of these unique students?

The research design began with the selection of four teachers to be primary subjects. Two of the teachers chosen are highly successful in working with at-risk students and the other two teachers have not been successful with at-risk students. My initial definition of success was based on classroom management, rapport with students, and failure rate. Using this criteria, teachers were selected by professional reputation, following a standard practice used by Peterson, Bennet, and Sherman (1991). Recommendations for my subjects came both from my mentor teacher, Nancy Baker, and Ms. Black, the principal of the school. My subjects consisted of two females and two males with two teachers described as the more successful teachers (MS) and two teachers identified as less successful teachers (LS).

Each of my subjects participated in a 30- to 40-minute interview where they were asked a series of open-ended questions regarding their teaching style, experience, and ability to work with students at the middle school. I also conducted two classroom observations per teacher, approximately 90 to 180 minutes in length. The first classroom observation was planned with the teacher's preference of date and class. The second observation was an impromptu visit with no prior notification.

As I spent my days sitting in classes and talking with my teachers, I began to wonder how the students felt about these four teachers. Did the students' perceptions of these teachers match my perceptions? I knew that in order to grasp what these teachers were really like, I would have to get input from their students. With the principal's consent, I facilitated a discussion–interview with two small groups of students. These students were also chosen by teacher recommendation.

The selected students had a variety of ability levels but were all considered to be at-risk (as determined by Frymier, 1992). Each grade level (6–8) was represented by at least two students, one female and one male. Every student had a class with at least one of the four teachers I had chosen as a subject. Students were asked to talk about their favorite teacher(s), their least favorite teacher(s), and to explain their reasoning for choosing a teacher. Because the most common at-risk students tend to be extroverts (Hanson, Silver, & Strong, 1991), these students were eager to express their thoughts and let their voices be heard. Even though the students had no idea that I had targeted four individual teachers for the study, they repeatedly mentioned these teachers' names throughout the interview. In fact, all teachers fell within their expected categories as predetermined by professional reputation.

- "We listen to outside experts to inform us, and, consequently, we overlook the treasure in our very own backyards: our students" (Soohoo, 1993, p. 390).
- "Who knows better about the teachers than the students who sit in their class everyday?"

Besides my teacher observations, interviews, and student focus groups, I have also kept a daily journal. This journal functions as a data source containing informal observations, conversations, and experiences that have occurred throughout my research. The information recorded in my journal synthesizes with my formal qualitative research, allowing me to be a participating observer. Quotes or scenarios that are not cited specifically were taken from my journal and are included to give the reader a more thorough and meaningful perspective.

During the last decade there has been a marked increase in publications addressing the issues of teaching at-risk students: "The publication of the document (A Nation at Risk) spawned a whole new generation of reports" (Crosby, 1993, p. 600). Abraham Maslow's (1970) hierarchy of needs was where I initiated my understanding of why these students were not succeeding in school. Maslow's hierarchy "is an attempt to formulate a positive theory of motivation" (p. 35).

In order to understand my students, I would have to learn what motivates them. The hierarchy begins with a lower level Maslow calls the basic needs. According to Maslow, most people follow the hierarchy step by step; without the lower needs being met, a person will not be able to move up the hierarchy. I now understand why students who came into my class suffering from hunger and sleep deprivation had little intention, motivation, or ability to learn. According to Maslow's hierarchy, if a student's basic needs (physiological, safety, loving, and belonging) are not being met, then the upper needs of the desire to know and to understand may be completely irrelevant. For an at-risk student to succeed in the classroom, a teacher must fulfill or account for most of these basic needs before the student reaches a higher level of motivation. The hierarchy of needs, according to Maslow (1970) are:

1. Physiological.
2. Safety, security.
3. Love and belonging.
4. Self-esteem.
5. Self-actualization.
6. To know and understand.
7. Aesthetic, creative.

- "I see them as an extension of my own family."
- "When I moved to an inner-city middle school I became a parent again."
- "No matter what we do to these students it doesn't make a difference because what they go through every day is much worse than any zero or suspension we could ever give them."

Frymier (1992) conducted a research project that reinforced Maslow's hierarchy of needs as it pertains to students. Frymier's study included over 20,000 students from various public schools throughout the United States. Frymier discovered that at-risk students had many common characteristics, and teachers that worked effectively with these students had four basic skills. Frymier, similar to Maslow, found that needs must be fulfilled in order. Therefore, when working with at-risk students, teachers who do not provide an understanding and nurturing environment first are not able to obtain academic success from their students. The four basic teachers' skills that Frymier found most effective with at-risk students are as follows:

1. Understanding.
2. Caring.
3. Cultivating a sense of responsibility.
4. Nurturing academic achievement and skills.

Hanson, Silver, and Strong (1991) based their knowledge of teaching at-risk students on the Jungian-based system. This system breaks up into two categories: one's perception (senses or intuition) and one's judgment (thinking or feeling). Their research concludes that "each person tends to have a dominant style that responds best to a specific type of instruction" (Hanson et al., p. 30). They further assert that at-risk students do not succeed in classrooms utilizing traditional types of instruction that emphasize facts, skills, and lecturing. Their research claims that today's society, as well as our education system, emphasizes the "sensing-thinking" and the "intuitive-thinking" learner that allows students who learn best through traditional modes of instruction to be successful. Natter and Rollins (1974) found that 99.6% of all students who drop out of school once they are of legal age fall into the "sensor" category. The neglect of teachers to focus on the "feeling" learners' style can cause these students to be at risk (Hanson et al., 1991).

- "These students aren't the kind of students who will sit and read a chapter or listen to a long lecture."
- "If we are to see the gifts of all of our students, we must first appreciate their learning styles" (Hanson et al., 1991, p. 34)

My first less successful (LS) teacher, Paul Simpson, is a veteran teacher. Paul teaches eighth-grade social studies in a traditional style. A daily lesson begins with a 10- to 15-minute lecture and then the students are to complete a worksheet. Paul considers the book supplied by the school to be "too hard" for the students, so his curriculum is based on a series of worksheets that he writes or copies from printed curriculum. He describes his teaching style as "aided practice with minimal evaluations." He believes that students should be homogeneously grouped. This belief contradicts the district and school policy of heterogeneously grouped students in academic teams. He feels that because students are not grouped by levels, he is unable to teach effectively. Therefore, Paul gears his curriculum toward the low-performing students.

Sherry: How would you describe the effectiveness of your teaching style?

Paul: For what I have to work with, the attitudes and work habits, I think my teaching style is about the best we can do.

Paul: I have to teach under those parameters (district policy) and those parameters have pretty much shut us down.

Student: All he gives us is worksheets . . . and says, "Here, do it," and doesn't explain.

The class sits in rows and the room has a very clean, neat appearance. The bulletin boards are covered with class schedules and administrative bulletins. On the front board hang discipline charts for each class period. The only posters that hang in the room are two computer-printed banners stating the district's theme for the academic year, "Let's Make It Happen!" These banners became somewhat ironic as I learned about Paul's methodology. Paul believes that "there isn't a way to have a successful class with these types of students." He also believes that if students do not come to school with their "head on right," well-fed, well-rested, prepared for class, and open to learning, then that student should be removed from the classroom.

After observing and interviewing Paul, I began to see the hostility that Paul exhibited toward his students, the administrators, district leaders, and fellow colleagues. Paul's views regarding discipline are not parallel with the administration and because he has voiced his lack of support and disagreement with school policies, he feels he has suffered greatly. Although Paul is not well-liked by most of his students, he seems to be a nice man who just knows that "this is not his place to teach."

Sherry: What disciplinary procedures achieve appropriate behavior in your classroom?

Paul: Not that much works. Good teachers aren't in inner-city schools.

Ronald Miller is the second LS teacher chosen for the study. Ronald is a young teacher who teaches seventh-grade English. A typical day in Ronald's class begins with a brief oral discussion and/or verbal instructions. Students are then left to work individually or in groups doing research or answering questions from the text or from a worksheet. Ronald's curriculum is mainly based on written projects. Because Ronald is an auditory learner, he usually teaches orally with lots of classroom discussion. Ronald feels that his strength in the classroom is his communication skills: "I am a good prober and don't let students off the hook." I found this to be a contradiction after observing two different classes. Students were very unresponsive to his discussion prompts and often times students would not even answer a direct question that required a "yes" or "no" answer.

Student 1:   Even the people who understand him won't speak.

Student 2:   We don't listen to him . . . we do something completely different than he asks us to do.

Like Paul, Ronald also felt ill-prepared to teach middle school or "to work with these students." Consequently, he has lowered his expectations and slowed the pace of his curriculum. This was evident even in the limited amount of time I spent working with Ronald. Over this span of time, I saw students working on one "project." The project included researching and writing an outline. Both times I visited the classroom, the front board still contained the same instructions, and there was no evidence that much, if any, progress had occurred.

Sherry: Why don't you like Mr. Miller?

Student: He gets to me.

Sherry: Why does he "get to you"?

Student: He doesn't know how to teach the class right, he stays on the same thing too long.

Ronald's opinion is that all teachers need a vision; although Ronald's vision "is for something else," and he will not continue teaching after this academic year. However, he does believe that the success of a teacher is based on his or her vision.

Paul and Ronald fit into a category of teachers who are merely "biding time." Their current placement or job is simply a holding place until they can be transferred to a "better" school or get out of the teaching profession completely. Although I did find some positive aspects in their teaching styles, classroom management, and personalities, their students' and fellow colleagues' opinions seemed to be fairly accurate as to their lack of success in the classroom. My biggest remaining challenge was to define exactly what about their personality or teaching style made them unsuccessful with at-risk students.

My underlying goal, as I started this research, was to establish good rapport with all four teachers, mainly in order to clearly observe their true teaching styles and personalities. This was a big challenge to overcome with the LS teachers. When I started to ask these two LS teachers about their backgrounds and teaching styles, they immediately became very suspicious of my work and the true intentions of my observations and interviews. One clear difference between the LS and MS teachers was the eagerness and willingness of the MS teachers to participate and accept me in their classroom. During all four observations of my LS teachers, I felt both teachers performed for my benefit, instead of teaching their class.

Sherry: I noticed that Paul is very curious about what I was writing. . . . I felt that I had to cover up what I was doing.

Sherry: Paul came to my room during his conference period to tell me that the next class period had gone better and he had found a way of teaching what he needed.

I found two similarities between Paul and Ronald's teaching styles: (a) neither of them used hands-on activities, and (b) their curriculum was quite traditional. Students were there simply to complete a worksheet, test questions, or a writing assignment. Both teachers incorporated "busy work" into their daily lessons. In Ronald's class, students copied an example of a four-page outline. Paul even explained that "today we are going to do some busy work." In both teachers' classes, I also observed an overwhelming amount of cheating: students copying answers from other students, textbooks, and research materials.

> Student: I like his class because I can cheat.

The LS teachers were both very critical toward their students. They tended to be judgmental and were very unwilling to repeat questions or empathize with any lack of understanding on the part of their students. I felt that most of their students felt very intimidated and uncomfortable asking or answering questions in class. Neither of the teachers focused on their lower achievers or students that simply sat because they did not understand. Nor did I observe either teacher making special efforts to check on a student's understanding of the lesson or general well-being.

> Ronald explained instructions on what the students were to do for the day and asked, "Does anyone have any questions?" There was no response and the assignment began. Jesse raised his hand in the back of the room and asked, "How do you do it?" Ronald simply replied, "You didn't shake your head 'no' earlier when I asked if you didn't understand."

> Paul: I don't help those students that are not eager and willing to learn.

During our interviews, students repeatedly expressed that the reason they did not like a teacher was because he or she yelled at the class or individual students. However, I did not observe either of my LS teachers raising their voices in class. Classroom management differed drastically between the LS teachers. Paul was implementing a classroom management plan that he had been advised to use by the administration. This plan consisted of five specific steps for Paul to record and account for misbehavior; each mark represented a negative consequence (i.e., warning, student conference, parent/team conference, lunch detention, and office referral). Ronald's management consisted of simply letting students do as they pleased until he felt they deserved lunch detention. It was not evident from my observations what exactly the rules in the classroom were.

In Ronald's class, I observed students who sat and did little or nothing for the entire period. This behavior was parallel in Paul's class; both teachers had a lot of "off-task" behavior. Students were combing their hair, writing notes, talking to peers, or throwing things about the classroom. Both teachers explained that all they do is "survive" each day. Paul explained that his days are spent "fighting to keep control." Ronald believes that teachers must "persevere" through each day and "come back fighting."

> Paul: I have gone to a survival mode, what can I do to get through the day and eliminate damage control? Just survive.
>
> Sherry: What kinds of things did you do in his (Paul's) class?
>
> Student: Throw paper airplanes.

The students interviewed showed little or no respect for either LS teacher. Students claimed that they and other students intentionally made fun of and acted defiant in the classrooms of my two LS subjects. The lack of mutual respect between the students and teachers was evident in both Paul's and Ronald's classrooms. The devaluation and basic lack of respect of students by teachers has been a vital complaint by students : "They treat us like kids" (Soohoo, 1991, p. 388).

> Paul to student: I am not going to talk to you anymore because I can see you are too tired.
>
> Sherry to student: Why did you call him "Mr. Fur Ball"?
>
> Student: Because no one liked him.

My conclusion regarding the similarities between my LS teachers was that neither teacher ever adjusted, changed, or just "threw out" their lesson or curriculum. The curriculum had a set timeline, and it did not allow room for adaptation. This was evident when I observed Ronald's first period class where students were very sleepy and unresponsive. Ronald proceeded to turn the lights off so students could copy off an overhead projector. I found myself in a dull stupor after 20 minutes of copying with the lights turned off. Paul explained to me that the next topic he planned to cover in class was too difficult for his students and he realized that most of the students were not ready to move on. Paul, however, still proceeded with the next day's lesson (worksheet), as the book prescribed.

Jane, my first more successful (MS) teacher, is recognized by her fellow colleagues for her work with at-risk students. She currently teaches eighth-grade social studies. Jane claims that there are "no typical days in her classroom." She does a variety of assignments including book work, reading maps, class discussions, and making three dimensional models. If she gives direct instruction, it is usually in a "miniformat" that is no longer than 10 to 15 minutes. She feels that most of her teaching is done while she is assisting and monitoring individual students' progress. Jane believes that her students should be doing most of the work in her class and not vice versa. Jane and her academic team are involved in the writing and implementing of interdisciplinary curriculum. She is always very eager to try new and different ideas.

Sherry: What do you consider your students' role to be in your classroom?

Jane: They are the workers and the learners; they need to be actively involved.

Jane's room was very organized and the place seemed almost like "home." Scattered throughout the room were big round tables that sat four students comfortably. In the front right corner of the room was the "living room." There was a couch, rocking chair, and a bookshelf filled with a variety of books. The walls were very decorative, and the room was covered with affirmative anecdotes or quotes, such as "We can work it out," and the positive consequences of her discipline management plan. During both observations, the agenda for the day and the instructions for the lesson were written in detail on the front board.

Jane is a very positive, upbeat person and she emphasizes courtesy and respect in her classroom. She rewards students verbally and also with personal attention. She gives a variety of rewards for perfect attendance, most improved, and good behavior. Jane enjoys being very involved and "hands-on" with students; this includes hugs and "pats on the shoulder."

Sherry: Why do you like Miss Neidorf?

Student: She gives us food and popcorn.

Sherry: Any other reason?

Student: She is easy to talk to.

Susan Peterson was the final teacher chosen for the study. Susan's MS status is attributed to her experience and knowledge of working with at-risk students. She enjoys teaching in inner-city schools and enjoys the challenge of working with at-risk students. Susan now teaches eighth-grade history. A typical day in Susan's class includes a variety of activities including a "bunch of laughs" and some storytelling. She requires her students "to be better thinkers" and is not interested in their ability to regurgitate a bunch of facts. Susan claims that her teaching style adapts to the needs of her students. Her class involves a lot of teacher–student interaction. She leads a variety of activities including group work, class and teacher-driven discussions, visual projects, research, book work, and map reading. Susan is also involved in the school project of designing and implementing interdisciplinary curriculum.

Susan: I want the students to find out that there is more to life than these couple of blocks around the school.

Susan: I like to address the kids' styles.

Susan's classroom is very small and comfortable. Her students sit in desks that are arranged in short tight rows covering both of the side walls. In the center of the room sits a big table that contains a map of the world and students' work. At the front of the room is the teacher's desk and two small couches. The room is covered with students' work as well as photographs of students. The crowded, cluttered room has a very lived-in look, and the students seem very comfortable in the tight space.

Susan is an extrovert and often can be very blunt. She "tells it like it is." She feels that her personality positively influences her teaching style. Being a mother and growing up in a single-parent home has also greatly influenced the way Susan teaches. She feels she can truly relate to many of the things her students are feeling and experiencing. Therefore, she expects her students to be active participators in her classroom and she encourages parental involvement.

Susan: They (students' parents) brought them into this world, so they can check their homework.

Both of my MS teachers were energetic women. Their love for their students and their job was evident from the moment that I began to interact with them. Both of the MS teachers chose to come and teach and enjoy the challenges, heartache, love, and joy they receive from their students. Jane and Susan love teaching. Susan feels that the key to a successful classroom is for students to really know that you like them. After observing their classroom and speaking with them, I realized that both of my MS teachers are "here for the duration."

Jane: One of the best compliments I ever got from a student came during the middle of the class when he hollered out, "Miss, you really like doing this don't you."

Susan: If you are going to be in a classroom, you better find a way to enjoy it because the work is too hard if you don't enjoy it.

Sherry: Why do you like Ms. Peterson's class?

Student: Because she is nice to me.

Sherry: Do you like social studies?

Student: No, I just like Ms. Peterson.

Both of my MS teachers spend most of their classroom time adjusting and meeting the needs of individual students. They explained that their lessons are fairly flexible. During one observation, I watched Susan focus a student's research topic so that the student would be able to cover the topic effectively in the allotted time. In Jane's class she took the first 10 minutes or so to explain that a guest speaker was coming sixth period and to answer any questions or concerns about the visit. I realized that they continually adapted their lessons to meet the individual needs of their students. Both teachers also explained that they spend a great deal of time assessing a student's weaknesses and strengths and assigning work to a student so that he or she can be successful. They also believe in giving the students a variety of ways to show their level of knowledge about a subject. This includes students giving answers orally to the teacher or into a tape recorder, writing a story, or drawing pictures.

> Jane: It doesn't matter what they do, within reason, as long as it demonstrates their learning.

> Susan: I often look at a student's ideas or concepts rather than the actual product.

Establishing discipline and being consistent with students is an important issue that both of my MS teachers address in a similar manner. Susan explained that she establishes the rules from the beginning of the year and simply expects students to abide by them. She thinks this expectation is what achieves appropriate behavior in her classroom. Jane explained that she sets up a parameter within which students are to behave. She does not believe in a long list of rules but instead has a behavior code that allows for leeway in the students' actions and her consequences. During my observations I saw little, if any, discipline problems in either Susan's or Jane's classroom. Susan and Jane both describe their discipline as fairly lenient but very consistent; however, both stress that students need enough structure and discipline so that students are able to learn and the teacher is able to teach. Both MS teachers explained how important it is, when working with young adolescents, to separate the student from the student's misbehavior.

> Sherry: Since I am studying to be a teacher, what things do I need to know or do so that I am a good teacher?

> Student 1: Don't let them (students) take advantage of you.

> Sherry: Should I be strict?

> Student 2: To a point . . .

> Student 1: Don't let students talk back to you. Tell them not to talk to you that way.

> Susan: I can really get put out with them but it doesn't mean that I don't love them or care about them or that I don't want the best for them.

> Jane: One of my students once told me that "you get real angry with us but you forgive us."

Both of my MS teachers repeated several times that the key to a successful classroom was mutual respect between the teacher and student. They feel that developing good rapport with their students makes all the difference. Jane is very courteous to her students and emphasizes respect a lot. During my observations, I noticed that Jane gets her students' attention by saying "excuse me, may I have your attention please?" I also noticed that she repeatedly thanked students for answering questions and for good behavior. Jane explained to me that she also expects her students to be respectful towards each other. She does not allow fellow students to tell each other to "shut up" or call each other "stupid." Susan is also very courteous and respectful toward her students. While observing Susan, I found her to be very encouraging towards her students' ideas and very complimentary about students' good work and behavior. Susan's and Jane's rapport with their students was also evident during the student discussion groups. Students spoke about them with respect and they were obviously well liked.

Although Jane's room was very well organized and Susan's room looked crowded and cluttered, the environment of their classrooms was one of comfort, stability, and caring. Their rooms did not look like traditional classrooms. There were no "graveyard rows." I observed students truly being themselves and enjoying the classroom. Therefore, I conclude that both MS teachers developed very warm and caring environments for teaching.

I also observed that Susan and Jane set high expectations for their students. They explained that students needed to be responsible for their actions and feel that it is their job to encourage and enforce responsibility. Susan and Jane challenge their students to be responsible and also challenge them academically. They want their students to be successful; however, they also realize that their students must be challenged so that they are not "bored." During my month of work with both teachers, neither teacher ever admitted that their students were not capable of learning something or that a topic was too hard for them. In fact, they were both very confident in their teaching styles, students, and lessons and demonstrated openness for me to observe or participate at any time.

Although my two MS teachers differ drastically in their styles, they both succeed in "winning over" their students. These two women are unique teachers who can work with these unique students. I feel that it is important for all teachers and administrators to focus on what qualities make a teacher successful with at-risk students. Many current studies developed lists or categories of personalities, teaching styles, discipline management, and a kind of curriculum that works most effectively with at-risk students.

After looking for similarities and differences among my four teachers, I set out to find the "key ingredients" to an effective and successful teacher of at-risk kids. My research illustrates examples of "what to do and what not to do."

Clarification of the real impact a teacher's personality and attitude had on at-risk students hit when one of my students shared with me how much an individual teacher affected her success.

> Melissa was very unsuccessful in school and had spent most of her time being in trouble, either with the school or the law. She informed me one morning that Ms. Fisher was her favorite teacher. Ms. Fisher is the in-school suspension coordinator. She explained to me that she would rather be in the Alternative Center (AC) with Ms. Fisher than in her regular classes. Her reasons were that Ms. Fisher really cared about her and understood her. Melissa explained, "Whenever I am in AC, I don't get in trouble; but when I am not in AC, I always get in trouble."

Melissa was willing to give up group work, hands-on activities, field trips, lunch with her friends, and any other privileges just to be with a teacher she knew cared for her and understood her. The bottom line is that a teacher's willingness to understand and care about a student is the most important issue to being successful with at-risk students. (Frymier, 1992; Manning & Payne, 1984; Porro, 1985).

It is important to note that both of the most successful teachers were female and both of the less successful teachers were male. In our society, women are usually characterized as more tender, compassionate, nurturing, and supportive. Men are stereotyped as unemotional and as rational, logical thinkers. Although these roles are breaking down, the issue that gender may play in working with at-risk students is significant.

Mutual respect and developing good rapport with students is very important when working with at-risk students, much more important than any discipline management plan or creative curriculum. If a student's respect is gained, they will try to succeed even if they "hate history." However, this respect requires a variety of issues. "It is hoped that this teacher self-awareness would result in a qualitative improvement in teacher–child relationships" (Manning & Payne, 1984, p. 11).

In conclusion, when working with at-risk students teachers should, therefore:

- Establish a fair and consistent classroom management (Lehr, 1987; Porro, 1985).
- Adapt lessons or curriculum to the individual students' needs (Peterson et al., 1991).
- Allow curriculum to be interrupted to deal with students' concerns or problems (Peterson et al., 1991).
- Set high expectations for students (Lehr, 1987; Peterson et al., 1991; Porro, 1985).
- Incorporate "hands-on" activities (Lehr, 1987; Peterson et al., 1991).
- Establish a warm, comfortable environment where students feel relaxed and safe (Peterson et al., 1991).

- Remain positive and patient with students (Lehr, 1987; Peterson et al., 1991).
- Use humor to overcome difficult issues (Porro, 1985).

Ultimately, the personality of a teacher is a key element to success with at-risk students. Therefore, one must show love and care to those children that enter today's classroom.

"They won't care what you know until they know that you care."

7

Don't Be Sorry. Just Learn It.

C8 ◆ 80

Heidi D. Anderson

My mother was the first person to really make me think about gender bias in my teaching. In August before school started, I mentioned to Mom the research the American Association of University Women conducted on gender biases in the classroom, published as the report *How Schools Short-change Girls* (1992). In general, I explained to her that boys typically receive more of a teacher's time, attention, and energy than girls do. I mentioned that boys are usually called on before girls and that boys dominate class discussions. Then I dared to tell Mom that I would never fall into this trap. As a female student, I knew what it was like to have boys dominate discussions in high school and middle school. I told Mom that I would be sure to call on just as many girls as boys and would never allow the boys to dominate the classroom.

But Mom disagreed. She felt certain that I would be inclined to call on boys first, to give them the attention they demanded simply because I have a younger brother with whom I am very close. She reminded me of all those times I had tutored him in math. Mom felt that I would be more in tune with these young men because of having a younger brother myself.

You know, Mom always knows best. Now that I have read the research and spent over 4 months in the classroom, I see that I, too, have fallen into the pit of gender-biased teaching. Despite the fact that I consciously call on girls and boys equally, the boys still manage to dominate the classroom and steal most of my attention.

Unfortunately, when teachers focus their attention on male students, girls are left by the wayside. I am especially worried about the gender gap that exists in high school mathematics. Why are boys outscoring girls in this subject? When I teach math, what can I do to entice young women to continue taking more mathematics courses?

99

It is important that we do encourage young women to take more math classes while in high school. Why? Because the subjects that girls study in high school make a difference for their futures. For example, despite society's great leaps toward gender equality in the workforce, men still continue to earn more than women despite equal years of education. However, these "wage differentials favoring men are considerably less for women . . . who have earned eight or more mathematics credits in college" (American Association of University Women [AAUW], 1992, p. 4). But our female students will never reach that level of equity if we do not encourage them to take more mathematics courses—now.

The obstacle, however, appears to be the girls' attitude that math (and science, too) is a "boy's domain." In this case study, I strive in part to show why girls feel this way.

To make the research more realistic to me and to verify that the written reports concerning gender bias were indeed legitimate, I observed 11 mathematics classrooms myself, as well as concentrated on my own work in the classroom. I chose to watch willing teachers of both sexes and various ages and years in the profession. I spent at least 45 minutes in each class and compiled data on an observation sheet that clearly indicates what features of teacher intervention and reaction occurred in each class. I found that these classrooms exhibited slight, almost subtle instances of gender bias. Not one teacher purposely inhibited or discouraged a young woman from learning mathematics.

Here I create a case study that includes aspects of events and characters across a number of classroom scenes, including my own. The case is a compilation, if you will, of the trends in classroom practice that manifest potential gender bias (see Sizer's *Horace's Compromise*, 1985, for a text based on summary characters and events) and is based on my observations, interviews, and analysis of data. This case study seeks to alert teachers of instances of gender bias and to suggest possible solutions. My hope is that the reader will at least take a few minutes of self-reflection to determine if the scenarios that follow have been repeated in his or her own classroom. I know they have been in mine. A teacher's heightened awareness may be all that is needed to give female students encouragement and support during their journey through high school mathematics.

ALISON

Meet Miss Thomas. She has that spark of energy that tells her students, "I love mathematics and I would love to share with you everything I know that's beautiful about mathematics." She cares about her students as exemplified in her numerous after-school tutoring sessions that she schedules throughout the academic year. At home, Miss Thomas carefully updates previous years' lectures, worksheets, quizzes, and tests to maintain their usefulness with her current classes. In the classroom, she wants each and every student to succeed so she tries her best to explain the concepts thoroughly through her tried-and-true lecture format. Clearly, Miss Thomas is a caring, exemplary educator. But each day, Miss Thomas unintentionally cheats her female students out of an encouraging, supportive, challenging education. We have much to learn about gender bias from her.

I observed Miss Thomas teach on two separate occasions, each involving a different collection of students. The first involved a group of young people of whom Miss Thomas is very proud. These students comprise her upper level math class. The class of 18, 9 boys and 9 girls, buzzed with the sound of minute activities: rummaging through bookbags, tossing snippets of conversations, giggling. I have walked in on the start of correcting the last 6-week test.

Initially, I am impressed. Miss Thomas has pushed her students to complete some complicated proofs, things I was not exposed to until college as a mathematics major. Verbally, Miss Thomas goes over the test and writes some answers on the board. But she is not at all personal with the students. She, in fact, appears to be talking to the blackboard with her back to her students. Meanwhile, her students are more concerned with comparing grades with each other than correcting their tests. But I excuse this lack of student interaction due to the fact that this is a relatively unimportant part of the day's agenda.

Once this drudgery is complete, Miss Thomas begins a discussion of the previous night's homework. "Any questions on this 6 week's first assignment?" The class stirs quickly to life, eager to rectify last night's confusions. The room swells with productive noise as students whisper disagreements, arguments, and supports of their methods of working the problems. Sally is the first to speak: "I don't understand number 12."

"Give me what you have so far. . . . Okay for that one spot. You got it. Good." That is the first of a total of three praises Miss Thomas lavishes on her students this period. Sally continues with her questioning of that particular problem, only to be squelched by Miss Thomas' irritated voice, "Now we're getting this." Interestingly, Miss Thomas later speaks in irritated tones, in both instances to girls. Why is she annoyed that these young women are attempting to sort out and make sense of the information?

Then Cassie, a girl seated in the very front, right where Miss Thomas stands, raises her hand to ask a question. She is called on, and the teacher begins to listen to her question. Suddenly, with a flurry of movement, a boy from the back of the room raises his hand and begins speaking loudly without getting called on. Obviously flustered, Miss Thomas listens to Tom, and simply allows him to finish his question. She does not correct the young man. Rather, Miss Thomas turns to Cassie and says, "I'll answer this question then get back to what you were asking me." From this interruption, Cassie learns that her questions are not as important, thought-provoking, or worth answering before Tom's. The message: Tom deserves Miss Thomas' attention first.

> Alison: Miss Thomas isn't completely aware of what's going on in her classroom. She needs to move at the students' pace. . . . She doesn't really take the time to explain things well, and that's when asking questions is crucial. If you don't ask questions in that class, she won't slow down.

After 5 minutes of an extensive explanation for Tom, Miss Thomas' attention returns to Cassie. Again, before she has a moment to answer, Tom speaks up again, "Do you think you could go over number 30 quickly?" Clearly, Tom is cognizant that he interrupted Cassie; he asks Miss Thomas to go over problem number 30 *quickly,* implying *before* getting back to Cassie. I am worried. Will Cassie ever get her question answered? Does this young man feel his question is more important than Cassie's? Fortunately, Miss Thomas says, "No, I don't think so. I had some others to answer before that came up. Cassie, what was your question?"

Believe it or not, Cassie is interrupted yet again, this time by a housekeeping question that Miss Thomas feels compelled to answer. But Cassie is quiet and patient, a model student, and she's not creating any disruptions; her question can wait. After another minute, Miss Thomas finally answers Cassie's question for her, but it is too late. Cassie's self-esteem has been chipped away with each minute spent answering someone else's question. For the remainder of the period, Cassie is silent. It is not worth asking questions in this class when a boy's question is interpreted as more important or crucial than her own.

Cassie's question has alerted Alison to another quandary. She asks, "Why do we multiply by two again? I'm sorry, I forgot." Without a word, Miss Thomas walks to the blackboard and with snide flair, writes then underscores the answer multiple times. Alison says, "Oh, oh."

Miss Thomas now shifts emphasis to the next problem with a general question. "Now do you recall the logical first step here? What do you get?" Tom shouts out, "One over x squared! One over x squared!" Miss Thomas ignores this incorrect answer and writes the correct one on the board. "Oh," says Tom. "*Negative* one over x squared."

Alison continues to struggle with the reasoning. "I don't understand why that's true." Miss Thomas begins disdainfully, "We're going back to *algebra,*" then completes the explanation. The comment is meant to chide students for not having brushed up on their algebra skills, but the manner of delivery is one of irritation. Alison does not let this irritation get to her; she plows onward, trying to apply higher level thinking skills. She wants to know if there is a better, more efficient way of solving this problem. "I don't understand how that makes it any easier," she challenges. "It may not," Miss Thomas replies. "It's just another way of doing it." Alison is now clear. "Oh, I see. I'm sorry. I'm sorry."

Miss Thomas did not respond to Alison after the apologies. Why did Alison feel she needed to apologize for asking questions that would ultimately lead to a better understanding of mathematics? Is it not true that teachers experience a small victory when their students ask questions to aid understanding? Then why didn't Miss Thomas alleviate Alison's troubles by saying something like, "Hey, no need to apologize. It takes courage to ask questions." Girls need encouragement to be aggressive and take control of their learning. And they should not feel they need to apologize for taking up class time when asking questions.

> During my observations of your class, you brought to my attention something very interesting. You spoke up in class and asked questions of your teacher, but you apologized for asking her questions. Why do you think you did that?
>
> Alison: I guess it's a way to cleanse yourself for any blame the class could give you if you put them all behind.

ADRIAN

One week later, I visited Miss Thomas again, but in a different class setting. This time she is teaching a lower level math class, difficult because the students are generally not interested in mathematics. In all likelihood, this class may be the students' last math course. Miss Thomas maintains her same dignity with these students, but I notice that she does not enjoy this class nor does she expect a lot of progress from this assortment of teenagers.

Students stroll into the room, continuing their excited chatter and laughter from the halls. They are more boisterous than the upper level class, even with only 14 students. A tall, husky young man saunters into class. He sits just as the tardy bell rings. He has a look about him that says, "I am unique. You will never teach another student like me in your classes ever again." This is Adrian, and I imagine he was placed on this earth to keep teachers on their toes. Adrian demands attention. He glances around the room, taking note of who is here and who has seen his entrance. Noticing a new face in the classroom, he immediately strikes up a conversation with me. Once he discovers that I am an intern teacher, he immediately rattles off a list of other interns that he thinks I might know. He is polite to me and seems to have a genuine interest in people. We talk and the background chatter continues.

The morning's announcements begin, but this does not stop the students' socializing. I alert Adrian to the fact that the announcements have begun and break off the conversation. He finds another willing participant with whom to continue his socializing. The students do not quiet down for the announcements despite Miss Thomas' warnings. As a reprimand and a method of calming the students down before the daily routine, she announces a pop quiz for which they must list two items they heard from the announcements. Additionally, Miss Thomas instructs the students to write a paragraph on their opinions as to whether the morning announcements are worthwhile. Surprisingly, they take the impromptu assignment seriously, and I see many put forth a strong effort.

Soon, Miss Thomas calls for the assignments to be passed toward the front. They are collected and the class proceeds to discuss the practice problems also assigned at the start of class. Two minutes into this activity, Miss Thomas dishes out the first of 16 reprimands for the 90-minute period. This one is directed at Adrian: "Adrian, we're going to go over this, so pay attention." Miss Thomas proceeds through this activity by calling on specific students to ensure comprehension. "Deena, how did you do number 4?"

But Deena has no chance to answer as Adrian loudly notifies the class of his method of solution. Miss Thomas realizes Adrian's need for attention, but she seems determined to allow Deena a chance to think and answer the question. Half-joking, Miss Thomas says, "I never knew you changed your name to Deena, Adrian."

"I did it over the weekend."

His comment, of course, sets the class in an uproar. In Miss Thomas' attempt to give Deena a chance to answer, Adrian once more steals the floor. He again receives teacher recognition and attention. But that's not all. Adrian is encouraged further to be aggressive, a quick thinker, a superstar in the class.

"Helen, how many inches in a foot. . . . No, not ten. . . . Yes, twelve. How can we remember that? Do you have a rap for us, Adrian? Sometimes rap helps us to remember." Here, Miss Thomas tries to connect with the students by mentioning a part of their culture, rap music, and suggests that a student come up with a rap to help classmates remember the conversion of inches to feet. Granted, this provides a certain amount of ownership and motivation in the class, but it is Adrian who is yet again placed into the limelight of the class. He receives more of the teacher's attention than all the students combined. For a girl who may already feel inadequate in mathematics, or determined that it is a "boy's subject," this incident reinforces those feelings.

> Alison: Boys need just one thing to be successful at math and math-related jobs. They just need to be good at math. But girls need *two* things. We need to be both brave *and* good at math.

Miss Thomas, however, is not purposely trying to deter girls from learning in her class. She is merely providing many opportunities for Adrian to vent his verbal hyperactivity. She knows that if she provides controlled instances especially for Adrian to speak out and demonstrate his wit, then she will have better control of the class—subtle discipline management. If she did not provide these opportunities, Adrian would deftly disrupt the class with his spontaneous, whimsical comments.

But even a veteran like Miss Thomas cannot predict when to give Adrian a chance to speak out, or to predict what he will say. I soon saw him receive the "evil eye" twice for laughing out loud during student discussions. It is distressing to those students who lack the self-esteem to ignore Adrian's laughter during their moments of speaking. Suddenly, the four students surrounding Adrian burst into laughter at another of his soft-spoken jokes. From Miss Thomas, Adrian now receives a finger pointed in his direction and says "Excuse me." Perhaps he has recognized the limitations to his teacher's patience.

Miss Thomas glides smoothly over Adrian's interruptions with subtle hand signals and facial expressions. She is calm and patient while preventing the class's attention to focus on Adrian. So far, she is stern but noncondescending in her reprimands for Adrian's social inappropriateness. He is yet to be reprimanded for any academic errors.

Alex is not that fortunate. She sits next to Adrian and seems to be the first person Adrian turns to with the next comical remark. After hearing about 30 minutes of Adrian's shouted-out answers and comments, Alex has gained the courage to shout out an answer to practice problem number 6: "It's D! It's D! The answer's D!"

In disapproving tones, Miss Thomas chastises Alex: "Alex, Alex. You think first, *then* speak." I noticed traces of that agitated voice that I first noticed in the upper level class. Why does Miss Thomas use this voice with her female students? Would not Adrian's constant disruptions deserve the same agitation? Why has she not spoken to her male students in this tone? Why did she not respond this way to Tom in the upper level class, who also blurted out an incorrect answer? My thought is that perhaps she did not want to discourage Tom from trying again.

Miss Thomas turns away from Alex. "Now say that again, Phil. What was your idea?"

But Alex will not be put down that abruptly, so she again offers her input to the discussion. Her comment is met with, "Alex, that's *not* what I asked for," and again the teacher's back is turned on her. Alex is shut out of the discussion.

Miss Thomas has left Adrian a little too long without direct attention, so she aims a question at him. "Adrian, how did you do number 7?"

Adrian begins by reading the question aloud, thus breaking the established class routine of simply giving the answer. But this is Adrian's game; he adds a twist to everything, even if it means doing extra work. Alex is fed up with her friend's larks. Loudly she exclaims, "That's not what she told you to do! You were supposed to just answer the question! You're not supposed to read *that!*"

Alex is swiftly reprimanded for interrupting Adrian and disrupting class. Each reprimand targeted at her is quick, intense, and public. Miss Thomas encourages Adrian to start where he left off. Alex is silent.

I cannot help but compare the two different types of reprimands used. First, Adrian, despite a few mathematical errors, is not reprimanded or belittled for his errors. Alex, however, is publicly chastised for her mistakes. I sense her frustration with her mistakes and her subconscious recognition that the boys in this class receive more attention. However, when Adrian made fun of other students by laughing at the presentations, Miss Thomas silently reprimanded him. Despite the serious ramifications that Adrian's laughter has on the esteem of his classmates, Miss Thomas did not correct this negative behavior. She only controlled it. When Alex attempted to catch Adrian for reading when he was not instructed to do so, her redirections from Miss Thomas were made loudly, clearly, and harshly. Alex learns that she must follow classroom rules, but Adrian is allowed to disregard them.

After dealing with Alex, Miss Thomas redirects the class back to the problems at hand. "Now Adrian, why were you going to say A is your answer? . . . Trey, what would you do with that problem? . . . Now do you see what I mean, Adrian?"

Adrian answers, "Yes. I'm sorry."

"Don't be sorry. Just learn it!"

My stomach jumped into my throat. Just one week prior Miss Thomas gets annoyed with Alison for asking questions and offers no reassurance or encouragement. However, she responds to Adrian by telling him not to be sorry, to "just learn it!" He has been challenged to be aggressive, to demand more explanations, to succeed. Why was this not provided for Alison? Would that extra push help Alison gain assertiveness and ownership of her education?

What sorts of students excel at math?

Alison: They would need to be like machines. Memorization like a scientist. Fast, speedy. . . . In math, it's as if you memorize then the understanding comes later. I'd rather not do it that way.

Miss Thomas allows Adrian to bring the stapler around to the students to staple their work together; Deena collects the assignments. The teacher transitions to the student projects that are due today. She describes what the students should have, using Adrian's project as an example: "You may have chosen to survey people on their favorite musical groups, as Adrian has." Again, I note another instance when Adrian receives teacher recognition. His self-confidence must be great in this class. He seems to own it.

The presentations begin but Adrian is oblivious. "Adrian, are you about ready there?" comes the stern voice of Miss Thomas. Oddly, the reprimand is in the form of a question. Adrian turns around to face the front of the class; he was talking and laughing with Alex. The presentations continue, but after 10 minutes Adrian is again reprimanded; this time with the raised eyebrow.

Alex is the next presenter. This is the first time she has spoken since her scoldings from Miss Thomas. As anticipated, the description of her project is short; she has been embarrassed in front of the class and she does not have much to say to her teacher. But Miss Thomas attempts to make amends and asks, "Alex, can you tell us more?" Alex refuses to play this game with a simple, "No."

Miss Thomas chooses Adrian to present next, as a hope that he will pay attention and behave. His project is the bare bones minimum, but Miss Thomas tries to make a better mathematician out of him. "How did you arrive at that conclusion?" Adrian does not accept the challenge; he is more concerned with making his peers laugh so he cracks a small joke. "That will be all, Adrian. Thank you."

Two more students attempt to report their findings, but Adrian continues his loud chatter. "Adrian, let's go to the door, stand there and be quiet." Miss Thomas' voice is tight with impatience and seriousness. Adrian is made to stand at the doorway, facing the class, and to be silent. Does this have any impact on Adrian? No, he is pleased at this extra attention and proceeds to grin and laugh. He mumbles humorous commentary toward the direction of the presenters, but it is not loud enough for the teacher to hear.

Estelle finishes her project and Miss Thomas asks her one higher level question. She cannot answer before Miss Thomas starts correcting Adrian again. She has caught him making faces into the classroom and instructs him to turn around three times where he stands before returning to his seat. But this is fun and games to Adrian! He asks for a clarification on the direction of rotation, grins, spins around three times, then takes his desk. Estelle is dismissed without the chance to answer the question posed of her. Correcting Adrian that moment was more important than checking the development of Estelle's higher level thinking skills.

With 20 minutes of the period remaining, Miss Thomas chooses four students to go to the board to solve a simple equation. She selects three boys and Alex. While the four complete their problem, Miss Thomas notices that Adrian is yet again acting up. "Adrian, you're really enjoying yourself, aren't you?" With this comment, Adrian is silent for the remainder of the period. Why did it take 11 reprimands for this young man to be quiet and on task? Why was it the 11th that worked? Why were his corrections more gentle than the ones Alex received?

Focused back on the students at the board, Miss Thomas checks over the students' work. "Trey, erase that last step. Do you see what you did wrong?

Good. Do it again and think. . . . Alex, that's not the form I told you to use."
Miss Thomas walks over to Alex's work and points, "Put the equal sign
there. Draw a line there. Subtract the 4 from both sides. Okay." With that
last comment, the bell rings, energizing the students, propelling them into
the hall.

WHAT CAN WE LEARN FROM MISS THOMAS?

Which of Miss Thomas' actions have created instances of gender bias in her
classroom? First, much of her teaching revolves around lectures and teacher-
driven activities. Lectures allow for students to shout out comments, questions, and answers, but this is not to a girl's advantage. Boys simply speak
out more frequently and more quickly in class, thus girls do not get a chance
to speak their minds. Instead, it is strongly suggested that girls be presented
with cooperative-learning opportunities in the classroom.

Dillow, Flack, and Peterman (1994) suggested that cooperative learning
be used "as a way of encouraging inclusion and acceptance and of teaching
female students to value their own 'voice' and achievements" (p. 48).
However, when using cooperative learning, the teacher must be sure to
assign roles to each student, otherwise the male students may become group
leaders. Whereas this helps to cultivate the males' leadership abilities, the
girls are prevented from developing theirs. Furthermore, girls often allow
boys to become leaders or problem solvers in group activities. Girls seem
willing to pass the challenge on to the boys due to lack of self-esteem or their
assumption that boys are "better at those things." All students can learn
various leadership roles when group roles are assigned and the teacher
instructs students on the qualities of being a good leader.

Second, Miss Thomas chastised Alex for not "playing by the rules." She
reprimanded Alex three times for shouting out answers and comments;
however, not once did the teacher reprimand a boy for doing the same. The
problem is that girls who play by the rules do not get the same sort of
attention from teachers that boys do (Orenstein, 1994). I think this is
evident from my observations of Tom and Adrian. Essentially, Cassie received little attention because she *did* follow class rules and raised her hand
to speak. To see just how much attention was given to the boys, I tallied the
number of answers boys shouted compared to girls. In one upper level class,
nine boys called out a total of 23 times, compared to 5 times from the same
number of girls in the class. Even in a lower level class the boys spoke out
more than the girls with 18 male "speak-outs" from eight boys and 5 from
the six girls. When a teacher acknowledges every answer from every student,
the boys clearly win the most attention from the teacher. When girls are
encouraged to follow the rules, the boys dominate.

Boys receive more positive recognition when a teacher specifically directs his or her questions at the males. Miss Thomas again falls into this trap, with most of her academic questions directed at the boys.

> Alison: If you hear any dumb questions, they're usually from a girl. A *particular* girl. . . . Looks bad for us other girls. Funny, the smartest girl in the class never asks questions and the smartest guys always say *anything*. But that's all they have. All they have is math.

Estimate what percentage of class time Miss Thomas spends correcting Adrian. This is the fourth lesson we can learn from the teacher. Adrian, in a sense, controls the classroom. The attention that he demands dictates how class time is spent. Due to boys' tendencies to be more aggressive, demanding, and disruptive in class, Miss Thomas, as do most teachers, spends a lot of her energy engaging boys in classroom activities and topics. For example, recall that Adrian was solicited to compose a rap as a memory device. And Miss Thomas kept Tom engaged by answering his question despite the fact that Cassie was interrupted and ignored. In a course already determined to be "for boys," girls lose even more ownership when they see that the boys receive the most attention.

The inequities increase when students are given independent work. Remember the board work assigned to Trey and Alex? Trey is made to look for his mistake then to "think." Contrast this with the help Alex received—in reality, none. Alex was told *how* to do the problem; Trey was made to think for himself.

Apparently, this is a common problem. The Sadkers (1994) in their book, *Failing At Fairness: How America's Schools Cheat Girls*, cite similar situations. During a visit to a Virginia high school, the authors spoke to students to determine their interpretation of such events. Surprisingly, the students were well aware of the inequalities:

> A tenth-grade Asian-American girl says, "I have found that teachers will help girls and tell them the answer. If boys don't know the answer, they will be made to solve it themselves.

> Ben, sitting in the back row . . . says: "That's right. It happened again last week in calculus. I was working on a problem, and I asked the teacher for help. He said, "You can handle this. Figure it out yourself." Then a girl asked for help on the same problem. The teacher went over to her desk, took her pencil, set up the problem for her, started the computations, and then let her do the last step. And I was still sitting there trying to figure it out. . . . I struggled with that problem and never did get the right answer. And that girl not only got help but she got credit for getting it right. She ended up with a higher grade." (pp. 156–157)

On the surface, Ben's incident seems to reflect an unfairness directed at the student himself. But actually Ben received the better education, as did

Trey. Again, boys seem to receive more attention in class through academic interactions with the teacher. In general, boys are pushed to be aggressive in the academic environment. They are encouraged to think on their own.

There are still other ways that boys receive more attention. As an intern teacher, I notice that I also contribute to this aspect of gender bias. For example, after I have set the students on their tasks, I walk around to ensure that everyone understands what is going on. I know that I stop by the boys' desks more frequently as a form of discipline management. I spend most of my energy coaxing certain boys to accomplish something, anything, before the bell rings. Also, I recognize the fact that I visit the boys more because they are vocal about not understanding. In general, the girls are quiet, so I assume that they do not need any extra reinforcement. However, everyone needs some academic interaction with the teacher for reinforcement and encouragement.

The only way we can hope to get more young women interested in the fields of mathematics and science is to reach them while they are in high school. We need to help them overcome their math anxiety by demonstrating that math is a girls' domain also. We must strive to build self-esteem and an aggressive search for knowledge in all our students, not just the boys. To do so, teachers need to start analyzing their own teaching styles and methods of discipline management in the classroom. We need girls to feel important in their mathematics classrooms and to take control of their learning. Teachers can help girls gain the courage. It starts with self-reflection.

FOR THE FUTURE

The following list suggests solutions we can implement to encourage increased participation of girls in high school mathematics courses.

- Form girls' mathematics clubs.
- Allow girls to read and try out math and science problems before they are covered in class to help narrow the "experience" gap between girls and boys.
- Insert the history of female mathematicians into the curriculum.
- Invite female speakers into the math classroom. This demonstrates that girls can partake in mathematics without being a "nerd" and that women have successfully penetrated the imaginary wall that separates women from math and science careers.

Alison: Women are now moving up in the world and working in placements that usually only men used to, like with math, science and technology. But, you know, it still seems that women aren't as accepted in these endeavors.

- Plan more activities and lessons that utilize cooperative learning. Cooperative learning, when implemented correctly, actually helps girls to better learn and understand information than individual work or listening to lecture in the large class setting. Plus, it gives them a greater opportunity to speak up.
- Purposely illicit girls' opinions or answers. A teacher could say, "Okay, ladies, this question is for you to answer."
- Give female students plenty of "wait time" after calling on them. Girls tend to spend more time preparing oral answers than do boys.
- Reinforce classroom rules about raising hands before speaking.
- Encourage girls to attend special mathematics and science conferences.
- Find and discuss more instances of when and how mathematics ties into the lives of everyone.
- Create a "Mathematician For A Day" week in which all students are paired up with professionals who utilize math in their jobs. Allow these students to "follow" these men and women for a day to see to what extent math is used in their careers.

Part III

Learning by Listening to Prospective Teachers' Voices

8

Foundations for Learning
From Inquiry

CB ♦ BO

This chapter examines in more detail the relationships and experiences that the five female scholar-teachers and I shared during the internship. Their voices and experiences, along with their final research reports and my interpretations and experiences, are all central to understanding the wide context for learning that existed in our lives and in our endeavors together. Our story reveals issues and events that provide a broader context for their research as well as for interpreting what they took away from their experiences of conducting research and participating in the internship. The foundations of our work together, how we related and what we experienced together as colleagues, provide the base from which to better understand the learning that went on in this situation, from both intern teacher and teacher educator perspectives. These foundations of learning signal these specific learnings for us, as well as suggest wider lessons for the fields of teaching, teacher research, and teacher education. A further discussion of the story surrounding considerations of defining the problem and method for the interns' studies is the subject of chapter 9; the specific learnings from this experience are the subject of chapter 10; and a discussion of the wider lessons for the field from our story are the subject of chapter 11.

JENNIFER

I learned a lot from the research project, even though I didn't think I would. I learned, for instance, that I hated it. And that I hated it while I was doing it. And I hated it while I wrote it. And the only thing I felt when I turned it in was just relief that it was over. . . . But when I put my paper into my year-end portfolio last week, I put it in there with pride. I revised it, and when I went back to revise it—to really read it and think about it again—I really thought it was worthwhile. And I was proud to put it in my portfolio, and I didn't put it in there just because you told me I had to. (Jennifer, interview)

From the moment I met Jennifer, I knew we would have a spirited relationship. She helped make up the cast of characters who met me at the doorstep when we arrived in town. She volunteered to help us move in. The boxes had begun to stack up in the room set aside for storage, so I asked Jennifer to take over the organization of all the boxes moved into that room. She agreed to do it. I think this proved to be one of my last easy encounters with Jennifer. My first testy encounter with Jennifer—filled to overflowing with hard questions, a quick wit, opinions—occurred soon after my request.

"Hey, that's the wrong pile. Get it right. That box goes over there," Jennifer scolded when I placed a box of Christmas decorations on the pile of boxes meant for books. I immediately moved the box to the right pile. What recourse did I have? I put her in charge and she did a good job. There were no boxes out of place on her watch. I had a feeling, however, that I hadn't misplaced my last box with Jennifer. I was dead right.

In fact, from the beginning of the internship experience, I found myself at odds with Jennifer because of several early and tense interactions with her (beyond those concerning box placement). She made me feel as though I had somehow misplaced myself. I stuttered and bumbled through complex answers to complex questions she threw my way. And because she was so very outspoken and asked hard questions both in class and one-on-one, I felt somewhat threatened by her. I sometimes wish I could go back and claim an easy, confident manner and give the best answers for her, like I probably could now.

But I guess I hadn't expected to encounter a student like Jennifer at the beginning. Some twisted, hopeful expectations had me assuming, in error, that all of our new students would go along with the project, in part because they might be glad that they had a full-time university liaison in place for their internship year, in part because I myself had been generally compliant as a student during my long apprenticeship of observation (Lortie, 1975). Besides, I figured they must have anticipated that there would be some changes in the program that they had come to know in their previous practicum experiences in the schools, in their interaction with school and university faculty, in their discussions with friends who went through the program, and in their recent orientation experiences at the schools in the spring. But Jennifer wanted things to stay the same; she liked the way things were. It was a known quantity and I constituted no such thing, and only a threat. Thankfully, as is often the case, Jennifer and I found some shared ground, developed a relationship, and became colleagues. Getting there, however, involved scaling some major hurdles.

I have struggled with myself with regard to Jennifer and others who openly criticized me and the research component in our internship experience. I am grateful, in retrospect, that I wrote the dissertation I wrote and that I learned something from it. My inquiry experience played a major role in shaping my application of knowledge and value in actual practice as a teacher educator. My dissertation study of a women's volleyball team and its experience of the curriculum centered in part on the women's negative perceptions of the coach as a person and as a teacher and the team's resulting dysfunctional relationship with him. Basically, the scene deteriorated quickly when the women realized that the coach would not ever listen to them, never take their suggestions seriously, and/or never change to save the situation (Poetter, 1994b). I resolved that I wouldn't let this happen to me (the coach ultimately resigned under duress); I decided to trust my students and colleagues while remaining firm in my convictions, and I vowed that this situation would work itself out and that I would still be standing with them at the end.

Jennifer's reactions to our first seminar meetings that introduced the research component set the stage for her disaffection for me and for the changes we hoped to make in the program.

> When you all decided to start those seminar classes early, I thought, "Oh, well, that's great, I'm teaching, I might as well be talking about it, and have these other people around." But we get to the seminar and we're not really talking about what we're teaching, we're talking about the fact that we have to do this research paper, and you're telling us to go buy this textbook (Glesne & Peshkin, 1992), and you're teaching us this lesson on how to do research the first day of class rather than asking us, you know, "What are your fears? What have your first few days been like?" I felt right off like I was being dumped on rather than supported. I felt a lot of anger, and I already felt overburdened. I already felt like there was so much for me to do that these mentors were having me do, and that I was told that I would be journaling, and observing, and I would be doing all this stuff, and then all of a sudden I had to do this paper on top of it. (Jennifer, interview)

And so Jennifer became overwhelmed the very first day, the very first week. It didn't help that her clinical assignment had her working in two different departments, in two different subject areas, with two different mentors. Compounding the complexities of her situation was the approach by Mr. Baker, her math mentor, of incorporating her into the daily activities of teaching, planning, and evaluating from the very first day. He took the notion of "partners in teaching" to heart, and gave Jennifer substantive responsibilities in the classroom from the start.

> Mr. Baker got me very involved very fast with teaching at the beginning of the school year. But I felt completely comfortable with it. It wasn't like he was pushing me too hard. Interns were asking me, "What are you doing?" And I'd say, "I taught all day today." And they'd say, "Oh, I graded some papers." I was kind of surprised that other people weren't doing what I was doing, because it felt right. But the problem was that our topics for the paper weren't due until September 20th so I got all involved in school, and then I figured out what my topic was, and then I had to start leaving to go do those research things. And I felt like I broke all these connections that I had made with the kids, that I had really gotten involved, and that they had started to see me as teacher, and then I was gone. And I think that's where a lot of the tension was.

It was just that I had gotten so close to my students so fast, and had really fallen into the role of teacher, and was very comfortable with it, and then all of a sudden I was forced into the role of student again—student and researcher—rather than teacher and being there. And at that point I still didn't see the value of the research project, so I didn't want to do it. But yet I had to. (Jennifer, interview)

Jennifer liked and appreciated Mr. Baker's approach. I did, too. It helped her to feel as though she was being grounded in the stuff of teaching from the very beginning and at a very high level with a lot of quality support from her mentor. But her immediate understanding of the hectic nature and demands inherent to her placement didn't leave much room for flexibility, and by no means for surprise. She wanted to do a great job in her classrooms, and she felt as though this nebulous research component threatened that. I don't blame her, I just didn't see the research as a threat, but only as a complement to the whole experience of the internship. We would continue to differ on this issue, as you could tell from the opening tag in this section, to the latter part of the year. Her mentor, Mr. Baker, and I went around and around about the value of the research component in light of Jennifer's experience; we came to an agreement later that the component is valuable and that his approach to immersion in teaching, with support, is valuable, too, of course, and the central, strongest point of our program.

A certain balance needs to be held, however, through the mentors' guidance in helping the interns appreciate from the beginning that: (a) there are other opportunities interns need to take for learning about teaching besides teaching (such as observing other teachers' work); (b) interns' resilient students will not be damaged by periodic absences; and (c) interns' research will open ways of seeing teaching and of being a teacher that they never anticipated or could have anticipated if this were simply a teaching apprenticeship, and not a teaching internship.

Jennifer's initial reactions do, of course, raise some other very important issues and problems that need to be addressed by anyone hoping to get into inquiry as a mode of activity and development with prospective teachers. Her feelings of being overwhelmed by her initial commitments to teaching, being in the classroom, interacting with children, and studying teaching (and in new ways) all at the same time cannot be underappreciated or overlooked, and the timing and methods with which inquiry activities are introduced in this milieu must be taken into consideration in light of her feelings.

Teaching is hard, demanding, sometimes troubling work. Getting acclimated to the demands of the work in terms of its assault on our normal patterns of mental and physical exertion, which hardly ever reach the heights in our "normal lives" that they do when we teach, is an enormous step. Paying attention to the hard questions Jennifer had such as "What are your fears? What have your first few days been like?" are first places for us to go as teacher educators and as students of teaching. Future first meetings with interns will not begin with a lecture on the merits and processes of becoming a teacher-researcher. There are other, more important, primary grounds to cover, as Jennifer and I so very well know now.

Also, great care needs to be taken by students, mentors, and teacher educators in the planning of the internship experience in terms of the types of activities and amount of focus in effort and time that will be devoted to each. A committee can't always put a timeline in place—a timeline might even constrict a student and the team instead of freeing it up to experience teaching and learning in the best ways for that team in that context. Yet, some agreement must be reached in order to frame the many activities that a student of teaching must encounter in order to have the most full and rewarding internship. When parties negotiate and agree on what these commitments and activities will be, the prospects for a successful internship are enhanced.

I respect the tension in Jennifer's experience over the conflicts that different roles produce for the prospective teacher—student, teacher, and researcher, among others. Although it is inaccurate at any point to see the teacher in only one of these three roles at a time, the goal is for the prospective teacher to approach the role of teacher with many of its various manifestations of responsibility and ability that are experienced by the prospective teacher in a teaching internship. The vision of teacher as an inquiring student of the art and science of teaching is a valuable and worthy vision. Sacrifices by acting parties that help get the intern on this path are worthwhile, too. I think, at this point, that the results of Jennifer's journey toward and on this path have been worth the inconvenient stops along the way.

One of the interesting, valuable, and natural side effects of Jennifer's and others' early disaffection came in the form of group cohesion among the secondary interns. They met to eat lunch in the teacher's lounge nearly every day at the beginning of the year in hopes of finding out more details about what was going on, for measuring other interns' experiences against their own, and for finding personal and professional support.

> It was kind of nice knowing that I wasn't the only one who didn't know what was going on. We clung to each other because of that. The first two weeks of school every day the interns had lunch together in the faculty lounge, and a good month and a half into the school year you'd be lucky if you could find someone for lunch. We'd all finally found our own niche and we were meeting with our mentors or our students, or with other teachers at lunch time. But the first two weeks we were all there for lunch and it was really nice. And I think we built that support system because we all needed it so badly. It was a way to ask others, "Do you know anything?" And if someone knew something, where we're supposed to be, or when we were supposed to be there, or how to do something, we would share all of that with each other. (Jennifer, interview)

There came a relatively early point when Jennifer and her closest friends in the program and her mentors resigned themselves to the inevitability of the research project and the real, pressing place of the work associated with it in the internship experience. Jennifer realized that she and others had overreacted at the beginning, and found some solace in our continued explanations of the project, especially in our insistences that the final product wouldn't have to resemble a thesis or dissertation. She did take up her research activities and began to make some connections to her experience as teacher through them. She found support from Mr. Baker, although it didn't come in the form I had hoped it would.

> Mr. Baker and I decided that if making time for this research project is what we've got to do, then the two of us will work together, and we will do the best we can to get through this, and we'll do it. And we worked as a team to do what you wanted, not because we understood it, but because it was what we needed to do. It was something we had to get done, and we would do the best we could to do it. And Mr. Baker was very supportive in that. (Jennifer, interview)

Yes, Mr. Baker and Jennifer worked together to make the research component work, though their collective hearts and minds were not in the place I hoped they'd be. I'd rather they viewed the project with less utility, and instead incorporated it into the way they acted and became together as a team. Instead of having Jennifer leave class and break from the valuable teaching routines she had established, which I thought were excellent, I wish they had decided to do most of the research together in their own classroom, to study their own work together, and not make the venture out to other classes into some sort of dramatic exodus. I still think that Jennifer's extensive observations could have been more easily incorporated into her schedule over time. I believe this would be the case now because of the shared ground and trust we all now occupy together. At the time, however, it all constituted utility and survival, things I hoped to move interns away from and wanted to help them avoid. I'm sorry for the lack of shared ground and the move to survival techniques that this team experienced, although her work and learning and product in the project were exemplary all along and in the end.

Another gap Jennifer highlights is the gap between the mentors and me about the place of the research project in the internship. Mr. Baker's position mirrored others' positions.

> I don't think that Mr. Baker ever doubted the validity of the research project. I think he was just angry at it being thrown on us so late. And the timing of it was wrong, and the mentors had the same problem we did: We didn't really appreciate it at the beginning; we didn't understand it. They didn't know what was expected of the mentors either. (Jennifer, interview)

I have given my early experiences with the mentors so much thought. We had a lunch meeting the first week of school where I took some time with the mentors to explain the project. I think I did a poor job explaining it, I was nervous and worried, and they could tell. I had already been through the wringer with the students and with Jennifer. No, the timing wasn't right for introducing the project, as I have said here earlier. We should have had earlier discussions about the nature of the project and how the mentors saw the project fitting (or not) the internship. And they didn't get it at the meeting and they didn't ask questions. And if they did get it, like Mr. Baker did at a later point, they struggled with understanding how it fit the other time demands of the experience and their own conceptions of what an internship in teaching ought to look like, maybe even conceptions that my department chair and others had hoped I would transform. And there developed this excruciatingly loud silence about the project. It just whistled under the surface until it had to sound, and it did.

This was all somewhat maddening, because instead of going after me and making me get it clear and helping themselves to see where we were going and maybe recharting our paths, the mentors and I let this all fester for several weeks until we met again to clarify things at the puppet show (which as you know, didn't clarify anything much, except that we were busy and good at pulling each other's strings). But this is the nature of groups just starting out, with new leadership, and old ways of doing things, and former leaders displaced or feeling that way, not wanting to alienate each other, or to take sides on the surface (although we all take sides anyway, at least covertly), and to protect me and themselves to some degree. So we let ourselves flounder, the mentors allowing me enough rope to tighten the grip, or loosen my way, however you choose to interpret, and me trying to convince instead of listen, hear, and adjust. We were getting somewhere that seemed like nowhere, very slowly, and very quickly, all at the same time. Now this all seems very odd, but very believable and so true in the course of interactions between stakeholders at the university and at the school who find themselves at cross purposes. We reached shared purposes, but the journey was rocky. In the end, the processes that we undertook together to decide how the internship would look with a research componenet served as ends in and of themselves, as signs of our becoming colleagues in a shared endeavor.

These foundational considerations paved the way for Jennifer's experience with the research component of her internship. As you can tell, not everything seemed to be in place. I hoped that things would become clearer over time. Thank goodness that they did.

CHELSEA

I had no preconceptions about this program at all because I wasn't involved with the education department as an undergrad. I wasn't friends with these people. I never hung out in the department. So I didn't know what the program was. I was not taken aback by this project. I was really excited to do it. (Chelsea, interview)

Chelsea took her baccalaureate degree 2 years before starting her internship, working as a journalist out in the "real" world. She had often thought about teaching, but wondered how effective she would be as a journalism teacher if she hadn't actually worked as a journalist first. But teaching was always in the back of her mind, and as teaching came to the front, we had a place for Chelsea as a "postbaccalaureate" candidate for the MAT. A certain number of individuals in each new class who haven't completed the undergraduate practicum and course requirements by graduation day participate in the fifth-year master's program as "postbacc" candidates.

Chelsea's lack of connection to the past and to the program as it was, specifically, proved to be refreshing in some respects. She didn't have an idea of "how things were supposed to be," so she seemed able to adjust to us as new professors and to new requirements quite well. After all, "new" applied to nearly everything she experienced as an intern. And this newness didn't prove to be so bad after all. Still young at 24, Chelsea had been out making a salary and paying the rent for a while on her own. Her experience paid dividends in this context as she confronted new challenges and adjusted to them on the fly. I'm not saying her situation, that is, not having participated in the preparatory portion of the educational undergraduate program, proved to be an advantage altogether. She simply had a different perspective than many of the others who graduated on a Sunday and started graduate school the following Tuesday last spring. Anyway, she caught up fast and proved herself a creative, thoughtful, and caring teacher from the beginning.

Her reflections on how things started include an insight about how she, too, although being pretty much on board with me and expectations for the year, fell prey to the *groupthink* that pervaded the intern group regarding the project, especially at the beginning. The interns used the word groupthink to represent the phenomenon where the interns would build on each others' somewhat emotional and sometimes irrational arguments against the research project.

> Negativism really does spread quickly. I think that was a big problem. Once one person gripes, everyone starts to think it and have it in their minds and they wonder, "Gee, this really is awful." I don't think I felt any of the negative feelings about the project until other people started talking about it, and I was influenced by their thinking. It was "groupthink" there for a while. Other interns were griping about how this is not how it's been in the past. And I didn't know that; I knew nothing. I knew we were being pushed more than other intern groups in the past and that made me a little bitter. I'm over that now because I know, for me, that I have worked very hard to get this degree and I'm proud of that. (Chelsea, interview)

Chelsea soon came around. I remember distinctly the day after our first seminar meeting about the research project when Chelsea called and asked me to stop by her classroom so that we could talk about the project. She wanted me to explain again what this research thing was and how she might go about doing it. I saw a glimmer of recognition and understanding in her eyes that day while we were talking. She kindly warned me that others weren't getting it and were mad. This information helped me search people out and address their concerns. I still appreciate the understanding and candor that she showed to me that day so early in the semester; as an intern, hers were very collegial acts.

Part of Chelsea's easier acceptance of the project and her excitement for it centered on the relationship she enjoyed with her primary mentor teacher, Glenda, who openly viewed the project as a good idea and let that be known to people around her. Glenda's open support for me and for Chelsea and for our work together helped ease the transitions between teaching and research activities so that they became mutual undertakings. This is a necessary advancement, I think, for creating an educational situation for teachers that is not disjointed in terms of activities, but continuous and sensible. Theory and practice mesh best under circumstances where a vision for learning is clearly articulated, understood, and supported. Chelsea and Glenda laid these grounds early in their experience together. Chelsea said, "My mentors were really great about supporting my research. When I got really stressed out about it, they tried to accommodate my needs, and if I needed to go visit a classroom, they tried to help me" (Chelsea, interview).

Chelsea refers to her mentors, here, for she, too, like Jennifer and several others in this intern cohort group, had split placements, or different mentors for different subject areas in which they were seeking certification. Chelsea's other mentor, Mr. Fletcher in journalism, however, did not stay for the entire school year. He took another teaching job in another district over the winter holidays. Chelsea was able, in effect, to take over Mr. Fletcher's classes after the winter holidays (while a permanent substitute was present) and performed so well that she was offered the position full-time by the principal for the next school year. Glenda continued to serve as Chelsea's mentor in her English classes, and acted as her primary mentor throughout the school year.

In retrospect, several areas regarding the project concerned Chelsea. For one, she struggled with the nature of the journal and how that document might fit and inform her practical experience as well as how it might inform her research study.

> We thought that we were writing the journal wrong at the beginning, I guess, instead of just realizing that all we had to do was keep writing, and we could keep venting if we wanted to as long as we tried to come to some conclusions and not just vent, but actually vent with the purpose of reflecting. (Chelsea, interview)

Like Jennifer, Chelsea had begun a personal journal focused mainly on venting, that is, "blowing off steam" or "writing off the cuff about reactions and feelings about the experiences at hand," the frustrations she met in her preparatory classes in the summer and during her first weeks in her placement. Our call for interns to recast their approach to the journal slightly in order to place more emphasis on reflective and observational writing threw her off for awhile. But she quickly got back into her writing and in the end was able to articulate the value of a journal balanced between venting and substantive reflection on experience and practice.

> Venting in the journal is good in one way only. It lets you get everything out of your system. But when you go back to reread your journal, venting material is not going to help you come up with what you can do to solve the problem or the frustration. All you are going to remember is how much you hated this certain thing that day. And who cares? That day is gone. So what you need to do is look at the next day, and the next day, and see how the situation changed, and how you changed and what happened. So venting only has so much value. In fact, in terms of helping you reflect, it has very little value, and I probably shouldn't have vented as much as I did in my own journal. (Chelsea, interview)

Like Chelsea, I believe the most personal venting has an important place in the journal and in the process of becoming a teacher. But balancing this venting with thoughtful, prolonged reflection about the deeper issues surrounding the situations we get into, the people we conflict with, and the ideas we develop about education, children, and teaching take us to another level of preparation. Dealing with the issues in our inquiry is an important step that certainly is grounded in, though it lies beyond, the first step of recognizing the situation or the person or the conflict on paper. In a sense, journals become action inquiry documents in and of themselves, the interns' forum for reflectively studying their own experience and practice as teacher. It would suffice to turn in an edited journal as a final paper for the project. Inquiry-filled journals can be powerful, insightful documents for developing teachers.

And this isn't the final step, but one important one along the way toward recognizing and deciding what's important to us, recognizing and deciding how to solve the problems we encounter and make, and recognizing and deciding how and why what we experience contributes to our growing understanding of self as teacher and of our links to a whole picture of education and life in school as student and as teacher. Chelsea did capture the spirit of this journaling enterprise and produced balanced accounts that informed her practice, her research paper, and her final portfolio document and presentation. She came to view the journal as a place to go by herself to encounter her feelings and observations as well as a place to go back and work things out and draw out new ideas. The document had practical applications, and aided in the connection between the practical and the theories of education that undergird situations, conflicts, and people.

I suppose the discussion about the journals and their purposes isn't over because the documents form such a vital part of the internship and now the research component. They constitute the link between the person who would become teacher and the reflections that shape the affections and cognitions of actual practice in the classroom. Therefore, their purposes and forms should be continually scrutinized and adjusted so that they serve the needs of the student and make a contribution to the formation of a whole teacher, one that recognizes the connections of self and other to the process of becoming teacher and to all of the various constitutive parts of that process.

Another issue that Chelsea encountered and has given much thought is the place of the mentors in the research process. She voices the concern that the mentors need to be involved more in the research from the beginning, possibly participating in the inquiry process somehow, at least being informed and interested in their own intern's project. I agree whole-heartedly with Chelsea. In fact, it was my intention at the beginning of last year to somehow incorporate the mentors by having them conduct their own inquiry, but when I dipped my toes in this water it was pretty hot. It would have been so very unwise to require an inquiry approach of some kind from the mentors from the beginning.

Some mentors didn't see themselves as researchers and didn't want to waste their time when they had so much else to do. The whole situation, as you know, produced negativism among some members of the mentor cohort. I backed off and made no requirements for the mentors regarding how they would or even how they might be involved in their interns' research. A few mentors didn't even know the topics of their interns' projects until the end of the year. At one level, it is crucial that mentors value the research component enough to support their interns with encouragement and flexi-bility in planning activities together. On a deeper level, inquiry has the potential for helping transform the teaching lives of mentor teachers, too. I would like for them to participate, at least in some limited (although not superficial) way, so that the benefits have a chance to stew and to accrue for them, as well, directly, and not just vicariously through their intern's experiences.

> It would help if all of the mentors were supportive. Even though mine were fabulous, there were other mentors who sometimes influenced my thinking because they were griping so much about the paper. Maybe it would help if the mentors themselves were involved in the writing process, and maybe wrote a reflective piece at the end. I think they would feel like they were really involved, that they weren't just housing an intern, but that they were becoming scholars, too. Actually the mentors' writings would be helpful not only for the fall semester project, but might even somehow tie into the portfolio. But I think they really need to get in there and feel what it's really like so they don't feel like it's worthless if we start griping. They'll say, "No, it's good." (Chelsea, interview)

So wise at 24; Chelsea's right on target. However, there is such profound resistance among the mentors to becoming involved officially in the re-search endeavors of our students or on their own. I don't know what the answer is in terms of getting the mentors involved in inquiry in a substantive way. I have encouraged several "research-friendly" mentors to keep journals and write reflective commentaries on their practice. So far this informal activity has helped build support and insight on the part of several mentors, and it is spreading. But this informal effort may not be enough. We need to continue to work together to find some common ground so that we can all grow as teachers and foster the further professional development of the intern class, which together, at least to me, ought to be our primary concern. It remains to be seen how we will manifest our commitment to others' inquiry through a commitment to our own inquiry. Again, only time will tell on this front.

Some have said that the endeavor is hopeless unless the teachers themselves first choose the way of inquiry as a professional development direction. I'm not so sure this is so. With the success of inquiry among the intern cohort, there exists the chance that the mentors will become excited about the study of their own and others' practice. The alternative is the continued dominance of an isolated, alienated way of being and a sometimes voiceless, plodding existence among many teachers. This is no way to go and no path to support. Jennifer's mentor Mr. Baker, who was most resistant to inquiry at the beginning of this story, recently told me that he wants to begin keeping a journal on how best to incorporate the intern into the teaching fabric of the classroom and school. I have been encouraging him all along and hoping for this move. All of my efforts are grounded in the belief that this great person and great teacher has something to offer the wider educational community beyond the walls of his own classroom.

Mr. Baker now says that he wants his legacy to be found outside the lesson plans that he has produced over his long career. He wants to make a contribution to the field of teaching, to have his voice and insights heard by other teachers. He has learned much about educating teachers and has decided to share that learning outside the classroom. No doubt this turn will enhance Mr. Baker's own teaching for his own students in his own classroom in his own subject. Any time teachers reflect deeply on their own practice, they continue to define their teaching styles and purposes, goals, and objectives in a most rigorous manner. I believe it is the university's role to offer ways for people to study and learn. It is the university's role to be involved in the suggestion and clarification of learning activities that can build professional development and collegial practice. Teacher inquiry is one avenue for moving toward these goals.

Maybe the most common conversations among teachers, as a result of a focus on inquiry in our everyday structures of experience and learning, will become discussions about pedagogy and learning. Maybe an excitement about the daily grind, and the sights and sounds of the old becoming new, the familiar becoming strange and wonderful, will spur teachers to share their great, abundant practical knowledge about classrooms with those of us who want to improve our own practice or simply to understand how best practice looks in classrooms today. In any case, inquiry can be contagious; and it is the university's responsibility to foster learning and the empowerment of teachers' voices and knowledge. I continue to encourage the support of inquiry among mentors and the pursuit of knowledge and the sharing of that knowledge as well.

SHAWN

Conducting inquiry sounded like the smartest way to become a better teacher. If you don't ever inquire about anything, how are you ever going to learn any more? (Shawn, interview)

Shawn gave me the impression from the very start that she understood what the research project meant to do for her as a prospective teacher. After a few weeks at the beginning of the year of hearing no complaints about the project from her or from her mentor, I asked her a point blank "Why?" She said she figured that there would be some kind of academic requirement for the course and that she might as well use her time to study her own practice, her own school while she worked in it. The project, it seemed to her, was a way to do that.

I'll confess that Shawn's support for the project made some of my early days in this job bearable. While Laura made great strides with the excited middle school interns, I struggled along defending the project against unhappy interns and mentors. I wish I could have been more examining and less defensive, but it just wasn't humanly possible. Shawn made me feel that we at least had a clue about what we were doing, that we weren't crazy, and that we could accomplish our goals for helping students connect theory and practice in education in part through the use of inquiry. However, helping her professor feel this way came at a sacrificial price for Shawn.

Her support for the project became a weighty tension in her life at school. Shawn had to step carefully around the issue when she suddenly found herself in conversations about the project with those who were complaining and venting. She wanted to defend the project and her professors and encourage her peers to move on, but she hadn't found the voice to do that yet. She remained conspicuously silent.

When I heard the other interns complaining about the project, I thought, "Am I supposed to be mad, too? Why am I not feeling this way? Is something wrong with me?" I had to think through why they might be thinking that way. And I isolated myself. I didn't start building relationships with the other interns, except for one or two of them, until that period passed. I wanted to say, "We're getting our master's degree. Yes, it's intense. When it's intense, that means you pretty much live it, so live it. It's just something you do, you get through it, you do your best, and you learn the most you can. You don't question what your professors do, because they're the professors and we're the students." (Shawn, interview)

But Shawn never said these things to the others. I don't blame her. In fact, I don't necessarily support the sharp distinction she makes between student and professor even though I, at times, have acted as though this were the ideal, as I did when assigning the project without input from others, then expecting compliance from them. But I'd truly rather land somewhere in between, as colleagues, and try now to make most of my decisions as a teacher educator collegial, shared ones. I recall that at one point soon after that awful Thursday meeting, I asked Shawn if there was anything she could do to help sway some of the other students, to support the project among her peers. I realized when I asked that, I had asked too much. It wasn't her place as a student to defend the course or the professors, I knew that. I quickly backed off as she revealed how hard it had been to stay silent while others railed. I respect her stalwart silence and appreciate the commitment and sacrifice that came with it.

Like Chelsea, Shawn understood a major difference between her conceptions of the course, the internship, the project, her professors and those of some of her peers who were most vocal against some of the programmatic changes they encountered early in the year to be a lack of extensive prior experiences with and expectations for the program.

> I knew full well that I shouldn't have any expectations about the program because I didn't know what was going to happen, what the year was going to look like. Whereas I think other people had talked to past interns, and maybe knew some of the past clinical professors better, and had an idea, and formed a picture. But I didn't have one. So when they came in and found out it was not going to look the same, they freaked out. (Shawn, interview)

It was easier for her to adapt because she had invested less in preparing for old routines in a program she thought was inevitably bound to change on the arrival of new professors. Shawn saw change in this context as the natural course of things, not something that threatened her experience or her year ahead.

> Everything was new at the beginning. How can a program be the same when different people teach in it? Taking Calculus with Dr. X is completely different than taking Calculus with Dr. Y. They're different teachers. It can't be the same. So I knew I would be teaching, and I knew that I was going to have classes at the university. I assumed that I would have books to read, just like any other class, and papers to write. (Shawn, interview)

I do have remorse about how distinctly the lines became drawn among some of the interns, those who supported the changes in the program with regard to the inquiry component and those who did not. As Jennifer put it, the group never did quite regain the level of trust that existed among the group's members up to Black Thursday. This trust gap affected interpersonal relations among interns at school and at the university, to the point that some, including both Jennifer and Shawn, didn't feel comfortable examining some of the deeper, harder issues and questions that surrounded their experiences as interns. Did we miss the opportunity to understand and support others because we thought if we brought up something, anything, we'd have a falling out and not ever get to the issue? No doubt, yes. I'm afraid that in this context this phenomenon occurred among these students and with me. Ideally, inquiry ought to free up people to question and inquire, and share and support each other as teachers and as scholars. Whereas the group reached some level of trust, we didn't quite make it all the way, and the inquiry project, for this group, may have been a major roadblock in our path.

The groundwork for building a conception of reflective practice and a reflective way of being as teacher, in part through the use of inquiry in the program—while we attempted to lay it—did not support the group adequately at the beginning of the year, especially in light of the interns' and mentors' misunderstandings about the research project, at least according to Shawn. The experience factor that allows a prospective teacher to value varying activities as necessary for developing a whole and critical conception of life in schools lies in the remote distance of time, down the road of experiencing several 6-week grading cycles, issuing numerous tardy referrals, and attending faculty meetings. As a result, the interns just couldn't make a positive leap toward embracing the research project as another cog in the journey toward reflective practice, in addition to the wealth of other experiences with which several interns put the research component in competition.

> We were too early in the whole program to realize that the inquiry project would make us more reflective because you don't have any idea about reflection as a prospective teacher. You're just so immature in your thoughts about what you're doing. You really have no idea. None of us had a clue what we were doing when we started. I mean, we could fake it, but that was it. But I think that will come, I mean, you told us a billion times, "Listen, doing this inquiry is going to connect your teaching and your pedagogics class together. It's going to be about real life in teaching." (Shawn, interview)

Shawn listened, and reaped the benefits of "getting it" at the beginning. She found that the research project stimulated thought in her teaching and made her excited about the next day at school, how she would proact and react in different situations, what she would do in response to her newfound understandings of and interactions with students and teachers. She became excited about the prospects of further applications of her work from the beginning, when I mentioned at one of the opening seminars that I planned to help some of them publish their papers and to write about their experiences as an inquirer myself. This made Shawn view the projects as "real"; the fact that someone else would value her work and seek to give it a voice out in the real world made her eager to pursue the study and the end product in writing. She couldn't wait to get started, I recall, and I found her interest refreshing during a time when most people complained.

> The first day you explained the project to us you said, "This isn't just another paper. This is something real." And that's what got me so excited. I said, "Well, if this is going to be important, well, then come on!" (Shawn, interview)

Indeed.

SHERRY

The research has to be in the classroom. It can't be just in books. That's what this whole thing is about. It wasn't about going to the library and reading some journals here and there. Yeah, I did read some journals. I did do some library research. But it was really about hands-on research. That's what it is all about! It's about learning how to teach yourself. It's about still being a student. (Sherry, interview)

Energetic, creative, friendly and maybe sometimes effectively frenetic describe Sherry, intern math teacher at the middle school. I didn't have as much day-to-day contact with Sherry as I did with the high school interns, but I did have the opportunity to work with her in our Pedagogics class and on the research project. She and the other students assigned to the middle school placement supported us and the research project from the very beginning. As I mentioned earlier, the middle school crowd, including the mentor teachers working with the three interns there, treated the research component as an important and reasonable expectation for their course-work component of the program. When Sherry uses "we," she is referring to the intern cohort at the middle school.

We viewed the research component as something that we could do, that was part of our masters program. We thought, "What a great idea. We get to see other teachers and do this paper." It was a very positive thing for us. We never saw it like some of the others did. They thought, "How dare the professors ask this of us?" And not just that, they thought, "We have other better things to do than to do this research. The classroom is far more important than this." (Sherry, interview)

Sherry touches an exposed nerve in her statement here. Her statements, although sometimes quite general, are effectively accurate regarding the way things shaped up with the entire group and between the two groups, the high school and middle school cohorts. The preceding chapters and the students' many various perspectives tend to support her positions and statements here. It is true that the contrasting views that the intern cohorts had about the research project and other educational issues sometimes reached a tense pitch. Although there were few sparks between the groups, tension grew at times when the camps aligned along the relatively well-defined middle and high school trenches concerning the philosophy and the delivery of education to students and to the public. Of course, the groups had completely different experiences as prospective teachers on a day-to-day basis. They worked in different schools, at different levels, with different populations, with different faculties, and in different school districts. They encountered different realities in terms of teaching, planning, politics, and priorities.

For example, the middle school interns found themselves wrapped in the practice and rhetoric of the middle school movement. They would get especially ruffled when discussions would move away from what they would interpret as a "student-centered" perspective on an issue or situation. The high school interns might sometimes take a "discipline-centered" line, and would get equally upset when challenged by the middle school interns. I think the high school interns believed that one could take both the student-centered and discipline-centered positions simultaneously—that they weren't mutually exclusive; I don't think the middle school interns believed this was a possibility. And so Sherry developed a very strong opinion about the actions and approaches of several of the high school interns and the group that built up over time and through their experiences together as interns. Yes, they sometimes found themselves at odds with each other. Sherry was oftentimes pointed and critical in her remarks, as she is here, about the different approaches the two groups took to problems, including those surrounding the research project.

> I think the high school interns sometimes thought, "I want to do what I want to in my room, and don't ask me to go outside and look at something. I want to teach. Don't ask me to do anything else." And we never viewed the research component that way. We never saw it as something that was taking away from our year. Some of the high school interns honestly viewed it as another professor trying to get a grade so he or she could say, "Look, we made our kids write these papers." But I know if you gave us the option, we would have done the paper anyway because we saw the value in it. You know, some people just don't like change and you asked them to change. And so they're not going to agree. (Sherry, interview)

Because of her self-professed commitment to a student-centered approach to teaching, Sherry found herself at odds with resistance to the paper on the part of several interns in the cohort. She bounced the group's discussions concerning the problems that many were having in tapping the motivations of their own students, especially in terms of getting them to try new approaches to learning, against the side discussions that many were having regarding the research paper. She sensed a hypocrisy when she tried to balance the two discussions.

> We want our students to try things. And we want them to change, and we want them to really push themselves. And then you ask that of us, teacher to student, and we are not willing to change. And we're not willing to be risk takers. So how hypocritical we are. We want that out of our students. But we don't want our teachers to ask that of us. That's where we weren't going to play that game. (Sherry, interview)

The middle school interns, according to Sherry, viewed the project as a way of enhancing their commitment to students by focusing on their own development as students of teaching. They saw the potential benefits of looking closely at others and at the self as teacher before they really understood what this whole process of conducting their own inquiries would entail. This leap of faith, if you will, matches the sort of approach they encourage their own students to take as they encounter exciting new ways of relating new material and of learning in their own classrooms and with their own students.

> A lot of it has to do with what your role is as a teacher. We saw the research as a way to educate ourselves to be able to see other things. Maybe the more student-centered we are, the more we'll look at our own profession and our own role as a student. Maybe people who aren't so student-centered are more into the "teacher" role. Many were saying that you asked them to be a student, and it's going to take away from being a teacher. And we thought, "No! What you don't realize is that being a student of teaching is going to add to your being a teacher." In fact, we never thought that the project was a separation from teaching. We didn't have to give up our teaching for 2 weeks to go and do the project. It was a *part* of our teaching. (Sherry, interview)

So on the one hand, the middle school interns, including Sherry, adopted a view of the project that allowed them to see their own development as teacher as being served by the academic inquiry they would undertake. This is exactly where we hoped students would land. But as Sherry so eloquently stated, the group did encounter some splintering. Whereas most could agree to disagree on many issues, and take a healthy dose of balancing from discussions and encounters that pressed interns and their mentors to evaluate their own practices and positions, some fell short of being able to come all the way back to the group following their own resistance to the project, in general, or from events such as Black Thursday.

Sherry knows from a relative distance as a middle school intern, as we all do from inside the experience of working at the high school, that the cohort group didn't exist in a perfect equilibrium ever after, where interns shared everything they needed to in their group or among other colleagues. The reason? The pain we experienced together over the project. Maybe this balance never happens with groups because of the many individual differences and personalities and experiences anyway. Maybe this phenomenon of disagreement and challenge gives bite and meaning to interaction. Maybe it is learning-filled. I don't know. Maybe the reality is that some mix will always be the case. At any rate, here's Sherry's take on it.

> You know, even if as an intern you didn't agree with the project, which many of us didn't, it wasn't approached in a very constructive way. It was bitter, and it built up, and then it blew up. So some had to back out because of the few people that were still going to fight it. Some people had to say, "I can't stand with you anymore." They broke apart from each other to keep their own sanity. (Sherry, interview)

It is important to emphasize here that Sherry gives great credit for her own and to her colleagues' approach to the course and to the internship to the mentors at the middle school who supported their educational endeavors at every turn, both in terms of the required coursework they encountered at the university and in the clinical requirements in the field. Mentor

support proved to be a crucial factor in the interns' success in the class and in the internship as a whole experience.
Our mentors completely backed us. They were willing to give us what we needed. In fact, they were like mothers to us, continually asking, "Are you all starting stuff yet? Are you guys going to do anything?" (Sherry, interview)

HEIDI

I would have become a reflective practitioner anyway without doing the research project, but I think I've become reflective to a higher degree, now that I've completed this case study and I've focused so intently for so long on gender bias in the classroom. I am anxious to do more research myself. (Heidi, interview)

Heidi's story is filled with the ups and downs of an internship year that on the one hand did not meet her expectations and on the other hand surpassed them. No one else who experienced the program this year, even Jennifer, took such drastic turns in response to how he or she felt about or responded to the situations at hand, especially with regard to the research project. Whereas remaining one of the most pleasant and interesting people with whom I worked this year, Heidi's rollercoaster ride through the first semester and the research process challenged me to remain steady and patient in my work with her.
From the beginning, I thought Heidi had touched on one of the more interesting and more practical and meaningful areas for a case study by choosing to look at the phenomenon of gender bias, especially as it may take root in the teaching taking place (or not) in math classrooms. Heidi's topic and her efforts in sorting through the literature and collecting rich data became fun to watch from the sideline and ultimately to participate in. But it wasn't always easy; Heidi's mind and heart conflicted soon after she heard the first words come from my mouth at the beginning of the term.

For the first ten seconds after you announced the project, I was excited. I felt honored. I had never done anything like this before. You don't do your own research in math courses and in education courses. We'd always written little 10-page ditties for papers. So I thought this was really a big deal and I was honored. Then I started thinking, "This isn't fair. This is not at all what I wanted this internship to be, and this is not what I'm paying tuition for this year—to do another paper that's going to be three times as long as what I've ever written before. And I automatically assumed that I would be spending all my days in the library, and that the process would have nothing to do with learning how to teach. And I was very bitter about it for awhile. (Heidi, interview)

Heidi scouted out the opinions of others at the beginning, from other interns and other mentors, hoping to find a way to make sense of what she had to do, why she was doing it, maybe even if she and the group could somehow get out of doing the project altogether. Heidi never spoke directly to me about her reservations about the project until that eventful Thursday night that has been noted here before on numerous occasions. Her own sense of up and down, hitting highs and lows, never hit home with me until that Thursday night—I hadn't anticipated her problems with the project until then. She seemed to be doing so well all along, studying and seeing applications of her reading and observing for her own work with students in her own math classrooms. I know that Heidi won't be the last student to surprise me, at least I hope I experience other more positive surprises. But I do hope that I don't misread others like I misread her at the beginning.

But I couldn't ever really worry about losing Heidi. She is just too strong, both in the classroom as teacher and in the classroom as student. Although she struggled internally over the project, she collected articles and observations that informed her growing conception of gender bias in math classrooms. She began amassing deeper understandings of herself as teacher and what it means to teach well, keeping questions that surround pedagogy and gender close in her planning and delivery of curriculum. I learned later that her reservations about doing the project rested primarily with her tension over one particular issue—spending time with her mentor Sandy, with whom she felt she lost significant contact time because of the requirements of doing the project.

> After feeling really angry and upset about the whole thing, I got excited about it again, and then it went up and down from then on until I began the writing process. I would get excited about the research I had read, and would think in my mind about instances that I myself had experienced or how I felt about it, and then I'd get excited about it, and I'd go observe some more. Then I'd get angry again because I had to write this stupid paper, and I didn't feel like it. Then I'd get excited about it again. Then it was also difficult with my placement with Sandy, because I did not want to observe her or my other mentor, Meredith, for my case study. I felt like I needed to be in someone's class that I'd never seen before for the study. I felt like Sandy and I got shortchanged in terms of growing as partners because I was out observing other classes and not spending time planning with her, and that was a shame. (Heidi, interview)

But true to form, this most critical issue with Heidi did not play itself all the way out in her experience. She reflected that even with regard to this perceived problem, the seeming lack of time spent with mentor Sandy, the experience balanced itself out in the end. She commented on her views of the total experience, including the research project, after having completed her internship.

> I wanted to be in Sandy's and Meredith's classrooms. But then I started thinking about it, "Well, wait a minute, I am in the classroom. And yes, I may not be up there doing my little show, but I am seeing somebody else and learning from him or her." So then I got over that, too. It's like I matured each way. At first I was complaining about the project. And then I started to realize that I was gaining directly from my research anyway. At first I thought the research was going to be indirect, just cranking out another paper, but then I started gaining directly from it, and that's when I changed. (Heidi, interview)

This learning process made a crucial contribution to Heidi's overall success in the program. It led to a very successful full-time teaching stint in the spring and to new conceptions of self as teacher that will help Heidi create a way for herself in the classroom whose boundaries lie outside its walls. As I have argued previously, this paradoxical position of being strong inside the classroom because one can see clearly outside it will stay with Heidi when times are good and bad in the field. She has experienced a new way of seeing more deeply into the hidden phenomena of school life and will always be able to reflect deeply on her own and others' practice as problems and joys arise in her own classes and school. Heidi came to see how important a culture of inquiry can be when it surrounds a teacher's practice in the field.

> Once I found out what the other interns were studying, I noticed myself looking for cases in my own classrooms concerning the other topics that we had dealt with, wondering about relationships with students and the use of technology in my own teaching. (Heidi, interview)

As another working example of her ability to reflect on educational scenes she experiences, Heidi is able to add these summative comments about the research project and me in terms of gaining ground in the program.

> The research component was so different, it wasn't just about researching Piaget again, because it had something to do with us as individual teachers, something that was dear to us in almost all cases. I felt like, "It's okay now. I agree with the added component." I think your particular problem was that you were the new kid on the block. And everyone had already been told exactly what was expected of them this year, and you came in with this new idea, which is great, but it threw everyone for a loop, and that's why there was so much resistance. You won't have that next year. But there was just resistance because no one expected it, and no one wanted it at the beginning. (Heidi, interview)

I can only hope that her perceptions and words will ring true for my experiences with a new cohort of interns and mentors next year. Heidi's struggles and successes have taught me much, especially how to remain patient in dealing with a student's incomplete understanding. I never expected Heidi to hit the lows that she did during the first semester. I know now that these low points weren't necessarily related to me or to the research project. Her work in the field as a teacher researcher proved to be particularly inspiring to me and to her colleagues. Heidi was able to make the project she conducted connect to her entire teaching experience and to her complete development as a prospective teacher. Out of her experience from our year together comes a model experience and a model piece of writing, as well as the beginning of a model career as teacher.

9

Considerations for Defining Problems for Study and Identifying Emerging Research Methodologies in Inquiry

ℭ ◆ ℬ

This chapter takes up the very substance of the interns' research activities, what they chose to focus on in their projects and why. It also attempts to give the reader some idea of how the prospective teacher–researchers went about conducting their studies and to address related methodological issues revealed by their experiences and work in the field.

JENNIFER

I must admit that I was very pleased with Jennifer's topic from the beginning. I thought that it had real potential to help her make connections between what she had been studying and would continue to study about teaching and teaching mathematics in her university coursework and how she might incorporate all of that into a working approach to teaching math in her very own high school classroom. Whereas Jennifer seemed to struggle in reconciling the research project with her understanding of the internship and even with understanding the assignment, she actually did have a clear vision for her own project from the start and set herself on a path of tremendous learning.

Jennifer found the problem she wished to examine in her study to be evident in her own classroom and in other math classrooms at the high school. Her understanding of the problem was that it had a tremendously general, wide-ranging impact on her understanding of the current state of teaching math in high schools as well as an effect on her perceptions of teaching and learning math in her internship. She says it better than I can.

> I decided that I wanted to learn about the teacher's use of manipulatives and technology in math classes at school because when I first got here, I was surprised that it wasn't happening in the school the way I thought it should. I had learned at college that teachers and students were supposed to be using manipulatives and technology, that all this research had been done, and kids learn better that way, so everyone should be doing it! And I was shocked that no one was using them, or it didn't seem like anyone was. And even my mentor, Mr. Baker, was asking how I thought that we could use manipulatives and technology in our classes together. But I thought, "Don't you know? I mean, you're the mentor teacher. Why don't you know?" (Jennifer, interview)

Good question. Jennifer had identified a very important area for concern and inquiry for teachers considering teaching in general and teaching math today. How do we interpret current research in terms of shaping and reforming curriculum and classroom practice? What is really happening out in schools? Do people know about certain advancements in research, in theory and practice? Do they care? How do classes look? What are the teachers and students and curricula like? Should we grasp change openly and with fervor or with closed caution? I preached with excitement from the beginning, over and again, that Jennifer's problem would lead her into a most valuable study and that it would greatly influence her own teaching. I still don't know exactly what role my encouragement (or persuasion) played, but I'm glad I took it on. She, in turn, took a set of understandings and questions into her study that would help her shape and guide her own inquiry and her own writing, her own process of learning about teaching from this experience.

> I had this feeling from the beginning that teachers aren't doing as much as the National Council of Teachers of Mathematics (NCTM) says they should be doing with manipulatives and technology...I think part of the problem is that math teachers love math, and they love learning math, and they love learning math the way they were taught it, which is not the way that it should be taught, which is . . . just from a perspective of, "Let's write it out in the numbers, not in what it means, not in what it means in real life or in a hands-on situation." When you start doing math, you use blocks. That's how they teach it. You add four blocks plus three blocks. . . . And teachers are willing to do that early, but at some point they totally switch to just the pure math, and it's a move to the symbolic. It's like the students have progressed and they are at the point where they don't need those manipulatives anymore, the concrete examples. And it often happens sometime in late elementary school. Teachers don't want students to use the manipulatives anymore, but then they start teaching all of this brand new math stuff in Algebra and Geometry, and they expect students to be able to do it symbolically, but they really can't and teachers have to go back to using blocks and those sorts of tools. (Jennifer, interview)

Jennifer began to develop early theories regarding her perceptions of the resistance teachers showed in their seeming unwillingness to take on new math ideas in practice. She speculated that several reasons produced the gaps she saw in the classrooms. First, the school's teacher and leadership culture didn't force anyone to do anything, accepting the differences in the ways people taught, regardless of style and perceived effectiveness. "At my school, they don't want to force anyone to do anything they don't want to do" (Jennifer, interview). This may be a great strength or weakness in the culture of school in this context, depending on your perspective.

Second, the lack of proximity to each other as a math faculty precluded a culture of sharing and peer coaching. "The department is so spread out that we're not even all in the same place. There are math teachers that I've never seen or had a conversation with this year. So it's hard to get people together to begin with, and when they do get together, they don't even want to argue about the differences" (Jennifer, interview).

These early perceptions shaped Jennifer's study, as she began to test them against her observations of different teachers and classes and studied the survey data that came in. She began to shape opinions about organization and leadership as a result of her study.

> I want to know that my students next year are going to come into my class and be able to use this calculator, but if they have a certain teacher they're not going to be able to use it, and if they have another teacher, they're going to be so comfortable with it that if I said, "Don't use it," they'd just go into shock. I think as a department we should have at least some common understanding. (Jennifer, interview)

Indeed, Jennifer began to pinpoint problems that have solutions, and her study began to illuminate ways that the culture of teaching in her field was taking shape at school. Ultimately, she would come to questions of most import, "Is what we're doing as teachers helping students? Can we do better? More?" We would all be better served if all students of teaching journeyed this path of inquiry in their chosen teaching field.

In terms of research methodology, Jennifer began formally by conducting a survey of the entire math faculty to find out the level of use and the reasons for use of manipulatives and technology in math instruction. About two thirds of the teachers responded to the survey. Jennifer visited seven teachers' classes and performed 10 observations for full-class periods (90 minutes), going back to several classes "to look to see whether or not the teachers were using technology and manipulatives, how they were using them, whether I thought the use was effective, if it really helped the students to learn it better" (Jennifer, interview).

An overall consideration for Jennifer in terms of collecting data for the study had to do with her use of her journal. And in fact, the journal really served as the starting place for her project as well as other students' projects, even before formal activities were put in place such as conducting surveys, observations, or interviews. All of the interns were required to keep a journal of reflections and observations, to some degree focused on their topics, the extent to which was up to them. They turned in their journals to us periodically and we checked that they were working on the journal and gave some guidance on topic related and method related issues that arose from the journal entries we read. This whole process placed Jennifer at odds with how the journal had been previously conceived in the program and by her. She had a difficult time reconciling the conflict, though she completed her assignments with regard to the journal and used the journal effectively as a data source for her final report.

> I was angry about the journaling all along. We were told at the beginning of the summer by the former interns that we really needed to journal because it would help us keep track of where we are and when we go to work on the portfolio we could look back on our growth. So we all started journals. And then you come and tell us that we're supposed to be journaling and kind of observing for this paper. That's what we're supposed to be journaling for, and that we need to have it on a computer disc. And all of us had kind of thought of it as kind of a personal journal, so most of us had bought these really nice personal books that we had been journaling in, and it was kind of like a diary almost about how we felt from day to day. But now we're not supposed to be journaling what we feel, as much as what we observe, and how it affects other things. More reflective than personal. So then I got angry. And I didn't want to switch the journal onto computer disc when I had made it personal, and I said, "Well, what am I going to do with this book journal? I don't have time to journal in just this anyway." (Jennifer, interview)

Whereas I believe that the personal and reflective approaches to journaling mesh nicely to form a cohesive and focused approach to writing about experience, Jennifer had her good reasons to feel that I had stepped on her conceptual toes again. We weren't so far off each other's bases in the final tally, but the fact that the journal's focus did shift slightly did have an impact, especially because time to journal became so preciously short. I had a hard time finding time to journal, too—like Jennifer I probably did less personal profiling than I did reflective, observational data-type writing in my journal. The tension? Good stuff for the paper and portfolio lay in the new, reflective and observational journals, but students didn't have the same sort of personal and emotional attachment to the journaling process as they did when they began journaling even before I arrived and before the academic year had started. I think an early discussion about this tension will be important and healthy with coming classes. I don't see the tension as irreconcilable. Jennifer worked it out; it just wasn't completely what she wanted. I believe both types of material can be incorporated nicely, although some sacrifice may be made in terms of personal focus.

Another important point of tension came for Jennifer in her perceptions of the opening seminar classes on qualitative research. Not only did she feel that we missed the more important pedagogical questions that beginning teachers need to address, "What have your first few days been like?" and "What are your fears?", but we also focused more on a skill approach to learning about qualitative research at the beginning than on giving a whole, clear, final picture of what the projects might look like. This was a very important step for someone like Jennifer, who isn't at ease with writing and pulling major projects like this together, and not many people are, I know. She stated that she didn't have a clear enough picture of the project to approach getting comfortable with it until we gave some written examples that modeled the types of writing we were after (Johnston, 1994; Porro, 1985).

> I don't think I really understood what type of case study you wanted until we started reading the samples. And we didn't do that until we actually started the fall classes, because the early meetings were all spent on how you research, how you read this book, how you interview. I didn't realize I was supposed to be writing this narrative, and sort of explaining it in a context, and raising questions, and writing notes. And I think if I'd realized that's what it was sooner, that I was kind of painting a picture, then it wouldn't have been so scary. And I think as I got to that point, I thought, "This isn't going to be that bad. I can handle it." (Jennifer, interview)

We chose Porro's (1985) work for our students to read as a model piece because of its informal, personal, story-like form and interesting, thoughtful insights about school life, school culture, and school children. The work is based on a limited time spent in the field, but also on a deep database and on a strong and creative narrative, interpretive approach. We chose Johnston's (1994) work as a more controlled, academic-style report that incorporated different sorts of data into coherent, well-organized, and well supported points. Both pieces represent types of work and styles of work that we as practitioners, researchers, and readers find helpful and informative for our thinking and working. Getting these models and others to students at a very early point will help assuage fears associated with the writing process, we think. The pieces aren't particularly long, they aren't written in unattainable prose, yet they tell the story of experience and inquiry in certain specific areas. Our prospective teachers could do similar, though less polished work, no doubt. Jennifer's insights have been helpful for identifying this gap in understanding the thought and mechanics of writing up a report, a very important methodological consideration.

CHELSEA

Chelsea confronted a very serious problem at the beginning of her research. She had intended to study the process of collaborating on a new curriculum with her mentor teacher in journalism. To this end, she thought that she and her mentor teacher would be working together, but she was basically left to her own devices in planning for the classes, so she felt that the paper would be about the absence of collaboration and that wasn't an appropriate topic to pursue. I agreed, and helped her adapt her conceptions of the scene into a workable project.

And her conceptions of the scene and the problem of choosing a topic went to deep personal issues. She had trouble developing a substantive personal and professional relationship with her mentor in the journalism classes. She found herself at odds with him philosophically and in practice situations. She found the notion of working on the project of collaborating on a curriculum to be an impossible one to take up. She wanted and needed the guidance for making this a successful teaching and learning situation, but Chelsea didn't find this in her journalism mentor. She had to find the resources within herself and from her other mentor, Glenda, and from me, and her intern colleagues in order to make it through the placement experience, let alone the research project.

But Chelsea came through, adapting her questions about the scene to the problems developing at hand. She set out on her own to understand how it is that an intern teacher creates an appropriate curriculum for journalism students given the nature of the classes and the students who often populate the desks in her rooms and the nature of the teaching practice and curriculum-making that had gone on before her.

> I wrote a paper about first-year journalism teachers trying to create a journalism curriculum. There is really a nonexistent journalism curriculum out there. Even though every high school has a journalism program, there isn't a set curriculum from school to school. So, I examined that issue, and talked about how to get one going, and how to know that what you're doing is right. (Chelsea, interview)

Chelsea's project could be described as an action research project, one designed not only to represent the scenes, people, and ideas in question but also to take action to better the scene. Chelsea charged herself with coming up with a workable curriculum for her new students, putting a learning environment together that more accurately and concretely fosters the skills and knowledges required for the success of beginning journalists in the program. I thought that her project posed a great challenge and marvelous learning opportunity. Chelsea would have the opportunity to struggle with the foundational questions behind the development of a new curriculum in her field, forge a new curriculum, implement new lessons, and judge the merits of her own and her students' work. Her work could contribute to our understanding of the issues around the development of curriculum in her field and the contributions this effort can make to the education of a new teacher.

Chelsea found early in her inquiry that the vagueness of the state's prescriptions for journalism curriculum left many holes to fill by the teacher in terms of addressing those prescriptive elements in classrooms. But this situation is also freeing, as Chelsea found in the liberty she had to try new approaches to teaching journalism.

> The state's prescriptions for journalism say that students must know how to do "this," and "this," and "this," but they don't say how you're supposed to do it. There is no way that you can cram four pages of state prescriptions into one year of basic journalism. The people who wrote the prescriptions don't know anything about journalism, what should be taught. And our state has adopted textbooks which guide us, but there are 18 different textbooks. Each school uses a different one. I have three different sets in my classroom that I can choose from, and each one focuses on different items. Some focus on writing, some focus on layout. So it's just hard to cram all that into one year for the kids. It's one big survey course, and we're supposed to hit everything. The dream is that the students will be ready to hit the journalism workforce by the time they graduate high school. (Chelsea, interview)

Chelsea gets a sense that the expectations for the curriculum are unrealistic, so she has to decide how to best meet the needs of her students in the context of the journalism program. Truly addressing the needs and problems of her students and program are the curricular challenges in this context. They are formidable, but manageable in light of Chelsea's inquiry approach to dealing with the problem in a constructive and positive manner.

The problem of how to challenge her students in an appropriate manner loomed as Chelsea got to know her students better. She found that most of them simply wound up in Journalism, placed there by their school counselors because they had no other elective choices that seemed to fit. She tells the story dealing with this fact in her paper, but she mentioned it in her interview time with me, too.

> Electives, in general, are "dumping grounds." I've gotten a promise from the principal that the upper division journalism courses next year, which are the production classes such as yearbook and newspaper, will not become dumping grounds. It says in the handbook that students have to have advisor approval. This year the counselors did not follow that, but they will next fall. Then we'll have lots more underdivision journalism classes for counselors to put people into and that will be the training ground for future staffs. (Chelsea, interview)

Chelsea knows how sensitive this issue of "dumping" kids is in the school. She did a tremendous job this past year, patiently reaching students who had no idea what journalism was when they entered her production classes at the beginning of the year. But to her it is unreasonable to expect the teacher of a production class to have to start from scratch with a student, especially if the student is placed there by default and doesn't possess the self-motivation or interest to request the class him or herself. She balances her view by opening her Journalism I class to all students, even upperclassmen. This way she can work intimately with productive and responsible

yearbook and newspaper staffs and give her best to those just trying journalism on for size in the beginning classes.

One of the issues that becomes central in the paper is Chelsea's struggle
with how the journalism teacher ought to come prepared for teaching at the
secondary level. Armed with her perspective as a journalist who actually
worked in the field before teaching and working in a teacher education
program, Chelsea struggles with the fact that many journalism teachers she
meets are former English teachers with no formal journalism experience.
She also wonders how effective professional journalists can be without any
teacher-education experience.

> Should the Journalism teacher be an educator or a professional in journalism, or a
> mixture of both? Should he or she be a theoretician or a practitioner? I do know that
> if you have not spent time in a newsroom that you cannot teach journalism. I've seen
> people who have gone through education programs, and read about journalism
> without really doing it, and they can't teach effectively. They don't know what they're
> talking about. But it's also a matter of how much practice you have. I only had one
> year of professional experience outside of college. So do I have enough? Do I have too
> little? I feel confident about my personal abilities. I guess it's more of a judgment call
> for each person to think about how much they know, and whether or not they need
> to keep working or go into teaching. (Chelsea, interview)

These are important, problemmatic questions for educators and for the
field of study of journalism in our schools. Chelsea attacks them head on in
her paper.

In terms of research methodology, one of the primary concerns for
Chelsea became the lack of available teacher respondents for her study.
Several Journalism teachers opted out of interviewing with her for a variety
of interesting reasons. She quickly fell back to focusing mainly on her own
scene, although not strictly by choice. Her dilemma speaks to the problems
teachers face in the field of journalism including isolation and paranoia.
Typically, there is only one journalism teacher on a high school campus who
is charged with an abundance of duties including the production pieces as
well as the bulk of the teaching load. Also, because the teachers are often
judged on the quality of their students' work, journalism teachers open
themselves up to critique, while also learning to protect themselves from
criticism. Chelsea encountered these phenomena as an inquirer.

> It was frustrating because I had planned on doing a lot more interviews than I was
> able to do. There are so few journalism teachers, for one, so I had a very limited base
> of people to interview. Then when I called certain people, they were reluctant to talk
> to me, because they were paranoid about what I was doing and thought it might be
> an administrator's observation in disguise or something. I had great hopes. And then
> I realized that journalism teachers did not work together, which also became an issue
> in my paper, and that they don't believe in collaboration, and they're very much
> isolated from each other since there is only one on each campus. (Chelsea, interview)

Chelsea uncharacteristically relies on gross overgeneralization here, but her observations are true for her own experience. She faced the prospects of not having much contact with other journalism classes and other teachers. She thought contact with other teachers and other programs should be an important aspect of her study as well as of her professional development. She, like Jennifer, thought that the looking she would do outside her own classroom might be very valuable. Although an abundance of outside interviews did not surface, Chelsea did not give up on other teachers of journalism, continuing to nurture a fledgling professional relationship with another young journalism teacher in the district. She made arrangements to talk with this teacher and to act collaboratively on some projects together as well as on her research project. This gave Chelsea renewed hope in the teachers in her field.

> Another young journalism teacher and I have done a lot of collaboration this year because she and I have both been frustrated about the lack of good materials out there, and she and I have vowed this summer to get together for a weekend to compile as much as we can so that we'll start to have common denominators from school to school. At least it's a start in our district. We read every textbook there is, and we take the best chapters out of each book so that the kids don't have to read everything. The hard part now is that we have so much it's hard to decide what to give to our kids, because we can't hit everything. (Chelsea, interview)

Chelsea's perceptions regarding the process of inquiry provide interesting pieces for reflection on inquiry. Her understanding of the act of writing and how it fits together with the processes of data collection inform us of the importance of writing often and well while we journal and observe.

> It was a key for me to write and to write immediately after an event had happened. That's when it was most meaningful for me. And that's when ideas started flooding in. Even though the journal was not always directly related to the paper, it still became a great factor. Writing is so much more powerful if you do it at the moment, and not wait until 2 weeks after the fact. You don't remember dialogue, and you don't remember emotions. (Chelsea, interview)

As a writer herself, Chelsea didn't need coaching on keeping up with her writing or reminders of how important immediate note taking and journaling are for the type of study she undertook. Her insights have helped me to understand how important it is for the teacher in a research context to continually urge participants to write as they collect data. This process helps bridge the gaps between the sometimes too distinct steps of data collection and writing, though Chelsea herself saw the two steps as separate to some degree, and even believes that she took different things away from each process.

I view this project in two parts, because there was the collecting data then there was the writing the final report. And for me those were very separate steps. So I don't think I can apply too much to my teaching from my writing. The collecting data, I can. I collected and I collected until I had my three-ring binder full of stuff, and then I wrote. And that's just the way I work. I value the writing part as something at a very academic level where it could influence other teachers, but not necessarily my students. I am tied to that paper in some respects. Because I did learn things as I was writing it, because new things came up to me as I was typing that I had not thought of before. I didn't feel that I had already done the project, and then I had something else to do. It was just two different steps. (Chelsea, interview)

This statement by Chelsea reminds me of something that Jennifer said late in the first semester while talking in my office about her final writing outline. She handed me her three-ring binder packed with journal notes, and student work, and observation notes, and survey responses, and so forth, and said, "Here's my project. Can I just turn this in?" I wanted to say, "Yes!" right off because I wanted to confirm Jennifer's feeling, and now Chelsea's, that there is much inherent value in the looking and that there already is a measure of learning that accompanies the foray into connoisseurship, learning to appreciate the qualities of things and incorporating those qualities into your own mind, knowledge base, and way of seeing the world. Perhaps this process of gathering data and looking at scenes holds the greatest value in the inquiry process for prospective teachers.

But, of course, I said, "No, you have the final step to take, sharing your data and your interpretations of it with an audience, even if that audience is only yourself. You must choose the important things and organize them in a coherent form." She knew that answer was coming, but I think she wanted to see the recognition of agreement on my face before I said it. I'm glad I let on. And I'm also glad that I pushed the players in this setting to provide a final portrayal of the things they saw, and that they shared their work with others. Whereas Chelsea perceives the writing and data collecting accurately as a simultaneous affair during her observation period on the one hand, her perception of the writing for the critical piece of the project as a separate step is altogether accurate on the other hand. The recognition of this tension is an important point of interest and teaching for the research leader in an inquiry context. I'll be sure to point out this possible interpretation of the process to students next time.

At the end of the project, once I really got into the writing, I realized that I needed more data. I didn't have enough to fill some of the holes that I had, and that's when finals started, and students' projects were being turned in, and I felt like I couldn't be there all the time for my kids. It was more of a timing issue for me. During the research gathering there were days that I really wanted to go visit other campuses and I couldn't because I had to teach that day. So there was conflict, but it's not like the project was this horrible thing that was completely separate from my teaching. There were just a few logistical problems. (Chelsea, interview)

Chelsea, too, acknowledges some of the timing problems that came with the project last fall. The timing of the project seemed to cause logistical problems, even when her mentors were so very supportive. The problem, reported as well by Jennifer, pervaded and must be addressed. There is no doubt, however, that there will be holes in the interns' databases. There just isn't enough time to get everything together in one semester. And although hoping that interns will do as thorough a job of looking as they can, it is important for them to know that I do not expect them to devote their internship to gathering data or to developing the skills of a professional educational researcher. Their education is to teach, to inquire, and to report out what they learned. Inquiry helps the teacher along this path; it is not meant to dominate or take over, but it is meant to share the stage with teaching so that theory and practice can wed in an emerging conception of teaching for the prospective teacher. As in Chelsea's case, inquiry and teaching constituted two sides of the same thing.

SHAWN

Shawn had little difficulty identifying a topic for study. She wanted not only to understand how it was that students and teachers often relate but also how she could do a better job of relating to her own students. Shawn hoped to approach the complicated but important field of relationships: "My project was on student–teacher relationships. I wanted to find out how to reach students, connect with them, and examine why it's even important to do that in teaching" (Shawn, interview). She, too then, like Chelsea, adopted an action approach to her project. One of the valuable aspects of qualitative inquiry in the teacher education context is the flexibility that it offers for students to study their own practice and action in depth and/or to encounter the practices of others. There are a multitude of routes that one could take in terms of topic selection in a teacher education context that are defensible in terms of their potential for making a substantive contribution to the prospective teacher's understanding of teaching, learning, and schooling.

Other teachers Shawn met had fallen away from a commitment to students and to relating to them, to meeting students and their experiences where they are in the overall scheme of things. Shawn, however, viewed a commitment to students as students and as human beings as a primary strength that she wanted to understand and to use better in her life as teacher.

I knew that I didn't want to have barriers between me and students as far as getting to know them, to asking them, "So, what did you do yesterday?" or "Were you out late last night?" or "Why did you have to go to the hospital?" or different things like that. (Shawn, interview)

Shawn made her commitment to students evident in her internship by supporting several student groups outside of class time (as did many of the interns in fulfillment of their school–community leadership project). Her ideas about teaching children centered on her positive experiences working with students in these contexts as well as prior experiences working with students in sports activities and camp situations. She—like many teachers who attempt to relate with students in a number of different activities not only to enhance students' abilities in varying areas but also to connect with them in unique ways in order to possibly enhance student performance in the classroom—wants to understand the complicated phenomena sur-rounding the relationships among students and teachers. How do students and teachers relate? How do relationships affect the teacher, delivery of curriculum, the students' choices in school? How can teachers better understand the varying roles they play in students' lives? What power finally rests in students to choose the nature of their relationships with teachers?

Several other interns examined the issue of relating with students. The concern that prospective teachers have about how to understand and successfully make the complicated transition from student to teacher (while maintaining their own status as student simultaneously) is prominent and important. Many prospective teachers struggle with becoming less a friend than a teacher to students, although all recognize the role of friend as an important aspect of relationships with students in many teaching contexts. Many interns find it easy to banter and relate with students as contempo-raries, and then get bogged down when they have to demand that a student refrains from talking during a lesson. An inquiry of this sort concerning student–teacher relationships has the potential for revealing some of the hidden questions and answers that may go unnoticed in this important practical area of consideration for beginning teachers.

In terms of research methodology, Shawn made inroads on her project early. Extremely organized in all that she did and excited about getting started on her project, she made her data collection and reading plans early and began working as researcher simultaneously with entering the field as an intern teacher. Her perspective on conducting her inquiry took shape early and carried her throughout the study; as a result, she encountered very few problems in her teaching and research in terms of activity or time conflicts. She attributes this to having a positive attitude and getting started early.

It's kind of hard to know exactly where the reading and data collection are going sometimes. But you just do it, and try to figure out as much as you can. Sometimes you'll find a topic in the process. As I began my early reading, I was picking out the important stuff. I thought, "Yeah, that is important, because students have said this to me." You just have to start doing stuff. Observing classes. Talking with students. Just thinking of some questions. You can't do it by sitting around and moping, and not doing anything but griping. If you fight it, you'll never find a topic. (Shawn, interview)

Shawn opened herself up to the project, knowing somehow that the work she put in would benefit her and her teaching. Her willingness to tolerate the tremendous uncertainty and ambiguity of the project during the first part of the year paid great dividends throughout her internship. The fact that her mentor supported her research endeavors made the scene more hospitable, even beyond Shawn's own commitment to working on developing a topic and beginning data collection activities. Her mentor made it possible for Shawn to get a great head start on the project.

> I progressed gradually into both my teaching and my coursework whereas some interns taught, took a break from teaching to do research, then taught again. So I think the fact that I was not completely teaching by the second week of school made the research component easier for me. Some of the interns were stressed out with four preps to plan for. And some people had to be outside of their class more for different observations and that may have contributed to their dissatisfaction since they were just starting to really know their students in class. If you start at the beginning, there might be a way to work the research in where it's not so traumatizing. (Shawn, interview)

Shawn benefited from having nearly everything in perfect order for a successful research experience. She had an action topic that would permit her to study her own teaching and her own students, cutting down the amount of time she would have to spend working on her research outside of class. Her mentor provided her full support, allowing Shawn time and space to move into teaching and research at her own pace. She was excited about the project and started reading and writing about her topic early in the semester. These factors seemed to make the process of connecting research with teaching possible and productive for Shawn.

A perspective emerged among some interns that is well-documented here that leaving the classroom to conduct observations or interviews or other research activities during the process of establishing the self as teacher in the classroom came at too high a cost. Interns argued that they were just getting to know their students, just getting a routine down, just getting comfortable in class and then they had to leave to do their research data collection activities or read in the library. Some even said it hurt the students in their classes, bouncing back and forth sometimes between the mentor and the intern from lesson to lesson. Shawn shot this all down; she didn't buy it one bit. On the contrary, she thought, the students adapted easily to a rich diversity in the classroom and were generally interested in the outside activities of the intern. She built her research into her relationships with her students.

> Leaving the classroom is more traumatic for us than it is for our students, and we tell everyone we're all worried that we can't go out of class because "we have to be there for our kids, they don't know what's going on." Actually, the students are fine. They're

used to it; but we're the ones who are traumatized. You leave for a week, you come back, the kids are still fine, they haven't been damaged psychologically. Besides, half the time the students are asking, "You're doing a research project? What are you doing it on? We want to know. Can we see it when you're done?" They want to know about what you're doing. They like that. (Shawn, interview)

Approaching the research process came easy for Shawn. But writing up the final report was not so simple. She built in several layers of comfort into her research, all designed to make the transition from data collection to writing it up less bumpy, not so scary. She feared looking over the precipice of her data and seeing nothing down there to write about. I told Shawn all along that most writers feel that way, but always have something to say in the end—they always meet the deadline. It somehow always gets done.

I would take a bunch of articles with me wherever I went, and read through them and highlight whenever I had a chance. I had a big binder with all my journal entries and articles inside. I started writing in my journal what I thought was all the important stuff from my reading. After I read all the articles the first time, and had highlighted some important things, I went back with note cards, and wrote even more important things, and then what I thought about them. And then through that came my paper. It just takes time. And it takes steps. You can't expect to have your paper written after you read your first article. You have to be patient to read all the articles once, get an idea, highlight all the important stuff, read them again, and pull out what you really like, and then figure out what you think about that. (Shawn, interview)

More valuable to her than any encouragement I gave were the times when Shawn was able simply to talk with me and the other interns about the data she was collecting. These momentous interactions allowed her the opportunity to begin formally sorting her ideas. She could take these discussions back to her journal and trust that what came out could be revised into her paper in the end.

You need to talk with people about your research. You can get a lot more insight and information that way and maybe not through reading that many more articles, but just by thinking about it, and talking about it. That's one of the best things. And one of the best things was me coming in early on and saying to you and to others, "Okay, this is what I think," then you asked me questions and I'd say, "Aha—I think this! This is why." Then we'd both say, "Hey! That's it!" (Shawn, interview)

It's funny how students will say in their own words how they feel about something and the listener finds that someone else out there has a similar insight, strength, or fear. I identified closely with Shawn's own picture of the writing act and the events that go into making it up. I, too, sometimes lament the idea that got away before I could sit down at the computer, or the supposed lost eloquence of my own thoughts that couldn't be recaptured at the keyboard. I suppose that making students aware of the phenomena surrounding the writing act is the best way of approaching the subject. Shawn said it better than I ever could.

I really felt like there were some real cool ways to say some things, but I couldn't remember how I said them. Or, you know, I said this to you just the other day, and I wish I had it taped because I can never get it out the same way. Once it goes, it goes. So writing is really hard for me. Seriously. It's really hard for me to gain things back, and I get so uptight because I come in and we have this great talk, and I have all this great stuff. And I know I said it perfectly in the meeting, and I can't ever get it back. That's real frustrating for me. It's happened with both my paper and my year-end portfolio. And I feel like whenever I finally get down and get the finished product, it's kind of a watered down version of my best conversations, because I can't get those cool words back or that neat sentence . . . you know? (Shawn, interview)

Do I ever.

SHERRY

We encouraged each intern to choose a topic that interested him or her, of course. Although this was the first time that most had encountered the formulation of their own problem or topic as an inquirer and then collected data in the field in order to look more closely at the problem at hand, we believed that interest would play an important role in helping the inquirer to stay with the project when the going got difficult and when making the connections between classroom experience and inquiry about teaching and learning. Sherry's topic fulfilled both of these demands adequately, and proved to be an important inquiry project not only for herself, but also for those surrounding her, including her mentors, mentor colleagues, interns, and student respondents.

When we first got assigned this project, I thought that I wanted to pick something that was important to me because I knew that the only way I was going to be able to do this project, and do it well, was if I really was interested in it. And especially having to write that long of a paper? You know, writing is not one of my strengths. It's something I almost dread, and it's very time consuming for me. It's just really hard on me. (Sherry, interview)

She chose to look at at-risk students in her school in order to get at what it is that these students believe is important about teachers and teaching in terms of helping them do their best in school. Because she had a number of at-risk students in her classes and school and because she found herself enjoying these students and the challenge of teaching them very much, Sherry hoped to approach a deeper understanding of how to reach them through her inquiry project. Now her dread doesn't bear itself out in the final product here, for her final paper is quite strong. But I identify with her and others who have commented here, especially Shawn, concerning the fear that writing itself or an especially big project can engender. I sometimes find myself staring at the blank page for what seems like hours, finding every possible thing to do in the house including cleaning (I hate cleaning) and calling the friend I could always call later.

Sherry laid out the problem and her general approach:

> My study is about at-risk students and their relationships with teachers. I picked four teachers, two of them who were supposedly very successful with at-risk students, and two who were supposedly not so successful with at-risk students. I chose the teachers with the help of my mentor teacher and my principal after I had talked to different people and found out who was really successful in the school with the kids, and who wasn't as successful. (Sherry, interview)

In terms of research methodology, Sherry found that her data collection focus changed as a result of her visits to her teachers' classrooms. She decided that she also wanted to include the perspectives of students in her study. She discussed this change in her developing conception of the project as a result of her early work in the field.

> I think the most important part of my study came after I got into the classroom, because that's when I found out that what I really wanted to do was talk to the students and to find out what they thought. I had already decided that I was going to use a student-focus group, but it was even more evident to me that was what I had to do. I really had to find out what the students thought, if maybe they were thinking the same things I was thinking about teachers. (Sherry, interview)

Her move toward including the perspectives of students yielded an important by-product from this study. The phenomenon of valuing some-one, in this case primarily the students as respondents, produced a new level of connection between the students and Sherry. Sherry could feel the positive effect of the research process on her student respondents. She described her feelings.

> The kids that I interviewed and I developed a special bond because I actually sat down and asked them about what they thought. And they got to speak about it. There's just a respect there that wasn't there before. And I guess it was the fact that someone actually sat down and asked them, "Well what do you think? Who's your favorite teacher? Why is he or she your favorite teacher? What do you think about this?" Nobody ever asks them anything. I can feel that respect between me and the students. I see them in the hallway and they stop and talk to me. (Sherry, interview)

The formulation of her strategy for interacting with selected at-risk students helped Sherry as a teacher. Her looking and asking and inquiring led to deeper relationships with students than probably would have been possible before under normal circumstances. She wonders why the educa-tional community doesn't ask students more and more often about their interpretations of school life, of curriculum, of teaching. She wishes that schools and teachers would listen, and try to get to the bottom of perceived problems by going to the most valuable, though least trusted, source for information and direction—students. In fact, she links her study with the assumption that listening to students is an important characteristic of good teachers and good teaching, something she and her students do see happening to some degree, but altogether too infrequently. "The people who really need to listen to the kids are the ones who aren't listening to them at all. And the teachers who are doing well and are successful are the ones who are listening" (Sherry, interview).

Her perspective highlights the importance of listening to students who aren't doing very well in school instead of writing them off, which we so often do, even when we seem to be well-intentioned in our efforts on their behalf. How we value students goes to our actions—do we value their experiences and their situations as students or do we disregard this data, if you will, as unreliable, subjective, their problem not ours, too difficult to interpret anyway? I know that Sherry has positioned herself as student-centered. What type of perspective does this give her, and how does it inform her teaching? Sherry explores in these directions in her study.

The pressing issues for Sherry in terms of methodology concerned her struggles with the ethics of sharing her work and the problems she encountered in facing the writing portion of the project.

As is the case for several of our interns, they felt that it was inappropriate to share their work with the respondents they studied, especially if their interpretations tended to be less than complimentary, and possibly critical. They were worried about hurting feelings, about violating trust. Maybe they violated this trust initially by writing pieces that could be interpreted as negative. Instead of building research circles and teams around the interns (as well as possibly guiding their papers away from a comparative approach) that were well informed about what would be happening with the projects, which would have included mentors and respondents and others who understood what educational research is and were dedicated to sharing the data and the write-up in process, the resultant products seemed unfit, in some cases, for sharing publicly. Of course, this degree of privacy doesn't completely fulfill Eisner's criteria for educational criticism as constituted by a public disclosure. It also makes the question, "Then what is the justification for including these studies here?", a very important one.

In response, there seems to be a distance, both in terms of time and anonymity, at work with this book. This distance is much further than Sherry felt soon after completing her writing. In her case, at that time, sharing the paper constituted too big of a risk. Her public disclosure, then, lay in handing the paper to her professors, and sharing her findings (anonymously) with the rest of the intern cohort. I think this type of situation is something that we as instructors of inquiry need to work diligently to avoid.

We can do it by making the public disclosure of papers to respondents mandatory, an up-front expectation, by checking drafts of work more closely, by guiding students' understandings of interpretation toward the more descriptive and positive, and by nurturing an atmosphere of trust and open inquiry. Respecting and honoring those who allow us to share the school and students as outsiders are at stake in this case. This consideration must be balanced delicately against the hope of opening up seemingly closed scenes to further inquiry and reflection about teaching.

Sherry reflects on her dilemma. "The reason I didn't share the paper with the respondent teachers is the fact that I'd labeled them, 'successful' and 'not so successful.'" (Sherry, interview). Maybe the categorization was flawed from the beginning and Sherry should have been steered away from the dichotomy and the judgment. Maybe a more helpful study would have been simply to look at teachers who are "successful" and then to share the findings with the entire faculty. I don't know. Would Sherry have developed as deep an understanding of students and of their conceptions of current practice if she had limited her study in such a way? I doubt it. Is it more important to challenge the prospective teacher to decide and to see, or more important to preserve and nurture the scene, to keep anyone from getting his or her feathers ruffled? I think there's a delicate balance to pursue. The ideal would be to work, teach, and write in an environment of mutual trust and respect, that was secure enough to allow the critique and the review of present practice among teachers. This environment would allow us to challenge our assumptions and increase our knowledge and reform/inform our practice.

Sherry struggled mightily, and mostly in private, with another concern—her fear of writing. As I have said, her final product doesn't seem to bear out those fears. But we all know, at least anyone who has tried to write, that the final product doesn't necessarily signal the terror that accompanied the process of sweating blood out one's forehead and onto the page. The structure of the research project, especially in terms of incorporating the journal into the data collection process, helped relieve some of the fears that Sherry brought to the page.

> I don't think I can be successful at writing; it's such a struggle for me that it isn't fun. I do enjoy journaling, though. But I don't enjoy writing when I have to produce something, so I struggle with it and I'm never satisfied with the quality of my work. I don't have the confidence in myself to say, "This is a great paper." (Sherry, interview)

I'd say this is a very common feeling and experience for young writers, and especially for those who hadn't intended to write, or to attempt to write at such a depth as that required for the final paper. But the possibility for success, from Sherry's perspective, came from the journal-writing requirement. The fact that we read and made reinforcing comments on her journal entries helped Sherry understand that what she had to say had worth and that she could say it in an effective, communicative format. This is a crucial developmental and professional growth issue for young teachers. Regardless of subject area, teachers need to be able to write and to communicate in a multitude of forms in order to be an effective teacher and teacher colleague these days and in the future. I suppose this has always been the case, but inquiry offers students the opportunity to test themselves and improve in a supportive and constructive environment. Sherry passed her crisis of confidence, and found strength and deep learning in the writing process.

The writing part of the process played a crucial educational role for Sherry, even outside and in addition to the learning she took away from studying her topic of at-risk students in-depth. She learned more deeply about what it means to be teacher and student through encountering her own fears and resistance to inquiry, to learning. She found a new respect and understanding for students who are challenged by the demands of school and sometimes sink because they believe they cannot succeed in the current order.

> I can really see how a teacher can just destroy self-esteem when you bleed red ink on papers. I try to write. And then I get something back and I get ripped apart. I don't even know where to begin, because it's bleeding. . . . It's dead. I know that's really stupid, but that's how writing was for me. I wrote a journal entry about the fact that I came into teaching and I knew I could do a good job, but then I had to write this paper, and here I am being graded on if I can write or not. It was about knowing how painful it is to feel unsuccessful, and how I could relate to my students in that regard. (Sherry, interview)

Sherry's efforts proved to be an important success for her and for her students, by extension. She conquered her fear, although she still recoils when she thinks about another major assignment. I joke with her when we talk about how the things she gets into as teacher would make great subject matter for another paper. Although this may not be an option for her, Sherry's joy in journaling and the success she has had on this project make the possibility for future success in curriculum writing and committee work in schools much less threatening and much more hopeful. I hope she uses her skills well in her work as an excellent teacher and as a school reformer.

Sherry gives credit to the use of examples in explaining the format for the final papers. As Chelsea commented, the writing examples showing different types of qualitative reporting helped her see that her research report could take the shape of a story. This empowered Sherry, took the threat of writing away, in part.

> When I read that paper (Porro, 1985), I thought, "That's the way I can write my paper." And I said, "I can do it. I can write this." I took it as a story. I took it as a journal-type thing instead of an "academic" paper. What hit home was the example, something that I could look at and say, "You know. I can do that." (Sherry, interview)

Another methodological issue that Sherry brought forth was that she felt as though she could have used more time and resources for gathering data. Although we helped the interns narrow their topics and confine their data collection activities so that they wouldn't overwhelm themselves or take away from teaching, most felt as though they got enough stuff to put together an accurate report. But Sherry, in her increasing energy for learning and sharing more, wanted to collect more, and not in order to delay the writing.

> I just feel like I could do such a better job if I had more data, more time. I would have really got to research them well and pick out some issues and stuff that I feel a little fuzzy on. It would be better if I could go back and really look at them again. Even now, a semester later, with more experience, more depth, more knowledge, more things read, I could do a better job. (Sherry, interview)

No doubt, Sherry could have done more and maybe it would have been a better paper over time. But she can always go back, or pick it up. Her work stands on its own merit for its own time frame. I count it, too, as a major success for her.

HEIDI

Heidi began to talk about gender bias in the math classroom almost from day one of our internship together. She began reading books and articles on the topic, finding lots out there that is new and interesting since the topic is so very hot and important in the field right now. Immediately, Heidi began to see how her work as a teacher-inquirer could pay dividends in the classroom. She sensed herself becoming acutely aware of how she treated individuals in the classroom, a more deeply reflective stance than she would have taken, typically, at such an early stage of her internship. She laid out the problem:

> The topic of gender bias concerned me because I had read the data from the American Association of University Women (AAUW), about how many girls were not continuing on in mathematics once they were in college. That concerned me, as well as how that contributes to women's lower salaries—they don't get involved in the technology and mathematic-based fields once they are in college. Plus I saw many of the girls fading out in my classroom, because you really do try to incorporate the boys because they're more disruptive. And although that's a method of behavior management, it's not really fair to the girls. So my project centered around these ideas, and I started looking at the reports and then I decided that part of my research would be to observe different classes and my own classroom practice to see if I could determine if there was any truth to these reports. (Heidi, interview)

Heidi found herself especially prone to being more attentive to the boys in her classes as a classroom management strategy. But she began to question this approach as she reflected on her own teaching and the teaching she saw around school. She asked, doesn't this approach reinforce boys' behaviors, in the end, and alienate and isolate the girls in the class, distancing them from the same quality of math education that the boys get? Heidi began to look at her own teaching in comparison to the teaching she saw in the field. She started to see how traditional modes of instruction remained commonplace in our schools today and how they had influenced her in her own learning and teaching. Recognizing a potential problem is a first step in moving toward some sort of solution. Heidi's research topic put her on this pathway.

> Boys automatically seem to feel more comfortable with the immediate feedback where the teacher fires a question out and the students respond. I think that appeals to the way society has brought up boys, and that the format appeals to the boys more. And I think that style of teaching is just natural for so many, and that might be part of the reason that girls feel distanced in classes. And I know that the same thing happens to me when I teach like that. (Heidi, interview)

Coming to a decision about what to write about wasn't nearly so easy as this scenario seems to suggest here. Heidi struggled with making the transition from thinking about research in its more traditional modes (in her terms), conducting statistical studies and/or a lengthy literature review, to a qualitative, narrative mode where telling a story about what one sees and learns about educational scenes is acceptable and potentially insightful and helpful to the writer and reader. In part, her mathematical training got in the way a bit, as well as her past experiences of conducting her own research. In those attempts, she reproduced others' thoughts or conducted minor experimental replications. I kept encouraging Heidi to look past these events and to tell the story jumping off the pages of her journal or her mind after considering all that she had seen and heard and read in the field.

> I think I wanted to use the notion of compiled figures and classes all along, but I was still floundering as to how to organize all the stuff I had found. And I realized that I needed to throw out the old model and make it a story. I wanted people to be glued to it. I didn't want it to be all stats. And once I decided to make it into a story, I knew I was going to use "Miss Thomas" as my focus. (Heidi, interview)

In terms of research methodology, Heidi visited a number of classes for observations, securing permission from several teachers to conduct observations of their classroom scenes. She didn't find evidence of gender bias lurking overtly and prominently and pervasively in practice everywhere, it was mostly subtle, and only evident to her, seemingly, because she had been studying the problems of gender bias and guarding against them closely in her own emerging practice.

In terms of adopting an interpretive framework for her study, Heidi found inspiration in her growing understanding of how educational phenomena seemed to be organizing themselves all around her. Instead of seeing and using a scientific model to understand and to interpret these events, Heidi began to sense the practicality and the power of a narrative frame.

> I think what I realized is that education is not about stagnant statistics. And that every single day you've got kids who come in and out of your classroom, and they're changing all the time. And I wanted my readers to read my scenario and be able to see themselves in this class. I just let it go, because this is what is happening, this is legitimate. Yes, it is a story, but it's a true story, and it's an example of what could happen. And I realized that the study didn't have to be just a spewing of facts, or a table of who raised their hands so many times and if the teacher responded to people for this long or that long. I wanted the reader to feel as if he or she were there. And that was the whole point of it. (Heidi, interview)

Heidi also became sensitive to the need for understanding the students' points of view with regard to the phenomena she witnessed in the classroom. She engaged several student respondents in order to get their reactions to the scenes she witnessed. She discussed how this focus emerged in her study.

> I thought that what I gained from the students I interviewed was the focus of my study, the girls' slant on things. This is where I decided I was building my story. (Heidi, interview)

Like Sherry, Heidi wishes in retrospect that she could have collected more data during the first semester of her internship. But, although I can understand why certain students would want to continue collecting data in order to strengthen support for their ideas and to learn more about their particular topic, the point, as I have stated often here, was not necessarily to enhance the students' learning in one particular area only and certainly not to make them into professional researchers whose foci may or may not be classroom practice. Instead, the point was to introduce prospective teachers to the means for becoming an inquirer and a more reflective practitioner as well as to the possibilities that inquiry holds for transforming the teacher's vision of self as teacher in the professional endeavor of reaching students in the classroom every day. It is still important to listen to Heidi, however, for this is an area that must be addressed early by teacher educators employing the use of inquiry during the practicum or internship year. It is crucial to find the fine balance between getting out of the classroom enough to see what is going on in other classrooms in the same school culture and gaining the practical experience of teaching in the classroom setting.

> I think I would have liked to observe more people. I look back now, and I think, "Wow, I wish I could have seen so-and-so teach." Even now I really don't have the time for it. And I think—as crazy as this sounds—that during this time when you have the case study going you need to really take advantage of observing a lot. (Heidi, interview)

10

Learning From Inquiry

ଔ ◆ ଚ

How do the interns' studies and their own reflections on their studies and experiences in the internship contribute to their understanding of the theory and the practice that undergirds their growing conceptions of teaching?

JENNIFER

Let me start by saying again that Jennifer and I became friends and colleagues despite our disagreements over the research component. I grew much from our interactions because Jennifer made me reconsider the value of almost everything I tried to do my first year as her teacher. I think Jennifer grew, too, as her reflective comments about her experiences in doing and in writing research show here. I found Jennifer to be an effective, very capable teacher in the classroom, someone who cared deeply about her work, about children, and about mathematics. This combination foretells great things for her and her career. Let's hope that these added layers of considerations brought to bear on her life and work through the research component add to the betterment of her life as teacher and to the achievements of her students.

Strikingly, Jennifer has shifted her ground nearly 180 degrees from her position regarding the research paper at the beginning of the year. Time and reflection and professional growth have been major factors in her movement away from her early resistance to the project and toward some measure of acceptance of it and, even to some degree, an advocacy for it.

> I didn't understand the project at all during the fall class. And it's not due to your lack of trying to explain it, why it was important, and what we were going to get out of it. I just really didn't appreciate it or understand how it was going to make me a better teacher, more reflective, a critical thinker, or how it would get me more involved in the school. Then this semester I really saw how I was using my research. I saw how I was using other people's research, because I got to hear about what other people had studied, and saw that I was actually thinking about their topics in my own teaching, too. (Jennifer, interview)

Jennifer showed the most surprising and complete turnaround in the group. Her response reflects the very goals we had for shaping a curricular component, the research project, as a vital tool for helping our students become more reflective, critical, and active in the school during their practicum. Approaching a more reflective stance in teaching practice requires that the prospective teacher learns to reflect on various levels of practice, including the planning, action, and evaluative stages of the teaching act. The goal is for the process of reflection, or reflection-in-action to become a pervasive, encompassing way of being and way of life for the teacher (*Mentoring*, 1994; Schon, 1983).

Jennifer found this reflective posture in the largest part through her practicum experience in the school classrooms under the watchful eyes and care of her students, master teacher mentor, and university liaison. She also gained another path to reflection through the domain and action of educational research by participating in it herself, both by reading it and by writing it. This opportunity had not opened itself to her before. Now she can be an inquiring teacher with the skills and the vision to look, or not. It's her choice now; before she had been shut out by a lack of understanding and by no conception of the relevance of educational research and the practice of it.

> My research was what I got to see, not so much why I was looking for it, or what I was looking for, but just the fact of seeing it. I got to see and talk to a lot of different teachers. I got to see how their classrooms were set up, how they taught different things. I got to see whether or not I liked the classes and decide if "I'm not going to do that whenever I teach that" or "I'd like to do that when I teach it." And I could choose to follow in someone's footsteps, or to just go someplace else because I was sitting in there and I was bored to death. And it was good, because some of those things I saw are probably things that I might have done, and sitting there made me realize how I hated that, and I didn't want to do that. So that was good. (Jennifer, interview)

This realization about the value of learning to look and looking at classroom scenes took Jennifer to another level of understanding regarding her work and her place in the career and act of teaching. Like many other professionals, including doctors and lawyers and clergy among others, the act of inquiring about practice produces untold layers of learning and opportunities for professional development. The act of inquiring about practice, and writing about it, and sharing the results with others gives voice and power to the participants and listeners in inquiry activities and allows for growth beyond the oftentimes private, isolated world of teaching practice. Jennifer developed a new way of envisioning her practice as teacher as a result of her experience as a prospective teacher inquirer. "And I learned that wherever I teach, I want to be observing other people. That's something that I need to fight for and that I need to try to do. And I learned that I want to journal, and that I want to be thinking all the time to keep myself fresh" (Jennifer, interview).

Jennifer's commitment to inquiry in the future is an important one. It will contribute to her efforts at maintaining a reflective stance regarding her and others' teaching practice. As a result, her more reflective and inquiring approach to teaching will better her own classroom practice and increase the quality of the classroom experience for her own students. It will make her so much less likely to accept the status quo for instruction and for her students, and make it more likely that she will stay abreast of developments in the field and possibly have a hand in shaping improvement in her own department and school as well.

Jennifer's commitment to inquiry will meet obstacles, as you may well know. She will meet the sometimes unreasonable demands of time and effort needed just for teaching and certainly for dealing with the structural problems inherent in the natures of school and of teaching that foster teacher isolation instead of teamwork, and closed communication instead of honest, open dialogue about teaching. She realizes these things, but hopes to overcome them. She already struggles with the age-old tension that metacognition brings to so many veteran teachers: How do I deal with the conflicting views and practices of teaching among my colleagues?

> I think after a certain amount of years of teaching, people just assume that they know it; they don't realize how much things change. And when I was doing my research, I realized that the earliest copyright dates on all this stuff telling me that I need to use manipulatives and technology was 1988. So a lot of this has happened in the last 5 or 6 years. And so from the project I learned that no matter how much NCTM says that something should be happening, it's not what happens. And that teachers are so isolated that they can completely reject suggestions, and they can make their rooms into bubbles. You don't have to do any of them. Part of that is kind of empowering. You have this classroom, and you have control, and you can decide. But at the same time, it's kind of scary that there are people teaching who can totally reject all of this, and there's not a whole lot you can do to them. (Jennifer, interview)

Indeed, Jennifer identifies a moral and ethical dilemma as it raises itself in the current milieu of public school teaching in many secondary schools. To what extent is the professionalism and decision-making ability of the single classroom teacher protected? When does the responsibility of the classroom teacher to adopt new ways of looking at old problems, despite his or her own seemingly "tried and true" methods or "outstanding" record of achievement, reach the stage of necessary change? Jennifer calls the potential for isolation empowering, though she recognizes how deceiving this power can be. It is a silent, unvoiced power, this bubble-like isolation. Her goal is a more open, sharing, and voiced power for teachers and teaching.

At the same time Jennifer recognizes the great contradictions and tensions in teaching, she has also experienced the resiliency and "get-it-done-at-any-cost" attitude that guides the lives of master teachers who don't have the support or materials that they need to get the job done in the most comfortable fashion. She has learned much from them.

The other thing I learned from the teachers that used manipulatives and technology, even though there isn't enough money for it, and even though there aren't the materials for it, is that they found a way to do it anyway. They got support from the community. They got their students to bring in materials. They made their own. And that really showed me that if I want to do something that I will find a way to do it. Because everyone says, "Well, there's no funding for it" or "We don't have enough calculators for everyone, so you just can't do it." And that's the wrong attitude. If you just work hard enough at it, it might not be exactly the way you want it to be, but you can do something. And people say that they're not trained adequately. And that's true. But a lot of people only go to the mandatory training, instead of going to everything they can go to. So I'm going to a graphing calculator class this summer. (Jennifer, interview)

The idealism that Jennifer has and shows in her teaching and work with students is refreshing. Participating in this idealism and contributing to it to some degree make my work very enjoyable. Teachers who know how structures affect them and work within them to change them and to get things done, simultaneously work to further their ideals, transform damaging structures, and help students learn better and more. We need teachers with reflective, inquiring, and "can-do" approaches to life and teaching. There is no phony or false or shallow idealism in actions that foster the result of children learning better and more and that make the structures that constrict us as humans and as teachers less damaging and in some cases nonexistent.

I know that Jennifer will make her way in this complicated and sometimes discouraging profession, through seeking answers to the many questions she has about who she is to become as teacher and what teaching and learning is to become in schools for students in the coming years. One of the ways that she can make her way is by continuing to have a voice, and inquiring about her and others' practice. However, she worries about roadblocks on this path toward voice. She worries, on the one hand, that her own colleagues will not be understanding of or value her interest in inquiry. And on the other hand, she worries that her experience in the field will distance her from the ideals of the university. Both concerns are legitimate.

I'd like to continue to observe and to research, but the problem is you're not always welcomed in classrooms. And I'm worried about that, because I know if I'm not here next year, I'm going to be at a school where I don't know what other people are teaching, and I'm going to want to know what other people are doing. And I'm scared that I'm going to leave and that I'm going to lose all of this stuff because I'm not tied to it anymore, tied to the ideals, and tied to everyone pushing me, and tied to everyone saying, "You need to do this!" I'm worried that I'm going to get out there, and I'm just going to stagnate. (Jennifer, interview)

Jennifer's fears and concerns are not unreasonable. Finding or making the structures that help the fledgling professional in teaching find voice and support is not easy. She may have to do lots of it on her own. But she has the skills and the frame of mind that will help her make it. As she continues to inquire, Jennifer will find ways to improve her own and others' teaching practice and to create avenues for expressing the voices of self and other, making contributions to the knowledge base in teaching practice through her own work and writing.

When Jennifer voiced these concerns to me in her interview, I offered to work with her and a group of her classmates who landed jobs in the area during their first year of teaching and beyond. Not only do I wish to offer support for their inquiries into teaching, but also to act as a support and resource person as they encounter schools and teaching and get entangled therein again. The university and the liaison need to stay connected in some way with teachers that go out into the field under their auspices, and it doesn't have to be strictly through credit-hour offerings. There's a calling there, and a moral obligation. These people, these new teachers, including Jennifer, are my colleagues and friends now and I want to support their successes and questions from the field. Trinity is educating a new brand of teacher—one that is committed to his or her new school and new students and to teaching, as well as to the university from which he or she hails. This enormous commitment and investment in time and resource to teacher education ought to be nurtured and not cut off. Here's to seeing new ways and to turning things around on a continuing basis. Thanks, Jennifer, for your inspiration and guidance. I look forward to seeing you on campus next year.

CHELSEA

Chelsea never once caused me to be overly concerned about her, as teacher or as student, never making me wonder if she had made the right choice to teach (like I wonder about almost everyone, including myself), or if she would be a great teacher altogether. She carried herself with style and grace, making the tougher parts of learning to teach look easy. She stood and spoke and listened confidently in front of groups from the very beginning, and dealt with students as a caring mentor when students plagiarized or rebelled briefly against her tougher writing standards for the newspaper.

She struggled during the spring a bit, finding herself fatigued and weathered by having to carry the journalism load and responsibility on her own for the most part after Mr. Fletcher's departure. But I never worried about her like I worried about the others sometimes, about whether she was getting it or making a way for herself. I think this feeling I had about her comes from her honest approach to people and activities. She came to me immediately when she didn't quite understand what I wanted her to do with this project. Then she flew with it. She stood silently among her peers while they debated a topic, listening, until the right moment came for her to speak and to point out the deeper issues that truly lay at hand. I think her qualities shine forth in her paper, as she takes us through the issues that circled her encounters with students, teaching, and curriculum. Chelsea has much to offer the field, including insights about how inquiry has shaped her growing conceptions of teaching.

In part, Chelsea learned about the underside of teaching and teachers in her field of journalism. The picture wasn't nearly in the focus she had hoped for.

> I learned that many journalism teachers wanted to quit within 5 years. They were burned-out. There's just more stress. You're in charge of a $30,000 budget every year with publications. There's just so much going on all the time that if you can't manage very well, then you'll go crazy. It was mostly the English teachers who had turned to journalism that were ready to quit so soon. They wanted to just have a set curriculum, and read a novel and talk about it, and not have everything change from day to day. (Chelsea, interview)

Chelsea's internship and inquiry experience gave her firsthand knowledge of the pitfalls that surround teaching journalism at the secondary level today. The experience of journaling and interviewing and writing up her story helped reveal to her the many demanding levels of her future work, and maybe the areas that she will begin working to transform in her next teaching position. My hope is that she will work to transform the structures that constrict teachers in the field.

In general, Chelsea credits the demands of the internship program, and the academic component of it including the research project, as fostering a higher level of thought and action from our students, her cohort, at least in terms of how she views her own academic work in college. She reflects on the pride she feels having accomplished so much in her internship—teaching her classes effectively, writing a substantive research paper, and facing the tough issues of teaching today by encountering them in practice and in discussion with peers.

> I have learned so much more during this 1 year than I did during all 4 years of college combined because so much more was expected of me. As an undergrad, I was able to float through. Nothing was that difficult. We were really taken to a higher level here. And it hasn't just been a fifth-year bachelor's degree, it's really been a master's program. (Chelsea, interview)

Chelsea's last statement points to a touchy issue in this scene, one that is not fully resolved as of this writing. One of my most controversial statements of the year came on Black Thursday when I said that students conducting inquiry during their internship had the chance to earn a "real" master's degree. I never should have said that publicly, because I value the people and the experiences that came before us and there really was no need, except deep within me as spurred by my insecurities, to draw a distinction between this course of study and past practice. The fact that I said this has hurt some people's feelings, especially those who teach at the high school and were former interns or mentors who had a substantive role in shaping the program in prior years, and most especially during that time when there was no university liaison working closely with them.

But I was hired, I thought with the knowledge of all parties involved, to do a specific job, and that was to shore up the academic side of the program. The principal, who had a major role in carrying the program while the committee searched for me, has said publicly on many occasions, "What we are doing now is so much better than what we have done in the past," although he, too, is hurt to some degree that I have made the distinction. But the students have to believe and to know that what they are doing is valuable. So, I am sorry. I am also making the point that inquiry has so much to offer prospective teachers that other approaches do not and that we must pursue a reflective and inquiring mode of being in order to fulfill our best selves as teachers and colleagues. Chelsea has benefited greatly from this approach, and in ways that other approaches would not have benefitted her (a skills approach, an apprenticeship, student teaching, etc.) for a number of reasons. She is straightforward in her reflections on the project's value for her.

> I think if I had not done this research paper, I might not have paid as much attention in my journalism classes. I would have taught, and reflected on why I was teaching it, but I would have not really analyzed it. Every day I walked into my classes and I had a battle plan. I knew I had to find out this research today, and I really looked at my kids and myself all the time, and analyzed what we were doing. (Chelsea, interview)

I am not satisfied with looking at issues only at the surface level, although sometimes that is unavoidable, either by choice or by ignorance. I have challenged our prospective teachers to look at events and issues for their deeper considerations, so that we are not a band of "take it-as-it-comes" practitioners, but a reflective and inquiring cadre of teachers who face change and make change head-on, with confidence and with care. I would not let students go through this project or their everyday experiences without challenging them to examine the deeper issues behind events and thoughts. Teacher educators must not sit on the sideline silently, but cheer and cajole and prod and coach in these complex milieus we call teacher education programs and schools.

> We weren't allowed just to come to class and talk about what we were doing, we had to write it down and make reflections on it, and then get analytical about it, then go even further when you'd say, "More, more, deeper, more. . . ." You made us go really inside of ourselves to create this product. So that nothing was surfacy after November, and we knew that. And we knew that we couldn't float through anymore because we knew that you'd be shouting, "More!" (Chelsea, interview)

Like Jennifer's mentor Mr. Baker, who confessed to me that he hoped that his legacy in teaching would extend beyond the ghosts and shadows of his classroom and his lesson plans and who subsequently took up journaling as a tool for reflection and inquiry, Chelsea wants her legacy as teacher to take a new shape. She wants to have voice as a professional, as a teacher who uses and creates knowledge in her theoretical and practical activities in classroom and school. Therefore, finding ways to manifest an inquiring way of life within the teaching act is a crucial undertaking. How will we support her and others in their efforts to better themselves and others through inquiry? Can we see that becoming an inquirer doesn't detract from practice or from students, but only enhances them both?

> I don't want to become a teacher and never produce anything again. I don't want my meaning as a teacher, and what I'm going to be remembered for as a teacher, to be my lesson plans. I want to be able to influence people's thinking other than my students. And now I'm trying to incorporate me as teacher and me as scholar and theoretician. But how can they combine without me going into a doctorate program? I don't want to do that. Yet, I really have the desire to write and be published because I know that what I'm doing is not fluff. There's just a lack of good articles about journalism educators at the high school level right now. (Chelsea, interview)

Chelsea is one of the best young candidates for making a way as teacher inquirer. But one doesn't have to be an exceptional writer or a first-year teacher. One simply needs the spirit to grow as an educator and professional. Jennifer's mentor, Mr. Baker, displays this spirit in his commitment to inquiry, even after his skepticism at the beginning. The obvious results in terms of increased reflection on practice and meaning in context and the empowerment that comes from the achievement of voice as a teacher inquirer are enough to draw people to the movement. These outcomes are the most crucial, pointed to as potential benefits in other studies, and brought to the surface in this context as tangible results of an inquiry-oriented way of life and practice.

> This program is not about us becoming good teachers; it's about us becoming influential teachers, and really supporting this movement for change in schools. Trinity has had such a great hand in changing schools, and then we get thrust into traditional schools, and feel that we don't have a voice anymore. And I don't want to lose my voice. I think inquiring will be a good way for me to keep thinking and writing. (Chelsea, interview)

SHAWN

Shawn's study immediately informed her growing conceptions of self as teacher and continues to do so as I write this and as you read. Her own paper is never far from being pulled out of her professional portfolio, browsed again, revised, and left out overnight to ponder. Shawn sees the document, in part, as a personal statement about aspects and processes of getting to know students as a teacher. Her study has informed her all along the way, helping her to think reflectively about the choices she makes in relating to students and about the phenomena surrounding student–teacher connections, in general. All of the activities involved in her research—proposal writing, collecting data, journaling, outlining a paper, and writing it up—have helped her organize and build a conception of the relational teacher from the very start of her practicum experience. She intends to continue the process by revisiting the piece often and building other projects from it and around it in her first years as a professional.

> The paper is there for me, ready. It's going to inspire me to go in and meet every individual student to try to see what I can do to make school better, make them learn more, to help them. You can lose sight of that so easily. I can make a little ritual of reading my paper once a semester, most definitely in the summer right before I go in for in-service. I'll read it as I go through the years, and say, "Wait a minute—here's another thing." And I'll write in it, and once it gets too messy, I'll retype it. I didn't do the paper just for it to sit there. Why spend all that time and work and research to do something that just makes your professor happy? (Shawn, interview)

Shawn truly wrote her paper for herself; she wrote it to help herself become a better teacher. She set out to understand her field of interest better, and to gain some working knowledge that might help her as a practitioner in the field. In this sense, she got the most out of the project that she could and that we could have hoped for as professors in teacher education. The acts of inquiring and reflecting are the goals at stake here; having reached them through her participation in the research process, Shawn is ready to pursue her former topic and others with even more fervor. She will constantly seek, I believe, to make herself a better teacher through a lifelong examination of relevant literature in the field of educational research and of her own extraordinarily effective practice as teacher and curriculum-maker in the classroom.

> My study helped me learn about students, and what they need, of course. But it also showed me where to go to find educational articles and how to do research. I can just go up to the computer—type in a subject —and find a bunch of articles and pick a couple out to read. Wouldn't that be a great habit to get into? What a better way to learn how to do that than to do it for real. And so this research experience was meaningful. (Shawn, interview)

Crucial, but sometimes overlooked, is the learning that comes simply from talking with people about a meaningful, important topic. Shawn found herself becoming more comfortable expressing her ideas to others and listening to others as a result of her work in the research process. Her growth in this area added to her confidence level in teaching contexts as well as in her university coursework.

I learned how to meet kids on their level more effectively. And maybe the research project helped in calming some of my fears about relating to students. Sometimes it's really scary, especially when you're so close in age to students, just getting to know them or learning how to react with them. So the project helped me to feel more confident with that. (Shawn, interview)

The project also grounded Shawn in what she deemed to be her strength as a teacher—relating with students on a personal level. She wanted to know what her strength had to do with teaching on an intuitive level and beyond, and the support she found for her talents in the profession of teaching through her research served as a springboard for a healthy, confident conception of self as teacher.

I became a teacher in the first place because I love kids, and I mingled and met with kids outside of school when I was an undergrad in various social-type settings. It's a little different when you're a teacher because you have to establish lines, but it really made me more comfortable with the kids. It's just the whole reason I started out, and I focused on that, and I can't neglect where my heart is—with meeting kids, and getting to know them, and figuring them out. (Shawn, interview)

Shawn sees the research component of her internship experience as a primary contributor to her learning about teaching and about herself as teacher this year. I saw Shawn's confidence growing as she made her way through the thicket of work and learning she set out for herself to encounter and to accomplish. She saw the big picture, if you will, of the research component and its possibilities for contributing to the overall experience in the internship from the very start, and this made her able to proceed with the minimum of impediments. She grew professionally from her experience as a reflective practitioner, both in the contexts of the classes she taught and through her research endeavors. "Now if there's anyone who can talk about reflection or professional development it'll be us. And we know how important it is because we've seen it and we've done it" (Shawn, interview).

I don't think Shawn is finished with her topic yet, or with looking at classrooms and students and teachers and herself more closely and more reflectively. I have high hopes that she will continue her inquiry and serve her students well in the near future.

My paper is there to remind me why I started teaching. And then when I find new ideas, I'll write them down or decide, "I don't agree with this anymore" and scratch it out. It'll be good to see how the paper changes. And who knows, maybe I'll be in some other type of program or project someday and I'll be able to say, "Well, I have this little thing. Maybe I ought to make it bigger. Maybe there's a lot more to this." I know it's not done, though, by any means. (Shawn, interview)

SHERRY

Sherry learned that her emerging theories about the importance of students' needs and perceptions were supportable. The students supported them as they answered her questions about school experiences and their lives with teachers.

> I learned how smart kids are. They told me exactly what they did and didn't like about their teachers. But most important, they showed that the personality of the teacher, whether the teacher was understanding and caring, was the most important part. They talked about curriculum and teaching strategies, but they taught me that if you care about the students, and you show that you're involved with them and you understand them, then they'll do anything for you. (Sherry, interview)

It is comforting and possibly inspiring to experience the success of other teachers, and then as teacher to feel as though approaching that success in your own practice is a real possibility. Sherry felt this way, I think, as she looked at other teachers and compared her own life and work to those fellow colleagues around her. She drew ideas and hope from those who committed themselves to bettering the lives of the students charged to their care. Out of her research emerged a formal conception of self as teacher, with foci on caring and understanding and meeting the needs, both personally and pedagogically, of the students in her classroom. This is where prospective teacher research has one of its greatest potentials—for revealing and supporting emergent conceptions of educational experiences in terms of their potential contributions for the development of the professional self.

The possibilities for our own learning that listening to others brings to us are great and attainable. What we need to do is to take the step of opening ourselves up to students and to others so that we can listen to what they have to say about their experiences in educational contexts. We can learn much from test scores. We can learn much from needs assessment tools and personality tests. But what can we learn from asking students and teachers questions about their lives in school? We can learn about and from the secret, hidden data that are real and meaningful and often untapped the things we need to know for helping us see what we are doing and what we ought to be doing better in schools for students as teachers. Unlocking the voices of those unheard helps them and us gain voice, and gives us the foundational springboard, the development of self as teacher, for making a way in the future as an effective teacher of students in schools. "This paper is not for you, it's all stuff for me. And I'm proud of it. It tells a story, and it's a good story. It may not be written in the best words possible, but it's a good story. And it's for me. If anything, it's for me" (Sherry, interview).

All along I had hoped that our student researchers and their mentors would see how powerful the educational tool of research could be for helping students develop their own conceptions and practices of teaching. In Sherry's case, the research process became a crucial experience for building confidence, knowledge, and a professional teaching style that could serve as the starting point for a successful, reflective career in teaching. She allowed herself to learn from her own thoughts and feelings and experiences as well as those around her, confronting her own fears about learning by facing the project and its demands head-on. Like Shawn, who talks of referring back to her paper periodically in the future, and Chelsea, who speaks of a sense of accomplishment and higher learning as a result of doing research on teaching, Sherry has found the research process to be a source of accomplishment, of achievement that may spur her on to even greater things in her teaching life.

I believe the bottom line to be that students in schools, by extension, will benefit from this heightened awareness of self and of a greater sense of accomplishment and learning on the part of their new teachers. A sense of confidence and hope and accomplishment tends to be contagious when shared by energetic human beings, teachers, who encounter others, their students, around the acts of learning and knowing more about ourselves and the world by engaging life and school life in meaningful ways together in classrooms. I contend that the possible overall success of students of teaching, like Sherry and the others, is heightened when they engage and increase their own learning about schools, students, and classrooms in reflective ways during their preparation programs.

There are many layers for accomplishing this in our program, not the least of which are the formal, focused looking and writing students complete in the exciting classroom environments they experience with their mentor teachers and students. Building effective layers for learning about ourselves and others as teachers and students ought to be the highest priority for teacher educators, teachers, prospective teachers, administrators, students, parents, and citizens. When we balance the experiences of gaining teaching skills with the gaining of practical knowledge of the complex issues surrounding teaching through reflective practice and inquiry, then we are well on the way toward educating teachers who have a great chance for long-term success in the field.

Sherry has a great chance for success. She has learned much about teaching and teachers and students and learning from her work as an intern, as a prospective teacher inquirer. She has found a friend in journaling, and through that writing process, in part, is conquering her fear of writing, and may employ it as a tool for continuing her reflective practice in the field during her first years. It will be up to her to find ways to continue the disciplined inquiry that she has started in her journaling activities. I hope that she will use it and strategies that prompt her own students' reflective looking and learning as they become educated in their classrooms together. "The journal is a way to reflect and see how I've grown; it's like a book of knowledge" (Sherry, interview). A key to professional development for teachers is filling gaps, in developing perceived weaknesses into strengths. For Sherry, continuing to write in her journal would be an effective way to continue her development as a great teacher.

Sherry spoke some of the most influential, powerful words I heard anyone say this year or in this study. Sherry's spirit for learning about teaching became infectious, as she carried her understanding of the project and its potential for helping her grow in the classroom into her internship experience with her colleagues in the cohort. She continued her pursuit of a teacher's persona and way of life by maintaining her status of student throughout, and by developing a conception of herself as teacher as a lifelong learner who sees the value of inquiry past the borders of her internship. Sherry's words speak volumes in support of enabling prospective teachers through a substantive internship to reach for a professional life that is marked by collegiality and inquiry. "It was really about hands-on research. That's what it is all about! It's about learning how to teach yourself. It's about still being a student" (Sherry, interview).

HEIDI

The turnaround in Heidi, with regards to her perceptions of the research project and its connection to her overall learning about teaching during the internship, nearly matched that experienced by Jennifer. Whereas Heidi did not display the pervasive skepticism and negativity that Jennifer exhibited toward the project for much of the first semester, Heidi nonetheless felt the conflict festering inside her as she experienced a roller-coaster ride of experience in terms of understanding or not understanding the value of her work on the project in her own internship and professional development. Regardless, the learning that Heidi encountered as a result of conducting this research and of teaching reflectively throughout her roller-coaster ride proved to be some of the most direct learning that any of the interns encountered. Despite some resistance to it, her research proved to be an important part of her development as a teacher. She relates how her project made a direct impact on her own learning about teaching.

> I have grown a lot because once I'd seen different types of gender bias in my research I was able to say, "You know, I do that. And I do that." And I've been trying to fix those ever since my study, trying to help the girls become more incorporated with math. And that goes to making sure that I visit everyone in the classroom, and not just the boys who seem to demand more attention because they're off task, and making sure the girls understand the concepts. Also the content of math needs to be more than boy-oriented, not just about skateboards and sports, and other things that society deems boy-oriented. I've been trying to teach in ways that help girls more. According to the research, girls learn best in a cooperative manner. (Heidi, interview)

And so having been profoundly influenced to reflect on her own tendencies as a teacher, Heidi has been influencing others around her. She has
made other teachers aware of teachers' tendencies that exclude women in
the classroom; she has raised both the awareness of the issue and the
understanding of how we can change our pedagogy in the teaching lives of
her colleagues. These effects are the manifestations of the potential that
inquiry has for shaping and changing teacher development and school
culture in positive ways.

Heidi's encounter with the potential benefits of teacher inquiry has
revealed a whole new world of questions to her that have taken firmer shape
as a result of her looking at classroom scenes with a more critical eye. She
seems to understand that it is the asking of questions that spurs knowledge,
and not necessarily the quick acquisition of answers. She has laid the
fundamental groundwork for her advancement as a thoughtful, caring,
experienced, and intelligent teacher during her internship by engaging
others, learning from dialogue and experience with colleagues and students
how best to go about planning and delivering curriculum in the classroom.

> I have mostly raised more questions, and I think that's because I don't really have the
> experience yet. I come up with more questions, but as I get older and as I get more
> practice in the classroom, I'll have more answers. In order to get the answers that I
> have, I found that talking to my mentor teachers and to others has really helped me
> because the sharing of minds is what I've really learned to value this year. (Heidi,
> interview)

Participating in the sharing of minds, of ideas and strategies and hopes
for teaching better, constitutes a worthy endeavor and outcome for any
prospective teacher engaged in a practicum or internship. It is this intellectual pursuit of what works, of the deeper issues behind success including
culture and structure, of who students are, of who we are, of what school
really is, that helps us stay on the path of continuous learning about teaching
and learning. We grow in confidence and knowledge and effectiveness when
we embark on journeys to reach these lofty goals. Heidi began to reach them
this year and set herself on the way to making further, continuous progress
as a teacher in the future.

> I've built confidence to really question things and analyze what I see and ask myself,
> "Did that work?" or "Would I be able to pull that off?" Also, as far as gender bias goes,
> it gives me confidence to go and look for more instances of ways to improve myself. I
> think it takes confidence to be able to say, "I'm really poor in this area" and to be able
> to go back and try and fix it. And I think that's what I learned from doing all of these
> observations of others' and my own classrooms. (Heidi, interview)

Far from being a harmful process that merely reveals our seeming foibles,
inquiry has the potential for taking us back to the realistic position that
grounds us in the facts that we are fallible, make mistakes, but can improve

as teachers if we are open to change, self-critique, and others who can share their insights about our work with us. Heidi claims these positions at the end of her internship and through her comments here. Being a part of an environment that supports the constant examination of self, both in terms of delivery of curriculum and the effects of our work on students and the school, becomes an important part of many young teachers' lives as they go through teacher-preparation programs. But how will teacher educators and school districts continue to support the desire and energy to know more about ourselves as teachers and the phenomena surrounding the teaching and learning acts inside and outside the classrooms of our schools?

I believe that it will take a fundamental shift in our priorities to support young teachers such as Heidi and the others featured in this text. These young teachers possess the initial momentum to continue their professional growth through inquiry and reflective practice. How can inquiry become a viable and acceptable part of school and teacher culture so that the sparks for personal and professional growth remain ignited in these young teachers?

These questions are important material for the closing chapter, Emerging Lessons From Inquiry. But, briefly, let me say that there are informal levels of reflection that might become institutional layers with the help of new teacher leadership. One avenue is to support "teacher-reflection circles," opportunities for young teachers to meet and reflect on their classroom experiences and personal development as teachers. I hope that these teach-ers will want to meet and to meet continuously, and ultimately gather a momentum together that helps them define their conceptions of teacher inquiry as they look and journal and lead in their new schools in the near future. As Heidi stated, she already has a plan for providing leadership in her new teaching environment next year. She will take on the role of initiator, asking questions and inquiring with her new colleagues about how to practice better.

> You have to make the first move in education. I think you have to go and sit down and talk to the teachers and ask, "How do you feel about this?" and be ready to realize that they're not going to ask you how you feel about such and such right away. But after you initiate some conversation with them, then they might be able to reciprocate and ask you how you do some things. (Heidi, interview)

I suppose it is fitting that Heidi makes one of the crucial arguments supporting the use of inquiry in teacher education programs. Despite the possibilities for resistance and problems to arise in any endeavor that asks people to take a hard look at what they are doing or what is going on around them, we have to start somewhere. Developing a culture of inquiry that trusts, supports, and pushes itself to create a better understanding of what schools and teachers and students are doing in classrooms as well as to improve those very events in terms of increased student learning and teacher effectiveness is a worthwhile goal all around. Getting on the path toward approaching the goal is an important step, one that all the players in this story took in some form or another. We need to educate new teachers who see the benefit in studying and reporting about their own practice. Teachers need to lead and define their profession by claiming a voice within and without. This small band of teachers enters the field with a spirit for reflection and inquiry and hope, believing that they can change schools and selves for the better for the benefit, ultimately, of the school children they will most directly affect as teachers.

11

Emerging Lessons From the Experience of Conducting Inquiry

☙ ◆ ❧

INTRODUCTION

I come to the end of this first year and the beginning of my second year as a teacher educator with mixed emotions. After surveying the reactions and perceptions of these five wonderful teachers regarding their experiences of conducting inquiry during their internship, I feel both a sense of accomplishment and of dread. I feel a sense of accomplishment in that these prospective teachers have grown a great deal; that they and their colleagues, including their mentors and students, have made strides in valuing and reshaping their conceptions of teaching and learning for the better; that they have prepared themselves adequately to take positions in schools as teachers, having experienced the deep rigors and challenges of everyday teaching and having looked closely and more reflectively at some of the pressing issues of schooling through the combination of their practice and coursework.

But toe-to-toe with these perceived accomplishments stand substantive feelings of dread. I sometimes wonder if I'm up to fighting any more of the battles like the ones we faced last year. I wonder if I can get up in front of another group and make the case for inquiry again or listen effectively without becoming angry or distanced. I wonder if I'm cut out for this at all; maybe I'm in over my head. Maybe I've done irreparable harm to those who must ultimately support our efforts, the teachers, by forcing them to support inquiry in their classrooms. Maybe.

These are some of the demons and doubts I must face this coming year. I know that almost everyone has them lurking somewhere in themselves, but that doesn't make it any easier to deal with them. Every year I find for myself that teaching involves, at root, the investment of self, the tireless wooing of others to a point of view or the enlightened agreeing to take someone else's position to heart, and the letting go of others to discover ideas for themselves. Recognizing these facts makes for a challenging and scary, yet rewarding, teaching life.

How well I deal with teaching and letting go of the various demons that plague many teachers (I hope I'm not alone) depends in part on how well things go at the beginning of this coming year. If I do a good job of listening and learning and reshaping my teaching practice to meet the needs of students and teachers better in this context, then the endeavors of the first year will have accomplished and contributed much. If the cohort of students seems stable and able, if the successes of the previous year win out in perception over the lows, if the new mentor cohort is supportive, then maybe we can turn it around for the better and for good. These are my hopes. I also hope that the resolve that buoyed my actions and spirit last year returns in due form in due time. I am counting on it to reappear and to carry me. It has faded in and out of presence during the course of this writing.

One intern last year said this about teaching: "I chose teaching over business or law because I knew that every day would be different from the last, that something new and exciting would happen every day in teaching." I find some solace in this statement, and as I've tried to make clear over the course of the book, these fine intern teachers and their mentors have taught me much. I sense here in this statement an attitude of resolve that encounters and wins out over the down days of teaching, the political battles for power, the seemingly senseless personality conflicts that sometimes get in the way of helping students or making school a better, more productive place for learning to occur. I am trying to be honest here; I don't look for failure over the horizon. I do know that persistence and patience can pay great dividends. I am a teacher and I intend to teach long past the events of this storybook. I only hope that I won't lose track of this chronicle, that it will continue to inform me over the course of my years as teacher, inquirer, and professor. I know that tomorrow will be another unique and challenging day. Making a contribution to the educational community, and ultimately to children, is an important endeavor. This is why I'm here; this is why I'll stay on.

SOME INITIAL LESSONS LEARNED FROM INQUIRY

The process of implementing the research component as a substantive part of our interns' experience this year resembled a roller coaster ride; we had several dramatic turns together this year. My experiences and my reflections on the experiences of the interns and their mentors in our shared culture have prompted me to pull out some initial lessons for my own development as teacher educator and might possibly be meaningful for others in the field. I believe that beginning teacher educators might especially benefit from interacting with this story and my reflections on it. These initial considerations are starting points that will be expanded on in the final part of this chapter.

First, I have struggled with whether we should have pursued this major change, even on a smaller scale, this first year. But the one question that pulls against me is, "How would we be perceived now as newcomer teacher educators if we had come in and maintained the status quo in the program?" I know that our department chair would not have looked favorably at a performance based primarily on the maintenance of the status quo. We were hired, in fact, to shake things up. I have the feeling that our interns wouldn't have minded the status quo, although their overall learning experience would not have been as rich, for not only would their academic experiences have been less substantive, but we as their professors would have been less excited about and invested in the curriculum.

The high school mentors are the tricky group about which to speculate. On the one hand, they had become fatigued by the responsibility of carrying the program by themselves and needed relief from a university liaison. On the other hand, they envisioned relief coming in only under their own terms. But they are crucial players in the success of any fifth-year program that includes an extensive, year-long field placement; they have much influence over the shaping of prospective teachers' beliefs and practices, and well they should. Their great contribution to this program is that they have agreed to grow together with me and the interns and to adapt. As a result of the learning we have seen from our interns in their research and teaching, we have our sights set on productive years to come. We have a shared sense of accomplishment and ownership of the reform now. This is ground we did not share at the beginning.

I would be remiss if I didn't mention how crucial the support of the principal became to me with regard to my relating and working with the mentor teacher faculty, all of whom were not chosen by me this first year. Remember, I was in Indiana when the selection of mentor teachers occurred. But our principal became a support and confidante to me personally, valuing me as a person as well as the work I was doing as a teacher educator from the very start. Although not always cheerleading for change or for me, this stance wouldn't have been prudent or effective for him, he nonetheless worked quietly behind the scenes helping to stall damage after some unfortunate misunderstanding or other by talking with individual teachers on my behalf. He took heat and took it off me in many situations, some of which I'll never know about. This sort of personal and political ally is indispensable. I don't know what might have happened if I would have been left alone without this most basic and crucial support.

Of course, this relationship and the situations that were enhanced by it point to the political nature of the everyday workings of school and collaboration efforts in teacher education. I recall, at this time, very few instances during my first year when I could really be myself in the field, unless you call the political animal that I have become my true self. Even when battling for the inquiry component as a valuable and indispensable component to the program, the struggle became more political than personal. I have had only a small cushion of time to help me understand the impact of the phenomenon of politics on my personal and professional lives in this context.

Second, I have come to realize and to appreciate how upsetting it was to the people I wanted least to upset—the interns and their mentors—that the change to doing research as a main focus for the Pedagogics course came exclusively from the professors. The interns had no choice but to take the course with us and to do the project. We were it, and there was no opting out if they wanted to graduate. Because the time frame for our coming from other locales was so short, there was no change process at all, no gradual implementation plan. Interns' expectations for the program, some long-standing, were swiftly changed. Others had no say. And we stormed ahead.

Regardless of the quality or quantity of my efforts to explain the virtues of doing teacher research, I hadn't taken into serious account where my students and mentor faculty stood and what their expectations were. And working with an established mentor faculty and prospective teachers that have a sense of ownership and pride about a program poses particular challenges to an inexperienced teacher educator coming in new, no matter how seemingly capable he or she may appear. It is not enough to have good ideas and to be able to implement them. It's not enough to appear well-liked or to impress others superficially. In order to make it in this type of teacher education environment—one where working closely with interns, mentors, and their students in the field is paramount—one has to build relationships, trust, collegiality, and respect a little bit at a time. It doesn't come all at once, and sometimes never.

The key is to be flexible, to adjust, to take to heart the insight of Fullan and Miles (1992): "Anxiety, difficulties, and uncertainty are *intrinsic to all successful change*" (p. 749). I was willing to adjust the details of the project, to negotiate with each intern and mentor how best the project fit the individual student's talents, interests, and needs. I do wish, however, that I could have been thicker-skinned in response to initial criticisms of me and the project. But I am human, and found out that my peers are, too. This isn't such a bad outcome; and it appears that having come to this realization has brought us closer together as persons and as professionals. We have come closer to expressing ourselves as opposed to trying to impress each other. This is a big step.

Before I began this job last summer, Chris and Mitchell and I had the chance to visit some friends for a short vacation. They had a visitor, a Catholic priest who had been teaching summer school classes at Notre Dame. I asked him if he had any advice for a fresh PhD starting the type of job I had just taken. He said very quickly with little thought, as though he had been asked the question before: "Seek to express, not to impress." I had little response at the time, for I found his answer to be both confounding and profound. I have referred back to it often, however, and it has spoken effectively to me. The key, I think, is to follow your heart, mind, and spirit into work and personal relationships, doing what you think best, but also remaining open to the practice of examining instead of defending positions and the self, and listening. I have been trying to express myself, therefore, and to constrain my will to impress others or myself. I intend this book as a product of expression and not of impression.

And third, I do know that several considerations may have eased the tensions and made things seem less severe than they seemed to the players involved in this story. I could have listened to the insights of Cochran-Smith and Lytle (1990), "Telling teachers they should do teacher research is an inadequate way to begin" (p. 10). Negotiating some version of the research component with the interns and mentors during the summer before the new school year would have been a good place to start. Even if the shared plan met resistance, we could have worked out a compromise, and at least interns and mentors would have been able to prepare and adjust their approaches to the first semester, especially to the first weeks. And I could have come off differently. I had to battle the "bad guy " image all term. I could have started out as a willing, flexible, and able teacher, which is who I think I truly am and how I would rather fashion myself.

Also, I could have better anticipated the concerns and fears that students have about educational research, what it is and how it can be done. James and Ebutt (cited in Kyle & Hovda, 1987) suggested that "there are two main obstacles to getting started: not knowing what to do, and not having enough confidence to begin" (p. 86). Interns and their mentors responded to former conceptions of educational research that haunt their personal experience with it: distant, not applicable, quantitative, hard to read, uninteresting, a waste of time. In response, I could have built a case early, using examples from the literature showing why and how teacher research is being carried out in exciting ways around the country in teacher education programs and in schools (Eisner, 1985; Gitlin & Teitelbaum, 1983; Gore & Zeichner, 1991; Goswami & Stillman, 1987; Teitelbaum & Britzman, 1991). I could show more clearly and earlier how relatively simple it is to act as a disciplined inquirer by keeping a journal filled with reflections and observations of classroom scenes. I could have shared testimonies of the impact that this type of inquiry process has had on the development of conceptualizations of teaching for participants in other programs. Making up the deficit in this area is a primary consideration for teaching next year's cohort of interns and their mentors.

Finally, I wouldn't trade this year and its trials for any smooth-sailing semester that will hopefully occur in the not too distant future. So much can be learned from the struggles we undertake together. I have learned more about teaching and learning from my interns and their mentors this past year than in all of my previous years of learning and teaching. This is the base from which I hope to build a positive, lasting relationship with them all as colleagues and peers. To make needed adjustments and to continue the positive energy of reform in this context will constitute substantive challenges and victories in our years of research and practice ahead—together.

LESSONS FOR TEACHING AND LEARNING FROM CONDUCTING INQUIRY

In conclusion, I'd like to offer an exposition of some further, more general lessons we learned as a result of our work together in this context this past year. First, I examine what I think we learned about teaching and learning as a result of our experiences of conducting inquiry. Second, I examine what I think we can learn about teaching inquiry and about doing inquiry during the prospective teacher's internship-year as a result of our experiences of conducting inquiry. Throughout the chapter I confront significant obstacles and address them as they pertain to these examinations and the initial lessons suggested at the beginning of the chapter. Here goes.

The most important case to be made for inquiry in teacher education programs rests in the experiences and perceptions of the prospective teachers who conducted their own projects in the schools. Their perceptions make clear, at least to me, that inquiry provides a deeper, much needed layer of reflection and analysis of practice and theory in education than only teaching does, as may be the case typically in an apprenticeship program or in a student teaching program for prospective teachers.

However, it must also remain clear that the main business of the internship year for prospective teachers must be the accumulation of numerous and varied experiences in the classroom. Teachers must enter their first full-time teaching position having witnessed and participated in the full range of classroom activities that most teachers face in their difficult work in today's schools. The chances for having a long career in teaching increase, we believe, when students have the opportunity in their preparation experiences to confront the realities of school life and teaching today while simultaneously gathering and testing strategies to deal with and transform these realities tomorrow. Inquiry balances and deepens the objectives of knowing what it's like out there and imagining what it might be like out there and changing what it's like out there. Inquiry allows the student of teaching to go behind and beyond practice in order to see how theory and thought shape and enlighten a teacher's development and practice.

All of the women in this study make the case through their remarks and experiences for the deeper, reflective value of conducting inquiry during their internship. They show how their views of students, classrooms, curriculum, social issues, and pedagogy have been shaped and transformed by looking at the phenomena that surround educational events they experienced with their students and with other teachers. They have had the experience of looking more deeply at what they are doing than most, reflecting on themselves and their practices and students and schools in order to understand what constitutes best practice and how they might meet those developing and internal standards in the future. You have seen these statements before, but I thought they might ring clearly again here, and support several concluding points:

> This semester I really saw how I was using my research. I saw how I was using other people's research, because I got to hear about what other people had studied, and saw that I was actually thinking about their topics in my own teaching, too. (Jennifer, interview)

Jennifer's remarks suggest the great hope of inquiry in teacher education: Inquiry can produce a culture of inquiry that fosters professional dialogue about teaching among teachers. Jennifer's involvement in an inquiry project, as well as in the process of sharing her work and listening to the issues raised by her colleagues, affected her decisions about practice. And these effects go to both the short-term questions, "What will I do in class today and what are the possible ramifications of my actions and my students' responses?" and to the long-term questions, "What does this unit or course (or school) have to do with anything? Is it connected in a meaningful way with students' lives and how will knowing this stuff help them in the future?" Jennifer felt the effects of inquiry on her practice, and began to see the effects of inquiry on her mentor, Jim, who began to journal and to inquire about the work of mentoring at the end of the year. Inquiry acts as an energy source, a structural beacon, for helping teachers look more deeply at practice, share their insights, and transform school scenes.

> I think if I had not done this research paper, I might not have paid as much attention in my journalism classes. I would have taught, and reflected on why I was teaching it, but I would have not really analyzed it. Every day I walked into my classes and I had a battle plan. I knew I had to find out this research today, and I really looked at my kids and myself all the time, and analyzed what we were doing. (Chelsea, interview)

Chelsea's remarks piggyback Jennifer's in that the specific outcomes of inquiry can affect the shaping of immediate classroom practice through the deeper analysis of classroom events. Chelsea's study helped her to examine the process of curriculum development and teaching in the complex milieu of journalism education, the journalism education that she tried painstakingly to make accessible and good for her students during her teaching internship. The presence of inquiry shapes the teaching day, incorporating reflection, discipline, and imagination through the acts of looking, questioning, and writing. Chelsea faced looking, and questioning, and writing daily—and this helped her to better understand the classroom scene, her students, and herself as teacher more clearly, and clearly for the benefit of all involved, especially her students, who received excellent instruction and personal interaction as a result.

> My study helped me learn about students, and what they need, of course. But it also showed me where to go to find educational articles and how to do research. I can just go up to the computer—type in a subject—and find a bunch of articles and pick a couple out to read. Wouldn't that be a great habit to get into? What a better way to learn how to do that than to do it for real. And so this research experience was meaningful. (Shawn, interview)

Shawn's remarks on learning from inquiry relate to Jennifer and Chelsea's in that she recognizes the great value of inquiry for helping teachers see and understand students better. But even beyond this, Shawn understands that conducting inquiry introduces the prospective teacher to the potential and real connections between educational research and teaching practice. Now her conceptions of educational research have been demystified. She has read meaningful articles in the field, studies that have helped her understand and question classroom phenomena more deeply. She has found educational articles to be accessible and useful, not scary, uninteresting, unintelligible (not that there isn't a lot of that stuff out there). She has experienced the benefit of reading and knowing in her field, of being current about present theories and practices regarding the relationships between students and teachers. She has also found voice, the chance to participate and conduct educational research, to make a contribution to the database in the field regarding her area of interest. The seeds are planted for growth; she may make major contributions to our further understanding of educational scenes in the future. One can only hope.

> "It was really about hands-on research. That's what it is all about! It's about learning how to teach yourself. It's about still being a student." (Sherry, interview).

Sherry's remarks reveal that inquiry can teach us how to be better students of teaching, and as a result, better teachers for our students. She understood that her internship would require her to balance many roles: the role of teacher, the role of family member, the role of friend, the role of student. She found great energy in and understanding from participating in the learning event of inquiry as a prospective teacher, balancing these important roles in her attempts to learn more about her students and teaching in hopes of becoming a better teacher. Her own learning journey as teacher inquirer helped her understand the plights of her students, the possibilities and fears that substantive learning attempts pose. She knows that her future success depends on nurturing the perspective of inquiry, for the best teachers are those who study their practice and seek ways to improve it continually. The bottom line take away from the experience of inquiring for these teachers: understanding and experiencing learning more clearly and deeply as teacher means better instruction and learning for students. Inquiry can take us toward this end.

> I have mostly raised more questions, and I think that's because I don't really have the experience yet. I come up with more questions, but as I get older and as I get more practice in the classroom, I'll have more answers. In order to get the answers that I have, I found that talking to my mentor teachers and to others has really helped me because the sharing of minds is what I've really learned to value this year. (Heidi, interview)

And Heidi suggests that inquiry takes us beyond the misguided notion that teachers can teach teachers to teach; instead, prospective teachers teach themselves about teaching, schools, students, and the multitude of issues facing them by confronting them and studying them through the "sharing of minds" in the field through teaching and researching with students, mentors, and university liaisons. Teaching isn't just a mechanical endeavor. It is an art, a craft, a calling. It is an undertaking that takes tremendous commitment and knowledge. It is, in the end, an intellectual undertaking, wherein the "sharing of minds" ought to be one of our primary purposes, not only in the lives of teachers, but by extension in the lives of our students.

No longer can we harbor the misguided hopes that we can somehow give prospective teachers what they need to be successful in classrooms in terms of teaching techniques (not dismissing technique as an important consideration). No longer can we dehumanize teaching by concentrating efforts in other places so that we might somehow make teaching a less important or vital function in our schools and society (like creating "teacher proof" curricula). We must not confine teachers to their own rooms and to talking only to themselves. No, we must encourage our teachers to transform themselves and others into thinkers, people who ask about, inquire into, and change teaching practice to meet the needs of students. When we engage in intellectual activity (inquiry) concerning our intellectual activity (teaching), we enhance our understanding of what we are doing and help our students receive the best instruction possible. In short, inquiry strengthens classroom practice.

Here are five conclusions about learning from conducting inquiry, drawn from my interaction with these five students and the field:

- Inquiry can produce a culture of inquiry that fosters professional dialogue about teaching among teachers.
- The specific outcomes of inquiry can affect the shaping of immediate class-room practice through the deeper analysis of classroom events.
- Conducting inquiry introduces the prospective teacher to the potential and real connections between educational research and teaching practice.
- Inquiry can teach us how to be better students of teaching, and as a result, better teachers for our students.

- Inquiry takes us beyond the misguided notion that teachers can teach teachers to teach; instead, prospective teachers teach themselves about teaching, schools, students, and the multitude of issues facing them by confronting them and studying them through the "sharing of minds" in the field through teaching and researching with students, mentors, and university liaisons.

It is important here to reemphasize and restate several points related to these five conclusions. First, let's not underestimate the value of inquiry for helping teachers more closely examine practice, both theirs and others. The skills, the arts of looking and listening to those things that happen every day in classrooms and that subsequently tend to be overlooked are invaluable to the teacher. It is so easy to peg one's self into the doldrums of hopelessness in school, the routines of day-to-day life in school along with the bureaucratic "mumbo jumbo" that don't seem to reflect who we want to be as human beings and what we want to do for children in classrooms. And yet beneath these structures, recognizable if we look and listen, beat the needs and interests and lives of students and teachers, nevertheless. We need to see them, and the only way to do this is to look and listen more closely to what is going on around us every day. To go on blindly accepting the present structures and events as natural and right without questioning them does nothing to enhance teaching and learning in schools or the professional development of teachers.

Second, how long will it take for us all to realize that teachers and other stakeholders, including prospective teachers and school students themselves, have so much to give to the community of learners all around them? I hope this book is a case in point. They live and study and teach in classrooms every day. They know the situations that society and children face daily. They experience what works, and work hard to counter mistakes and irrelevance in learning materials, and in the curriculum, and in their own pedagogy. As Corey (1953) argued so long ago, launching the formal interest in what teachers and other stakeholders have to say about what goes on in school through research of their own, "Our schools cannot keep up with the life they are supposed to sustain and improve unless teachers, pupils, supervisors, administrators and school patrons continuously examine what they are doing" (p. viii). The voices of teachers and other stakeholders can inform us about schools and teaching and learning and also improve these endeavors. Somehow structures need to support their inquiries and actions. Teacher education programs are a sound place to start. Trying to understand what one is doing when learning to do it is a vital and noble pursuit. It suggests that the person and the institution care about what is going on at present and what might go on in the future.

Third, several good habits for teachers are fostered by the experience of conducting formal inquiry in schools. The student of teaching sharpens the skills of looking, listening, and writing when he or she engages in research.

Shawn found the experience of doing research "for real" to be an important introduction not only to finding a voice for herself in the field as teacher but also for adopting an intellectual life that gives the body of literature about educational issues for current practice a place in the teachers' planning and teaching lives. Inquiry allows for an initial experience that may transfer to the professional life of full-time teaching. Good teachers know what's going on around them in the field and think about how their voice may add to the debate, either on a narrow scale (in their own classroom or school through classroom lesson plans and projects and in-service programs) or on a wider scale (in district, state, or nation through presentations or published reports).

Fourth, there is lots to know about teaching, and education, in general, as well as in the disciplines of instruction for teaching in secondary schools. The databases on classroom management and curriculum organization and teaching techniques grow by leaps and bounds daily, as does what we know about the Battle of Gettysburg or learning to write well. Do teachers fall back into the posture of relying on the university to tell them what is essential to know for beginning teaching and about these topics? I think this is an untenable position to fall into, because university types don't have the vaguest idea about what is absolutely essential for teaching (if they do, they are fooling themselves and hurting others). The notion of "expert" has drifted away into the past, when someone may have been able to grasp the handle on everything of worth being studied, taught, or tried in the field. It's not possible anymore. Instead of relying on the university for answers, universities, schools, and prospective teachers need to look within—by studying how to produce the best teachers they possibly can given who they are and who they want to be—and they need to look without—by giving students of teaching the skills and confidence to dive into the databases and into their own knowledge creating activities of teaching and researching.

Some may call this a cop-out on the university's part. I don't think it is. I think people always learn best when they determine their course of study and follow it with interest and perseverance. When students are invested in their study, they will learn to learn more than we could ever fill them up with in classes. Hopefully this tenet will go to our prospective teachers' conceptions of what it is to teach in schools, recognizing that their own students' needs and interests can be tapped and energized by engaging them in meaningful inquiry activities inside and outside the classroom. I have high hopes for our new teachers, and I trust them to continue learning more about the field they have chosen to teach within, more about the natures of learning and teaching, and more about the lives of their students and the structures of the institutions and cultures they serve. If they inquire in these areas and engage their own students in such learning, we will all grow and prosper much.

Fifth, and last for now, inquiry opens up avenues for dialogue that didn't exist or wouldn't have existed previously. Teaching and the business of schooling often take place in isolation, without the support of others' ideas and resources. Teachers and students so often make do on their own, without sharing in the greater intellectual pursuits of the school or the culture. Why? Because we tend not to examine ourselves and each other often or with any depth. We have created a teacher and school culture that protects us from looking. This so-called freedom or professional distance between and among teachers and administrators and students and parents and community stakeholders, typically, sometimes produces inaccuracies and ignorance among everyone. We don't know what each other is doing or why we are doing it. When we close ourselves to looking, we close off an avenue for growth and improvement. Looking and talking about practice scares teachers. But it can also truly liberate them, and help them grow for the benefit of themselves and ultimately, and most important, for their students.

The day after I wrote these previous pages I discovered one of the first articles reporting the use of research with students of teaching. Beckman (1957) reported the use of action research with student teachers at Wesleyan College in Georgia. The similarity of my conclusions and his are somewhat haunting, somewhat reassuring; the test of 40 years is that conducting research during the internship in teaching produces marked benefits for the prospective teacher. My thoughts, therefore, aren't necessarily original, though they came independent of my knowledge of his particular project and words. I want to give him and others credit for having pioneered in the field. Also, I want us all to ask, given the real benefits for students conducting research during their teaching internship or student teaching, why hasn't the idea caught on across the country, not just as a fad but as an important and accepted structural component of our institutions and programs of study in teacher education?

> The value of the experience (of conducting research) is broader than the specific understanding which a student derives from a particular project. It involves a practical induction into teaching with the viewpoint of the experimenter. It provides the framework for developing sympathetic attitudes toward research and the methods of making "common sense" judgments valid. It strengthens the skills of critical analysis which a professional leader requires. (Beckman, 1957, p. 372)

Maybe our unwillingness to move into research, empowering new teachers to voice and test their concerns about teaching, lives in the substantive lessons of the next section, "Lessons Learned about Teaching Inquiry and about Doing Inquiry." Maybe getting to these lessons, experiencing them and growing from them, is too messy. Maybe none of it is worth the bother, the pain, the hard work of collaborating and communicating and sharing that connote the best of research learning environments in education. Maybe.

LESSONS FOR TEACHING AND
DOING INQUIRY

Let's start here with a conclusive lesson drawn from earlier in the chapter. The inquiry teacher needs to make clear the nature and scope of the research project to take place during the internship. There are many important competing events for time and passion during an internship of this sort. Interns want to concentrate on the how's of doing teaching. They want to get mixed-up in the fray of classroom life as teacher and find out if they have what it takes to make it day-to-day in schools. This is a strength of our program, but only a strength, in my opinion, when it is balanced with a thoughtful attempt to help the prospective teachers study and reflect on what they are doing, what the students are doing, what the school is doing, and what the long-term affects of these actions are, what their perceived and actual purposes are, whether they want to be a part of them or help to reform them.

Oftentimes student teaching, or an apprenticeship in teaching, risks the loss of the student's autonomy and control over his or her own learning. The responsibility falls to the university instructor or to the mentor in the field to model appropriate practice and for the student to mimic that practice and digest the mechanics of teaching, the essential information about teaching and learning that comes from on high and that cannot be weaved in and out of the new teacher's own emerging conceptions of self as teacher. But mimicking, even modeling, isn't the type of learning performance that young teachers need to exhibit. They need to tap their own talents, their own ideas and thoughts, and their emerging knowledge of the realities of practice and of research in the field of education for today's classrooms in order to form their own original teaching philosophy and style. This is the stuff of a teaching internship, in which the intern and mentor and university liaison are all partners, striving through practice and inquiry to make themselves better at relating themselves and material to young people inside and outside of classrooms. Teacher research, as I've already pointed out, can play a vital role in transforming the prospective teacher into learner and teacher.

And so the prospective teacher engages in inquiry: journaling about field experiences, noting insights from classroom observations, telling and testing stories of experimental lessons and strategies for improving student motivation and learning in the classroom, talking with other interns and mentors and teachers about problems and successes in the everyday experiences of teaching, reading and discussing ideas garnered from focused and disciplined study in the database of educational research on general and chosen issues and topics. These activities complement the activities of curriculum planning and teaching and managing a classroom. They can and should be combined to create a whole picture of learning about teaching that focuses

on the connection between theory and practice of education. The internship experience and the school day are designed by each team to reflect the
balance among these tasks, with the emphasis, of course, focusing on how
all endeavors lead to better teaching. This explication underlies the rationale for doing inquiry. But there is also the matter of what data collection
and the final write-up should look like.

There is no doubt that the mention of research sometimes upsets prospective teachers, even graduate students. They have a conception of what
it is, and are reluctant to believe that there are alternatives to their
conceptions and that they can participate and learn from participation in
the research base and their own inquiries, to boot. But it is possible, and the
evidence of this transition by other students in the field or even in their own
program from previous years should be presented early on in the internship.
Of course, teachers of inquiry will want each new cohort to come up with
their own ideas for studies, but looking back at fruitful studies of others,
including those of the previous cohorts and from the literature base of
qualitative inquiry, and talking about what the research activities entailed
constitute soothing, calming activities that can help prospective teachers be
less scared of taking up an inquiry project of their own.

A concern for the interns and their conceptions of research also lies in
the effective building of bridges between the purposes of the university and
its general support of research endeavors of this sort, and the school
community, which may tend to see research as a waste of time or even as a
threat. How does the university liaison, or the university if it makes a
continuous institutional commitment in its formal curriculum to inquiry,
introduce teacher research? In our case, we included inquiry as a part of our
syllabus. We had the right and the permission to do so. But were we right in
not testing the waters before jumping in? Did we put our purposes ahead of
all others, and in effect, disregard what had gone before? Can professors
work well in an environment where they are charged to do something that
isn't complete, and doesn't help prepare the best teachers possible, such as
work with teachers in a placement where people do not support in idea or
in resource the notion that the best teachers study their own and others'
practices on a continuing, and often formal basis?

In a word, no. But would I do things differently if I had a chance to do
them over again? Yes. And I would start by at least making an earlier
declaration and explication of our intentions so that interns and mentors
would have a bigger time cushion to prepare and clarify before jumping in
cold at the beginning. Maybe a warming up (or cooling down) period would
have served us all very well. Maybe the incorporation of the mentor teachers
into the fabric of the endeavor, and supporting heartily the ones who resisted
early, is a potential approach. Chelsea makes it clear that mentor support is
crucial to the overall success of the research component and, of course, to
the individual intern. Building this bridge will take much discussion and

collaboration, and I think much pain, but it must be done. Passing over the requirement in silence will help no one, and only hurt the program.

I do know now, better than I knew before, that there are certain risks associated with conducting qualitative criticism as opposed to other forms of educational research, such as action research. Several of the studies included here could not be shared initially with the respondents studied. How does this help build collegiality or shared knowledge? It doesn't. I suggest that the best approach, therefore, especially in a sensitive milieu in which teachers are not typically enamored with the honest critique of their practice and of others, is to focus on the interns' own practice by helping them to conduct action research projects on their own practice. The dilemma here is the trade-off that several of these students would have to make in their own learning. Those who looked at others took away a knowledge of practice in the field that they didn't have before and that deeply informed their emerging conceptions of practice. Is this type of looking necessary, should it be salvaged in the research process, can it be gotten in some other component of the program?

I do know, at least for our next cohort and given the current climate regarding the research project among the mentor faculty, that we will encourage our students to study their own practice through action research. If students choose to look outside their own classrooms, they will be charged to build structures into their research that create value and benefit for the respondents in the study. For instance, if a prospective teacher wants to look at the four "best" English teachers in the school and try to tell how or why they are the best, the prospective teacher would share the focus of his or her study immediately with respondents; he or she should share his or her observation notes as a matter of course with each respondent; the prospective teacher should conduct updates with respondents regarding tentative conclusions and judgments and follow up with respondents for help in clarifying these for the final outline and paper; the students should share their final paper with each respondent immediately on its completion and allow an opportunity for respondents to discuss the document with the student.

Building research circles marked by procedures that guarantee openness, honesty, trust, and helpfulness through dialogue are essential for qualitative criticism or some types of action projects to make a substantive contribution not only to the student's learning but also to the teachers and the school focused on in the study. Qualitative criticism is a powerful learning tool that helps the research describe, interpret, and evaluate classroom scenes; it ought to equally empower those who participate in the study.

In our program, teachers and university liaisons and students of teaching had moved far away from acknowledging the formal role of student in the internship. The student part of teaching came primarily in debriefing about the practice of teaching. I think this is one of the most important processes in the internship experience and ought to be steadfastly guarded as an integral part of the program. In the fall and spring for instance, Thursday afternoon sessions are usually devoted to debriefing. But we lost the continuity in this aspect of group and individual development this year when communication broke down on Black Thursday.

I want desperately to rebuild the debriefing component this coming year as an integral, continuous part of the program, including both teachers and students of teaching. However, whereas our programs offer the chance for our students to try on comfortably the role of teacher, I believe we must maintain the rigorous role of student throughout as well. We are all students who are well served by looking closely at what we do. It is important for teachers of inquiry to address the tensions that students of teaching encounter when they are at once charged with the duties of teacher in the classroom and with the duties of student at the university. This can be an exciting period, as Sherry has so passionately and eloquently stated here. It should be a goal for teachers to help their students reach the sort of balance that Sherry was able to reach in her weighing of roles in her experience.

Teachers of inquiry to prospective teachers must also maintain a realistic awareness that although the research component is an important part of the teacher's learning, he or she is not being trained for a position as a professional researcher in education nor is he or she expected to produce something that is publishable. Instead, focus should be maintained on how the inquiry process fits with practice in the classroom. The teacher skillfully negotiates with individual teams the time commitment, the scope of the project, and the philosophical and meaningful place of the research in the internship throughout the process, maintaining flexibility and understanding for the demands of the internship. If the student planned to do six observations and can only do three because of other time constraints, then three it is. If the data will be too thin as a result, is there any way to complement the data with another more accessible data source? If the student planned to interview two students and subsequently wants to have a focus group of six students who participate in two interviews as well as five more separate individual respondent interviews, does this load fit with the time demands of teaching an upcoming unit on Huck Finn? If not, then what is a reasonable approach? How will the data collection activities complement current practice?

The research project that prospective teachers conduct is not meant to be a thesis or a tool for indoctrination. It is meant to serve as a means for students of teaching to understand the connections between research and practice, to participate intimately in the formation of their own teaching philosophy and style by giving voice to them in class discussions and in a paper, and to reflect on the deeper issues of schooling that lie at the surface and just below the surface of our everyday observations, ideas, and biases. Others have hoped that inquiry would introduce students of teaching to ideological frames in the hopes that they might be won over to said frames. I don't agree with this approach, but I do support efforts to encourage students to look at issues of justice, race, social class, gender, and so forth, in education. We must support the production of a culturally aware and society-sensitive teacher. These kinds of teachers will make a true difference in 21st-century schools in America.

I thought I was entering the business of educating prospective teachers for long careers in classrooms and schools when I started working with this program last fall. But I'm doing more than just this, I'm working and educating current teachers as well. We need them. And they need me and they need the university. I totally underestimated how important I would be to the mentor teachers last year. I totally overestimated how selfless they would be with regard to the education of their interns. Teachers are human beings, with definite ideas and experiences that support how things can and should be done in teacher education.

Teachers, and especially our mentor teachers, are full partners, and deserve to be a part of the debate and to have their voices heard. Although I do not feature them in this text, I don't think they are the bad guys or that they don't deserve to be heard. On the contrary, they are always on my mind and will probably be the focus of my next book. I believe they are the driving hope for reform and change and good in our schools and for our children; they do a great job in classrooms against great odds every day. We must find a way to incorporate teachers in a substantive way into the life of the research component in the program. Without them, the project has little overall meaning. With them, there is real hope for transformative change of practice, school culture, and personal understanding of what education is and can be.

The realistic possibilities are that teachers could share in the journaling activities of their interns, or act as a resource person on studies of certain topics of interest in which they may have expertise, or even conduct their own projects. But what are the rewards for teachers to spend their time this way? More money? The possibility of being published? Climbing the teaching or higher education ladder as a result of their research efforts? I don't know, but there must be something at stake in order to encourage, and not to force, teachers to participate. The coming cohort of mentor teachers is extremely supportive of the research component, but I want them to be involved in a substantive way. I believe it is up to me to provide some suggestions, but ultimately it is up to them to decide how they might become further involved.

And can research become institutionalized as a substantive structural reform effort in teacher education? Can we go beyond the mere inclusion of the requirement in our syllabi and even in what we do? Should it be a part of our recruiting literature? Can we construct places or functions that support research on an ongoing basis such as a department published collection of the year's best reports, or public presentations of findings that all students would conduct as part of their internship? This is a next step to solidifying prospective teacher research in the fabric of teacher education, at least in our program. The lesson is, I think, that it should be institution-alized, or it may fade away. This would be a great loss to future teachers and to students of teaching and to schools. Now that teacher research is beginning to be valued, how will we assure that their work doesn't just fade away like the work of Beckman's (1957) and Perrodin's (1959) student pioneers not so long ago.

Lastly, some schools and some teachers are ready for the challenges of research. They will support and excel in it, just as the middle school group did this past year. Other groups pitch, they need time to adjust, they wonder what the motives are behind the research, they wonder how it will change or tax them for the better or worse, and sometimes these considerations keep them from getting on with the business at hand. I think we are well on our way after some important stops along the way. I believe the research component will be stronger in coming years because we listened to teachers and students and tried to meet their concerns head-on not only in dialogue but in our actions on their behalf. Time will tell how inquiry will change (or not) the nature of teaching in the schools, for instance. I know it has changed the conceptions for the interns and mentors who participated in the internship year last year. The high school hired five of these nine interns to work full-time beginning this year. The seeds of change and transforma-tion have been planted.

Appendices:

Intern Research Proposals

.

A CASE STUDY OF MATHEMATICS EDUCATION: THE USE OF MANIPULATIVES AND TECHNOLOGY IN THE HIGH SCHOOL MATHEMATICS CLASSROOM

by Jennifer Pierson

Introduction

Due to declining national standardized test scores and various international reports that insist American students have inferior mathematics skills, there have been a multitude of reform movements within mathematics education over the last decade. Two of the more popular movements are the Reformed Mathematics movement and the Constructivist movement. Each of these movements emphasizes the use of manipulatives and/or technology to make mathematics more meaningful to students. The Reformed Mathematics movement is based on the notion that as America becomes a more techno-logical society, these tools should be available for student use to promote both technological skill and better conceptual understanding. Supporters of the Constructivist movement, which began in mathematics but has since spread to other disciplines, believe that students learn best when they actively construct knowledge for themselves rather than receive knowledge passively through lecture. Each of these movements would like to see manipulatives and technology in the hands of every mathematics student. Thus, in the past few years mathematics teachers have been bombarded with these different "tools" (software, graphing calculators, algebra tiles, geoboards, etc.) and ideas about how they should be used.

As a future practitioner of mathematics education, I am very interested in the topic of manipulatives and technology. Are mathematics teachers really using these tools or are the manipulatives and graphing calculators sitting in a closet somewhere collecting dust? If the research and literature are correct and these tools are so wonderful, why do some teachers choose to use them and others do not? For those classes that do use them, which manipulatives or technology do they use and how often are they being used? How do the teachers incorporate them into the different courses? Is their use meaningful? Do they promote/facilitate understanding or are they just seen as neat toys?

Theoretical Framework

There are several texts that deal with the issue of using manipulatives and technology in mathematics: *Everybody Counts: A Report to the Nation on the Future of Mathematics Education; Teaching and Learning Mathematics in the*

1990s: 1990 Yearbook, Reshaping School Mathematics: A Philosophy and Frame-work for Curriculum; Results from the Fourth Mathematics Assessment of the National Assessment of Educational Progress; Calculators in Mathematics Education: 1992 Yearbook. The majority of these texts present the reasoning behind the push for increased use of manipulatives and technology in the mathematics classroom. Some of them show how this is currently being done in different settings. A few of the texts also set goals for the future of mathematics education in the United States. These texts as well as articles from NCTM's *Mathematics Teacher* and other journals will serve as the basis for my research.

My goal is to compare what I find in my research to be the recommended practices for the use of manipulatives and technology in the high school mathematics classroom to what is actually being implemented at my school. In this endeavor, I hope to analyze the differences between current recommended pedagogy and actual classroom practice so as to better understand my role as a teacher of mathematics.

Research Design

I will use qualitative methods of data collection as described in the Glesne and Peshkin (1992) text *Becoming Qualitative Researchers: An Introduction.* Specific approaches will include: (a) a mail survey of the 18 members of the mathematics faculty of my school; (b) three observations each of five select members of the mathematics faculty at my school (as well as some one-time observations of faculty from other high schools, if possible); (c) open-ended interviewing of the five selected mathematics faculty members, the administration, and the secondary mathematics coordinator of the district; and (d) a survey of the students in two mathematics classrooms.

A large part of my research will be based in the classroom of my mentor because that is where I am serving my internship. This situation will of course lend itself to bias. However, four other teachers will also be chosen as part of the study. Hopefully, these teachers, along with my mentor, will be representative of the variety of views and practices of the mathematics faculty. The initial survey of the entire mathematics faculty at my school should also provide information on the diversity of manipulatives and technology use at the school.

Possible Results, Conclusions, and Implications of the Study

I hope to see how and to what extent the current recommended mathematics pedagogy is being implemented in the high school classroom. This report may help me understand both the difficulties and the benefits of such implementation. It may be that teachers do not feel confident in their use of manipulatives and/or technology, and therefore, do not use them with their classes. Or, it may be that the manipulatives and technology they feel would be most useful have not been made available to them. Or perhaps it may be that teachers feel the time or structure difficulties of using such tools outweigh their usefulness. Hopefully, this study will shed light onto these issues and may serve as a catalyst for department discussion.

Possible Results for the Intern Researcher

This project will make me a better teacher in several ways. First, it will force me to do research on the current pedagogy in my primary teaching field. In doing this research, I will also learn the goals for the future of mathematics education in America so that I may strive to meet them in my own classroom. Second, I can see how and to what extent different teachers implement this pedagogy. Third, it will provide me with an opportunity to see several different teachers practice and to speak with them concerning their opinions about mathematics education. Finally, I will get to see how manipulatives and technology are being used (or not being used) in the classroom so that I will have different options, which I will have already seen in practice, when I prepare for my own teaching.

A FIRST-YEAR TEACHER'S INQUIRY INTO JOURNALISM CURRICULUM: AN EXAMINATION, ANALYSIS, AND CREATION OF INTRODUCTORY JOURNALISM CURRICULUM AT THE HIGH SCHOOL LEVEL

by Chelsea Caivano

Introduction

Although the state has compiled and published a skeletal outline for journalism curriculum that governs what areas and topics should be taught, and although the school district has adopted a fine textbook and teacher's guide for use in its introductory journalism class, little other direction is available for instructors. Individual journalism teachers are left to put together their own curriculum, resulting in an autonomous structure with minimal continuity between schools and among teachers.

The lack of a specific journalism curriculum is particularly detrimental to first-year teachers. A typical journalism teacher serves as both publication advisor and educator of at least four different sections of the discipline: yearbook production, newspaper production, photojournalism, and introductory journalism. Because the deadlines and production output demands are often overwhelming, it is easy to see how natural and common it is for a journalism teacher to focus his or her energies on the publication and print classes while virtually ignoring the introductory journalism class. Yet, it is in this introductory class where future reporters, editors and designers receive their initial training. If the introductory journalism students do not learn the basics, do not improve their writing skills, and do not become interested in journalism, there might not be a qualified yearbook or newspaper staff the following year.

The obvious focus of this research project is to create a practical, publishable, usable introductory journalism curriculum. Whereas creating a unit is the overriding goal, three other issues must be studied during the process:

1. The qualifications of the educators. *How much professional experience should a journalism teacher have? Should educators or professionals decide what needs to be taught in high school journalism classes?*
2. The real-world needs of the students. *Are high school graduates meeting the performance expectations of their college professors or newspaper editors? How can current journalism curriculum be altered to help students meet those expectations?*
3. The demands of the discipline. *What are the most important goals and topics for the introductory year? What techniques and activities can a journalism teacher employ to better reach those goals?*

Theoretical Framework

Several academicians and professionals have influenced this study. Under the question of teacher qualification, Hernandez (1994), Schaub (1993), and Stein (1993) have written powerful arguments. Finally, Mills (1994) and McKeen and Bleske (1992) have published various techniques and activities to utilize in journalism classrooms.

Research Design

I plan to build a substantial database using a variety of research methods that will collect information from both primary and secondary sources. These methods include:

- Analysis of applicable articles published by both journalism educators and professional journalists.
- On-site class observations and open-ended interviews with three local high school journalism teachers.
- Open-ended interviews with two college students, who will reflect on their own high school journalism experiences.
- Open-ended interview with one local journalism professor who worked as a professional journalist for much of her career.
- Most important, a detailed account and analysis of my own introductory journalism class, noting which activities were beneficial and which were not useful.

Possible Results, Conclusions, and Implications of the Study

Journalism is a fascinating and ever-changing profession with scores of facets and subdivisions. I want to transfer my passion about the discipline into an exciting curriculum for introductory students. Moreover, because the field of journalism is so far-reaching, I want to set goals for the introductory-level classes and focus the curriculum around reaching those goals rather than giving the students an overall and overwhelming survey course.

This study is not just an individual project, though. I plan to share the results with other local journalism educators, with the hope that they will employ some of the ideas and techniques in their own classroom. Journalism teachers may begin to build a cohesive introductory curriculum that will provide continuity among the schools.

Conclusion

If I am hired as a teacher of journalism next year, this research project will in a large part serve as my curriculum. Because I will have spent this year in preparation, I will not experience some of the stress and anxieties many first-year teachers have. In addition, through my interviews and time spent with other journalism teachers, I will have compiled a bank of activities from which I can draw to vary my teaching according to the needs of my students. Finally, by experiencing first-hand the thought process and rigors of revising and creating curriculum, I will be more prepared to develop and hone curriculum for my other discipline, English. After spending this year evaluating existing curriculum, I will never blindly teach what I have not critiqued.

THE EFFECTS OF STUDENT–TEACHER RELATIONSHIPS INSIDE AND OUTSIDE THE CLASSROOM AND HOW TO MAINTAIN POSITIVE, HEALTHY BONDS THAT FORM IN THE SCHOOL ENVIRONMENT

by Shawn Stanley

Introduction

Relationships between students and teachers are commonly formed in the classroom. In fact, it seems almost difficult not to form relationships with students whom teachers interact with everyday. Each party has much to offer each other as they work together in the classroom, learning and exploring together.

Often in today's society, children are neglected or not exposed to the kind of nurturing or guidance that they need or that would be most beneficial for them. Sometimes the teacher is looked on to provide this role. It is important to fill this role completely.

I have had some very meaningful relationships with past teachers during my education. They helped me, taught me, and ultimately shaped my life. Isn't that a large part of why we are educators? We want to contribute to society. How do we do this in the most meaningful way? What can we give to our students that will help them in their future lives?

What are the effects of personal relationships between teachers and students on the learning environment, and on the development of the students as active participants in society? Issues including advantages and disadvantages of student–teacher relationships and aspects of forming these relationships will be investigated in this study. The following topics will guide the study.

1. The role that relationships play: "Do students and teachers need personal relationships with each other? Why or why not?"
2. The effects of relationships: "What are the benefits and drawbacks of these relationships?"
3. The active process of relationships: "How are these relationships established and maintained?"

Other related topics such as traits that are appealing to each party, breaking down barriers between each party, and what may be done outside the classroom to encourage these relationships will be studied, as well as aspects involving how gender, skill level, and affluence affect the kind or extent of student–teacher relationships.

Theoretical Framework

In a first glance, there are several theoretical frameworks that may inform my report (Juhasz, 1989; Medina, 1990; Soohoo, 1993). I hope to use the information in this study to better understand what goes on between teachers and students emotionally and to implement in my teaching career ideas and processes that may affect the manner in which I conduct myself so as to benefit my students most, both in and out of the classroom. The information I learn may affect my attitude toward the students and, in turn, affect their attitude toward teachers and learning. I hope to learn how to maximize emotional support as well as teach my subject area, enabling my students to be more free and able to learn. The knowledge gained from this study will help me and others to relate to the students so as to allow teaching a subject area to the fullest and giving the students positive experiences that are more on a relational level (e.g. support, encouragement, unconditional care, etc.).

This study will show the advantages and disadvantages of relationships with students and how different personalities impact the process, allowing other teachers to think about their relationships with their own students.

Research Design

I will be using several methods of data collection in this study. These include (a) observing student–teacher interactions in classrooms and situations at school, (b) observing extra curricular and outside school activities between teachers and students, (c) conducting open-ended interviews with selected respondents involved in the education process, (d) and analyzing written data, journals, reports, case studies, and so forth, on student–teacher relationships.

I will be involved in a school counseling program. By being a mentor to a couple of students, contacting them every day, and participating in various group sessions set up for students dealing with similar issues by the counselor, I will be able to collect a great deal of data without being just an observer but a direct participant. My journal and observation notes will reflect this.

My involvement in the program and actively teaching in a classroom will place me directly in the middle of the field that will be studied. Care will need to be taken as to how situations are viewed and how issues are thought through. I hope to view situations as an outsider, yet still have the advantages of insider knowledge. I acknowledge the possible biases I may possess considering my desire as a first-time teacher to establish relationships with students, but I will attempt to put my personal wants and needs aside so as to truly grasp the real purpose and consequences of student–teacher relationships.

Possible Results, Conclusions, and Implications of the Study

Teachers have a great opportunity to get to know students well as they interact with them in class. Both positive and negative effects of student–teacher relationships may present themselves in this study. The impact of both on students will be interesting to discover. There are some dangers in forming or having relationships between students and teachers that will be encountered as well, and much care needs to be taken in these situations. Positive and negative qualities of relationships may emerge as well as constructive mannerisms that are conducive to forming student–teacher relationships. This report may also lead into other aspects of teaching in the classroom besides subject areas that may need to be dealt with, such as morality, manners, personal skills, and so forth. The traditional role of the teacher could well be a role of the past.

This Project Will Make Me a Better Teacher

This project will make me a better teacher by helping me to understand my role and the possibilities of my affect on students' lives through actions, words, and other aspects of influence so that I may better effect my students with greatness both in subject matter and in person.

Note. The proposal just discussed is the basis for my thought process and my inquiry into areas of teaching that I wish to discover more about. Through this, and through discussion with Dr. Poetter, I have narrowed and slightly changed my topic from the previous.

Many people have theorized what helps students to relate or connect to the teacher or subject matter. Teachers are taught different ways to teach and react to students and are told they must find which methods work for them. These decisions often, however, do not take into account the students' perceptions of these methods.

It is most often the case that teachers want relationships with students. The question is does the student want this personal connection, or is the student going to shut the teacher out? When it comes down to the decision of establishing a connection or relationship, it ultimately lies in the student's hands to make the final decision.

The following questions will be answered from a student's perspective: What do students need from teachers in the classroom? What teacher mannerisms or traits are liked or disliked by students? What can a teacher do in various situations to encourage students to connect with them?

To investigate these questions, I will be choosing four students. I will follow each student once over a 4-week period of time. I will observe periods one and two, then get back with the student to observe period three. An appointment will then be set up with the student for the next day to discuss my observations and the students' reactions to them. The students will tell me what they felt or how they perceived situations that occurred during the observed day. A review of current literature on student perceptions and student–teacher relationships will also be conducted.

This will be a great opportunity for me to compare my view of class situations from a teacher perspective to the student's point of view. This will allow me to discover what truly works in the classroom in establishing connections or relationships with students.

A STUDY OF TEACHERS AND THEIR RELATIONSHIPS WITH AT-RISK STUDENTS

by Sherry Hughes

Introduction

Soon after beginning my year-long internship, I realized that there is a certain culture to this inner-city, Chapter I school. The students that walk the halls each day were not "typical" middle school students. Most of the students came from broken homes, where they often lacked the basic needs of food, shelter, and clothing. I began to consider that these unique students needed unique teachers. The recognition of this need for such unique teachers led me to question what types of teachers work best in a school with such a large population of high-risk students. As a result, my research will focus on the pedagogics, personalities, and teaching styles of teachers who are successful with at-risk students. My essential question will be, "Do at-risk students benefit from certain types of teaching styles?" My research will explore three additional questions:

1. Are there certain similarities in teaching styles among teachers who are most successful with at-risk students? If so, what are these similarities?
2. Do differences exist in the areas of pedagogy and personality between these teachers and teachers who work poorly with these students?
3. How can teachers adapt their own teaching style, pedagogics, and personality to best meet the needs of these unique students?

Theoretical Framework

I will begin my research based on Maslow's (1970) hierarchy of needs. In Maslow's hierarchy, basic needs must be met before learning, a higher need, will occur. For example, curriculum and class may be irrelevant to an at-risk student whose basic needs of food, clothing, shelter, and belonging are not being met. My intentions are to show that through a teacher's teaching style and personality one can fulfill or account for some of these needs, therefore promoting the learning process. Hanson, Silver, and Strong (1991) stated that "each person tends to have a dominant style that responds best to a specific type of instruction" (p. 30). They further assert that at-risk students often do not succeed in classrooms utilizing traditional types of instruction. Through my research, I would like to determine what teaching styles and personal qualities at-risk students are most responsive to.

Research Design

Using qualitative research methods, I will observe four teachers throughout the semester; two that work well with at-risk students and two teachers that are not as successful with at-risk students. These teachers will be selected based on recommendations from my mentor-teacher and the principal of my school. Formal observation will consist of two open-ended interviews and two classroom observations per teacher. The first classroom observation will be scheduled with the teacher; the other will be an unannounced visit to the classroom, agreed to by the teacher. I will ask teachers to complete a Teaching Styles Inventory, provided by Hanson, Silver, & Strong. Additionally, I will observe each teacher's interaction with students outside the classroom (i.e., the lunch room, between classes, after school, etc.).

With approval, I will also facilitate one qualitative discussion with a focus group consisting of five to seven at-risk students. These students will be hand-picked and will include: (a) at least two students from each grade level, (b) students with a variety of ability levels but formally recognized as at risk, and (c) a balanced ratio of male to female students. The discussion will focus on teacher personalities and styles that students consider to be successful in the classroom as well as those that are less successful. Students will also be asked to fill out the Hanson–Silver Learning Processes Inventory.

I hope to establish good rapport with my four teachers so I can clearly observe their teaching styles. Being a member of the faculty and considering the nature of my research, I realize the importance of looking at each teacher's style objectively. I must make each teacher feel that I am observing his or her teaching style and not critiquing it. Interviews with my student focus group will have to be very structured, and questions will have to be preapproved by my mentor and faculty liaison. Because I will be working with at-risk students, additional precautions may need to be taken. For example, I must be prepared for some reluctance with regards to student participation and parental consent. Guidelines will also need to be provided to students specifying behavior expectations for the discussion so that "teacher bashing" will not occur.

Possible Results, Conclusions, and Implications of the Study

With the rise in the number of at-risk students in our school system (Stevens & Price, 1992), the increased need for teachers that can work well with these students is evident. I hope to pinpoint the personalities and teaching styles that allow at-risk students to succeed in the classroom. I also expect to find significant correlation between the Teaching Style Inventory and the

Learning Processes Inventory. I want to provide future interns and current faculty with a base of knowledge regarding at-risk students so they can evaluate and effectively adapt their teaching styles to better work with students at school.

This project will make me a better teacher by allowing me to observe a variety of teaching styles and see what is most successful with students. My intention is to teach at a school that has a high rate of at-risk students; therefore, through my research, I will be able to evaluate my own teaching style and personality and use my findings for personal improvement.

GENDER BIAS IN THE MATHEMATICS CLASSROOM: HOW TO INCORPORATE GIRLS INTO THE DISCUSSION OF MATHEMATICS

By Heidi D. Anderson

Introduction

It was in 1991 that 60 *Minutes* brought the issue of gender bias to the nation's attention. Surprisingly, this edition of the television show did not explore issues of gender bias at the work place. Instead, 60 *Minutes* centered on gender bias in American classrooms. Focusing on an abundance of research demonstrating that the nation's teachers give more time, attention, and encouragement to boys than girls, the show highlighted much of the study completed by the American Association of University Women. This study entitled "Shortchanging Girls, Shortchanging America" is of much importance to my report. I am intrigued by this apparent subconscious favoring of male students in the classroom and propose to conduct similar research during my internship year. My research, however, will concentrate solely on mathematics classrooms and any gender biases that may develop.

I will focus my exploration on the following questions. One, is gender bias a problem in mathematics classes? Two, what are the manifestations of the biases towards the boys, both obvious and subtle? Three, what causes, behaviors, or situations within the classroom contribute to the apparent calling on, correcting, and encouraging of the male class participants more? Four, what are the effects on the girls of the class? Five, and most important, how can a teacher best remedy the situation? And finally, can specific curricula or lesson plans be written for the express purpose of educating both boys and girls equally?

Theoretical Framework

I plan to base much of my introductory readings of this intriguing situation on *Shortchanging Girls, Shortchanging America*, a study conducted by the American Association of University Women (1992). I will also support my background information with a text written by Myra and David Sadker (1994) entitled *Failing at Fairness: How American Schools Cheat Girls*. Currently, my theoretical framework is developing from my readings of *Building Gender Fairness in Schools* by Beverly A. Stitt (1988). Consideration will also be given to selected current education periodicals, journals, and other professional papers (such as those recently published in *Gender Tales: Tensions in the Schools* edited by Judith Kleinfeld & Suzanne Yerian, 1995). Finally, I will take a look at personality traits of males and females in general that may contribute to biased instructional methods (see "Sizing Up The Sexes" by Christine Gorman from *Time*, January 20, 1992, pp. 42–48, and "Biology, Destiny, And All That" by Paul Chance from *Across The Board*, July/August 1988, pp. 19–23). A combination of all these resources will hopefully provide a strong foundation from which to begin analysis and synthesis of my gathered data.

Research Design

I will utilize methods of qualitative data collection for my case study. Specifically, these methods will include three observations each of four mathematics teachers. I plan to observe two male and two female teachers, and have already completed one of my observations on a class taught by the male veteran teacher participating in my study. Open-ended interviews of no more than four male and four female students in these particular classes will also serve as important means of qualitative data collection. However, I believe that I will need to collect some quantitative data, such as tallying the number of times a teacher calls on a boy to answer a question, in contrast with how many times he or she calls on a girl. Another important statistic to note might be the number of times a teacher stops the lesson to correct or praise a boy, as compared with a girl. Later, I may also want to interview the participating teachers about certain consistent behaviors that I noticed while visiting their classrooms, being careful so as not to offend any of the participants.

Possible Results of the Study

After my research, I might conclude that math teachers are very in-tune with their teaching practices, and that I could not find any instances of biased instruction in the classrooms of the four participant teachers. Or perhaps I might find consistent or typical displays of biased teaching that could now be easily remedied. I would hope that my research and observations would be shared with other interns and teachers who are concerned about giving equal attention and educational opportunities to both male and female students in their mathematics classes. Most important to me, I hope to produce results that will help educators mend any unfortunate biased situations that may exist in their classroom.

Making Myself a Better Teacher

I feel that this case study of four mathematics teachers, in my place of clinical study, will help me to become a better teacher because it will open my eyes to situations that I may never before have noticed. I will learn the subtle ways that girls get "turned off" of education and mathematics, and I will learn how to avoid these detrimental practices. Developing lesson plans for increasing female participation will be of the greatest benefit to myself, as it will teach me to write curriculum and plan for the inclusion of all students.

References

CS ◆ ⏀

American Association of University Women [AAUW]. (1992). *The AAUW report: How schools shortchange girls.* Washington, DC: AAUW Educational Foundation.

Beckman, D. (1957). Student teachers learn by action research. *Journal of Teacher Education, 8*(4), 369–375.

Berenbeim, R. (1993). *Corporate support for mathematics and science education improvement* (Report No. 1022). New York: The Conference Board.

Boomer, G. (1987). Addressing the problem of elsewhereness: A case for action research in schools. In D. Goswami & P. Stillman (Eds.), *Reclaiming the classroom: Teacher research as an agency for change* (pp. 4–12). Upper Montclair, NJ: Boynton/Cook.

Brunner, D. (1994). *Inquiry and reflection: Framing narrative practice in education.* Albany: SUNY Press.

Chance, P. (1988). Biology, destiny, and all that. *Across the Board,* 19–23.

Cochran-Smith, M. (1994). The power of teacher research in teacher education. In S. Hollingsworth & H. Sockett (Eds.), *Teacher research and educational reform: Ninety-third yearbook of the National Society for the Study of Education* (pp. 142–165). Chicago: University of Chicago Press.

Cochran-Smith, M., & Lytle, S. (1990). Research on teaching and teacher research: The issues that divide. *Educational Researcher, 19*(2), 2–11.

Cochran-Smith, M., & Lytle, S. (1993). *Inside/outside: Teacher research and knowledge.* New York: Teacher College Press, Columbia University.

Connelly, F., & Clandinin, J. D. (1990). Stories of experience and narrative inquiry. *Educational Researcher, 19*(5), 2–14.

Cooney, T. J. (Ed.). (1990). *Teaching and learning mathematics in the 1990s: 1990 yearbook.* Reston, VA: National Council of Teachers of Mathematics.

Corey, S. (1953). *Action research to improve school practices.* New York: Teachers College Press, Bureau of Publications.

Crosby, E. A. (1993). The 'at risk' decade. *Phi Delta Kappan, 74*(8), 598–604.

Dillow, K., Flack, M., & Peterman, F. (1994, November). Cooperative learning and the achievement of female students. *Middle School Journal,* 48–51.

District Mathematics Curriculum Guide. (1994). *District goals for mathematics outlined.* San Antonio, TX.

Dvorak, J. (1990, Spring). College students evaluate their scholastic journalism courses. *Journalism Educator, 45,* 36–46.

Eisner, E. (1985). *The educational imagination: On the design and evaluation of school programs.* New York: Macmillan.

Elder, D. (1994). Different climbs. *College English, 56*(1), 568–570.

211

Erickson, F., & Shultz, F. (1992). Students' experience of the curriculum. In P. Jackson (Ed.), *Handbook of research on curriculum* (pp. 465–485). New York: Macmillan.

Ferguson, D. L., & Patten, J. (1993). *Journalism today!* Chicago: NTC Publishing Group.

Fleischer, C. (1995). *Composing teacher research: A prosaic history.* Albany: SUNY Press.

Flores, H. (1991). Please do bother them. *Educational Leadership, 49*(4), 58–59.

Frymier, A. (1994). The use of affinity-seeking in producing liking and learning in the classroom. *Journal of Applied Communication Research, 22,* 87–105.

Frymier, J. (1992). *Growing up is risky business, and schools are not to blame* (final report, Vol. I). Bloomington, IN: Phi Delta Kappa.

Fullan, M., & Miles, G. (1992, June). Getting reform right: What works and what doesn't. *Phi Delta Kappan,* 745–752.

Gitlin, A., & Bullough, R. (1995). *Becoming a student of teaching: Methodologies for exploring self and school context.* New York: Garland.

Gitlin, A., & Teitelbaum, K. (1983). Linking theory and practice: The use of ethnographic methodology by prospective teachers. *Journal of Education for Teaching, 9*(3), 225–234.

Glesne, C., & Peshkin, A. (1992). *Becoming qualitative researchers: An introduction.* White Plains, NY: Longman.

Goodlad, J. (1979). *Curriculum inquiry: The study of curriculum practice.* New York: McGraw.

Gore, J., & Zeichner, K. (1991). Action research and reflective teaching in preservice teacher education: A case study from the United States. *Teaching and Teacher Education, 7*(2), 119–136.

Gorman, C. (1992, January 20). Sizing up the sexes. *Time,* pp. 42–48.

Goswami, D., & Stillman, P. (Eds.). (1987). *Reclaiming the classroom: Teacher research as an agency for change.* Upper Montclair, NJ: Boynton/Cook.

Hanson, J. R., Silver, H. F., & Strong, R. W. (1991). Music and the at-risk student. *Music Educator Journal, 78*(3), 30–35.

Hernandez, D. G. (1994, April 2). State of high school journalism: Poor. *Editor & Publisher, 127,* 14.

Hollingsworth, S. (1990). Teachers as reseachers: Writing to learn about ourselves—and others. *Quarterly of the National Writing Project and the Center for the Study of Writing and Literacy, 12*(4), 10–18.

Hollingsworth, S. (1994). *Teacher research & urban literacy education: Lessons & conversations in a feminist key.* New York: Teachers College, Columbia University.

Hollingsworth, S., & Sockett, H. (1994). Positioning teacher research in educational reform: An introduction. In S. Hollingsworth & H. Sockett (Eds.), *Teacher research and educational reform: Ninety-third yearbook of the National Society for the Study of Education* (pp. 1–20). Chicago: University of Chicago Press.

Johnston, S. (1994). Experience is the best teacher; Or is it? An analysis of the role of experience in learning to teach. *Journal of Teacher Education, 45*(3), 199–208.

Joyce, B., & Weil, M. (1992). *Models of teaching* (4th ed.). Boston: Allyn & Bacon.

Juhasz, A. (1989). Significant others and self-esteem: Methods for determining who and why. *Adolescence, 24*(95), 581–594.

Kleinfeld, J., & Yerian, S. (1995). *Gender tales: Tensions in the schools.* New York: St. Martin's Press.

Kramer, R. (1991). *Ed school follies: The miseducaton of America's teachers.* New York: The Free Press.

Kyle, D., & Hovda, R. (1987). Teachers as action researchers: A discussion of developmental, organizational, and policy issues. *Peabody Journal of Education, 64*(2), 80–95.

Lehr, J. (1987). *A final report of the Furman University Center of Excellence.* Greenville, SC: Furman Press.

Lewin, K. (1948). *Resolving social conflicts.* New York: Harper & Row.

Lindquist, M. M. (Ed.). (1989). *Results from the fourth mathematics assessment of the national assessment of educational progress.* Reston, VA: National Council of Teachers of Mathematics.

Lortie, D. (1975). *Schoolteacher: A sociological study.* Chicago: University of Chicago Press.

Manning, B. H., & Payne, M. (1984). Student teacher personality as a variable in teacher education. *The Teacher Educator, 20*(2), 2–12.

Maslow, A. (1970). *Motivation and personality* (2nd ed.). New York: Harper & Row.

Mathematical Sciences Education Board & National Research Council. (1990). *Reshaping school mathematics: A philosophy and framework for curriculum.* Washington, DC: National Academy Press.

Mathematical Sciences Education Board & National Research Council. (1991). *Counting on you: Actions supporting mathematics teaching standards.* Washington, DC: National Academy Press.

McKeen, W. & Bleske, G. L. (1992, Summer). Coaching editors to coach writers with team teaching approach: Drama asks editors to learn to respond to reporters. *Journalism Educator, 47,* 81–84.

Medina, J. (1990). *Managing the at-risk student: A problem-solving approach to discipline.* San Antonio, TX.

Mentoring. A resource and training guide for educators, 1st ed. (1994). Andover, MA: The Regional Laboratory for Educational Improvement of the Northeast and the Islands.

Merrill, J. C. (1978, July). Do we teach ethics—or do we teach about ethics? *Journalism Educator, 33,* 59–60.

Mills, P. (1994, Winter). On method and madness: Teaching writers to write. *Journalism Educator, 48,* 67–70.

National Council of Teachers of Mathematics. (1989). *Curriculum and evaluation standards for school mathematics.* Reston, VA: Author.

National Council of Teachers of Mathematics. (1991). *Professional standards for teaching mathematics.* Reston, VA: Author.

National Research Council. (1989). *Everybody counts: A report to the nation on the future of mathematics education* (Mathematics Sciences Education Board, Board on Mathematical Sciences, & Committee on the Mathematical Sciences in the Year 2000). Washington, DC: National Academy Press.

Natter, F., & Rollins, S. (Eds.). (1974). *The governor's task force on disruptive youth: Phase II report.* Tallahassee, FL: Office of the Governor.

Necessary, J., & Parish, T. (1993). Do teachers' attitudes and behaviors, as well as students' behaviors, relate to one another? *Education, 114*(1), 61–62.

Orenstein, P. (1994). *School girls.* New York: Doubleday.

Overly, N. (1979). *Lifelong learning: A human agenda.* Alexandria, VA: Association for Supervision and Curriculum Development.

Perrodin, A. F. (1959). Student teachers try action research. *Journal of Teacher Education, 10*(4), 471–474.

Peterson, K. D., Bennet, B., & Sherman, D. F. (1991). Themes of uncommonly successful teachers of at-risk students. *Urban Education, 26*(2), 176–194.

Poetter, T. S. (1994a). Making a difference: Miss Conner and Bunker Hill School. *Teaching Education, 6*(1), 149–151.

Poetter, T. S. (1994b). *Making meaning in the experiential domain of the curriculum: A case study of an intercollegiate women's volleyball team and its experience of the curriculum.* Unpublished doctoral dissertation, Indiana University, Bloomington.

Poetter, T. S. (1995). A novice researcher's journey through time: Making a way in the fieldwork setting. *Teaching and Learning: The Journal of Natural Inquiry, 9*(3), 16–29.

Poetter, T. S. (1996). From resistance to excitment: Becoming qualitative researchers and reflective practitioners. *Teaching Education, 8*(1), 109–119.

Poetter, T. S., & Van Zandt, L. (1996). Introducing prospective teachers to the scholarship of discovery: Connecting research and practice through inquiry. *Teacher Education and Practice, 12*(1), 1–17.

Porro, B. (1985). Playing the school system: The low achiever's game. In E. Eisner, *The educational imagination* (pp. 256–274). New York: Macmillan.

Ross, D. (1987, Part 2). Action research for preservice teachers: A description of why and how. *Peabody Journal of Education, 64*(2), 131–150.

Rudduck, J. (1985). Teacher research and research-based teacher education. *Journal of Education for Teaching, 11*(3), 281–289.

Ruenzel, D. (1994, October). Past imperfect. *Teacher Magazine, 32*–37.

Rupp, R. (1994, July–August). Do girls really lose their academic edge as teens? *Utne Reader, 66,* 20–22.

Sadker, M., & Sadker, D. (1994). *Failing at fairness: How America's schools cheat girls.* New York: Macmillan.

Salinger, J. D. (1951). *The catcher in the rye.* Boston: Little, Brown and Company.

Schaub, L. (1993, December 18). High school journalism programs need support of professional journalists. *Editor & Publisher, 126,* 56.

Schon, D. (1983). *The reflective practitioner: How professionals think in action.* New York: Basic Books.

Silverman, R., Welty, W., & Lyon, S. (1991). *Case studies for teacher problem solving.* New York: McGraw-Hill.

Sizer, T. (1985). *Horace's compromise.* Boston: Houghton Mifflin Company.

Smith, J. K. (1993). *After the demise of empericism: The problem of judging social and educational inquiry.* Norwood, NJ: Ablex.

Smith, J. L., & Johnson, H. (1993). Control in the classroom: Listening to adolescent voices. *Language Arts, 7*(1), 18–30.

Soohoo, S. (1993). Students as partners in research and restructuring schools. *The Educational Forum, 57,* 386–393.

Stein, M. L. (1993a, June 5). Reeducating the educators. *Editor & Publisher, 126,* 38.

Stein, M. L. (1993b, August 28). Revamping journalism education. *Editor & Publisher, 126,* 12–13, 35.

Stevens, L. J., & Price, M. (1992). Meeting the challenge of education: Children at risk. *Phi Delta Kappan, 74*(1), 18–20, 22–23.

Stinson, S. (1993). Meaning and value: Reflections on what students say about school. *Journal of Curriculum and Supervision, 8*(3), 216–238.

Stitt, B. (1988). *Building gender fairness in schools.* Carbondale: Southern Illinois University Press.

Teitelbaum, K., & Britzman, D. (1991). Reading and doing ethnography: Teacher education and reflective practice. In B. R. Tabachnick & K. Zeichner (Eds.), *Issues and practices in inquiry-oriented teacher education* (pp. 166–185). Philadelphia: Falmer Press.

The Holmes Group Report. (1986). Tomorrow's teachers. E. Lansing: Michigan State University.

Thomas, C. (1993). Community within diverse settings: Reflections on school success. *Education, 114*(2), 233–241.

U.S. Department of Education, Office of Educational Research and Improvement. (1993). *Improving math and science teaching: a report on the secretary's October 1992 conference on improving mathematics and science teaching and instructional resources.* Washington, DC: U.S. Department of Education.

Wasserman, S. (1993). *Getting down to cases: Learning to teach with case studies.* New York: Teachers College Press.

Wishnietsky, D., & Felder, D. (1989). Assessing coach–student relationships. *Journal of Physical Education, Recreation, and Dance, 60*(7), 76–79.

Zeichner, K., & Gore, J. (1995). Using action research as a vehicle for student teacher reflection: A social reconstructionist approach. In S. Noffke & R. Stevenson (Eds.), *Educational action research: Becoming practically critical* (pp. 13–30). New York: Teachers College Press, Columbia University.

Author Index

ᗥ ◆ ᗪ

Subject Index